The Theology of Everything

The Theology of Everything

Renaissance Man Joins the 21st Century

KEITH EYEONS

Ellis &
Maultby

Ellis and Maultby
Cambridge
England
enquiries@ellisandmaultby.co.uk

The cover photo on all editions is by Daniel Parks.
The author photo on the hardback edition is by Perry Hastings.

ISBNs
978-1-9997631-0-7 (ebook)
978-1-9997631-1-4 (paperback)
978-1-9997631-2-1 (hardback)

My thanks go to my teachers, to my students,
and to all who have joined me in pondering the themes of this book.

I am very grateful to all those at Downing College who responded
to the talks and discussions which assisted in my writing,
and to my wife Mel for her proofreading and patient support.

Contents

Chapter One
Three Views of Reality

REDISCOVERING THE RENAISSANCE

Five hundred years ago, one man's accomplishments included designing a helicopter, sketching the anatomy of the human heart, and painting the *Last Supper*. Leonardo da Vinci is the most famous example of a 'Renaissance man', a person whose learning spanned the whole landscape of human knowledge. The books he owned covered a wide range of subjects, including what we would now call science, medicine, poetry, grammar, Christianity, ethics, history and philosophy. His own revolutionary achievements stretched across the arts and the sciences, in areas which we now regard as completely separate. He succeeded in extending the realm of human knowledge on multiple frontiers.

Today, we might be suspicious of a distinguished painter who also claimed to be a pioneer of aeronautical engineering. Leonardo was a great genius, but he did have an advantage over the people of the 21st century. It was much easier to master so many subjects in an age when people knew so much less. Our world is now awash with ideas, making it impossible for any of us to keep on top of them all. Today, we can search the internet to learn about anything from the classification of snails to the age of the universe, or from Egyptian poetry to the history of toast. But no one person could assimilate all this thinking. No individual reader could even keep up with the daily rate at which new content is added to Wikipedia. The ambitious thinkers of the Renaissance had a great confidence in the potential of human beings to make sense of the whole of reality, but they would be amazed by the amount which their successors have learned. The British Library and the Library of Congress own more than 150 million documents each.

Renaissance man would stumble along their many miles of shelving in astonishment.

Our great success in amassing knowledge in so many fields has brought an unexpected disadvantage. The more ideas we develop, the harder it is for us to get a sense of what they all mean together, leading many to wonder if they mean anything at all. The best we can usually hope for is to become an expert in one narrow subject. But back in the Renaissance, people had a great confidence that reality as a whole was coherent, intelligible and meaningful. They felt that they were at home in the centre of a divinely-ordered, purposeful cosmos. So they took great delight in the religious search for harmony and interconnectedness in all truth. It was much less surprising to them that someone who understood the mathematical principles of engineering would also know how to make a painting look beautiful. Aesthetics, geometry, physics, spirituality, ethics, love, astronomy and music were all closely interrelated in their Christian vision of the world.

In fact, throughout most of the history of western thought, Christianity provided the big framework which held all of our ideas together. It inspired the ways in which people established universities, built hospitals, developed laws, created art, composed music and studied science. But that great project of seeking knowledge and developing civilisation has been so dazzlingly productive that people have now largely lost sight of the underlying vision that energised it for so many centuries. Our collection of detailed information has expanded so rapidly that the old framework has long since burst open, scattering pieces in all directions. Christianity itself has fallen towards the margins, becoming one among many fragmented ideas. And faith is now widely regarded as one specialist interest among a great multitude of pursuits, rather than as powerful way of putting all the other pieces together. Even the most enthusiastically religious people now tend to home in on one or more areas of specialist religious interest. They focus on particular concerns, such as the aim of going to heaven when they die, rather than seeking a way of making sense of the whole of reality as we currently experience it. In doing so, they often lose sight of what could be the most compelling reason to believe in God in the first place. There is much that we could all rediscover from the breadth of vision of the Renaissance.

A RENAISSANCE VIEW OF PEOPLE AND GOD

The text often described as the 'Manifesto of the Renaissance' is the *Oration on the Dignity of Man* by the philosopher Pico della Mirandola (1463–1494). He declared that God had given to human beings the role of being able to 'reckon up the reason' of the cosmos, 'to love its beauty and to wonder at its greatness.'[1] This Renaissance vision has two aspects which mirror each other, and I will argue for both of them in this book. One aspect is the idea that the whole of reality has a divine order, beauty and purpose. All that exists makes sense together, because the whole of reality is shaped by God. The other aspect is the idea that human beings have a greatly privileged position in the universe and an exalted vocation, being made in the image of God. We have the abilities and the opportunities to investigate the rationality of the cosmos, to marvel at its beauty, to find meaning in life, and to grow in love.

Pico refers to a widely-felt experience of wonder: a sense of awe at the glory of creation, and of feeling of astonishment at our place within it. Among the texts he quotes is Psalm 8, which expresses the joyful amazement of being human in a cosmos of marvels.

> O Lord our Sovereign,
> how majestic is your name in all the earth!
> You have set your glory above the heavens…
> When I look at your heavens,
> the work of your fingers,
> the moon and the stars that you have established;
> what are human beings that you are mindful of them,
> mortals that you care for them?
> Yet you have made them a little lower than God,
> and crowned them with glory and honour.

This *Theology of Everything* will show how both aspects of that Renaissance vision of reality can still work today. I will argue that the

---

1   Pico della Mirandola *On the Dignity of Man*
     (p. 4 in the translation by P J W Millar, published by Hackett, 1998)

universe is a purposeful and creative space, a consistently structured environment within which rational creatures can evolve. It is a meaningful environment, within which consciousness can develop. And it is a moral environment, within which we encounter good and evil, and where we can develop character and virtue as we learn to build loving relationships and civilised communities. Underlying the whole of this beautiful, rational, creative universe is one divine mind, a loving consciousness who seeks to enable people to flourish and to grow in love. I will describe how such a theology can help to make sense of all areas of human experience, and to bring them together in one big picture.

In talking of the *Theology* of Everything, I have adapted a term which is most commonly used by scientists: the *Theory* of Everything. Mathematicians such as Stephen Hawking use the name to describe the search for a unified theory which will combine all the laws of physics into one set of equations, bringing general relativity into unity with quantum mechanics. Theirs is an important and exciting project, which has often been called the holy grail of modern physics. However, I am talking about an even greater quest: the search for a vision which can embrace the whole range of our human experiences, including the discoveries of science but not limited to them. I think that the physical properties we can investigate in laboratories are fascinating, but they do not themselves add up to the whole truth about reality.

Science is extremely successful at building an agreed understanding of the things that we can measure together, such as the melting point of copper or the size of Jupiter. However, much of human life revolves around things which are a lot more subjective, a lot more complex, and a lot less quantifiable, such as love, community, trust, the beauty of music or our empathy with the personalities of our friends. I believe that these experiences are connecting with genuine and important aspects of reality, and that a true Theory of Everything needs to pay great attention to them.

All of our faculties have evolved in response to the universe around us, and I believe that they all have genuine and important things to tell us about reality. Our highly evolved skills include our physical senses and our abilities to make scientific measurements. But I will argue that it is equally important to take seriously our appreciation of beauty, our ability to love and to form relationships and communities, our awareness of good and evil, our sense of spirituality and meaning, and our experiences of our own consciousness. The very sophisticated faculties in this second category are often dismissed as subjective and unreliable, relating to individual tastes rather than universal truths. However, I will argue that they convey vital insights about humanity and our place in the cosmos. And I will show how Christian theology can still provide a way of making sense of them together, within a single, unified theory about the universe.

A belief in God is a uniquely strong reason for expecting there to be a rich harmony between all forms of truth. It indicates that the whole of reality is created and sustained by one divine, loving intelligence, who is the source of all that exists. God is rational, and is the basis for the order and structure of the laws of physics, enabling us to develop as rational creatures who can investigate a rational cosmos. God is social, and is the basis for the universe's potential to bring forth creatures who enjoy consciousness and relationships. God is loving, and seeks to enable people to flourish as moral beings, in an environment where we have freedom and can learn to choose good and to reject evil. Physics, friendship and ethics are therefore three examples of aspects of reality which connect with God.

These examples demonstrate how theology can offer to support all other endeavours by affirming their true context, meaning, dignity and value. It is theology which can tell scientists that they are thinking God's thoughts after him and investigating his works. It is theology which can tell poets that their explorations of human consciousness are engaging with a phenomenon which is at the heart of the purpose behind the universe. It is theology which can tell parents that their hard work in nurturing their children is joining in with the creative love of the Father of all. As I shall describe in the coming chapters, Christian faith can give perspective and encouragement to all human activities which pursue truth, goodness, beauty, civilisation and the flourishing of all people. All of these aspects of reality find a harmony and meaning within the mind of God.

The seven chapters of this book will therefore travel across the wide and fascinating realm of human knowledge and experience. I am going to talk about science, beauty, goodness, evolution, consciousness, rationality, love, relationships, community, galaxies, personalities, crime, equations and symphonies, among other things. Along the way, I shall show how they can indeed make sense together within one coherent picture. But the rest of this chapter will first explore some more of the intellectual resources which inspired the Renaissance, and then start to examine the conflicting views of the world which have caused us to lose sight of their sense of the unity of all truth.

GOD AND THE HISTORY OF WESTERN THOUGHT

The great thinkers of the Renaissance did not believe that they were starting from scratch, but were in awe of the tradition of learning which they had inherited from the ancient world. Among the Greek philosophers they admired, Plato (c. 427–c. 348 BC) wrote about subjects ranging from agriculture and politics to the nature of the soul, while the many topics discussed by Aristotle (384–322 BC) included astronomy, metaphysics, elephants and rhetoric. Early Christian theologians then borrowed enthusiastically from Greek thought, and the resulting marriage of religious and secular learning flourished through the Middle Ages, when the first universities were founded. C. S. Lewis has described the 'tranquil, indefatigable, exultant energy of passionately systematic minds bringing huge masses of heterogeneous material into unity.' The result was 'the medieval synthesis... the whole organisation of their theology, science, and history into a single, complex, harmonious mental Model of the Universe.'[2]

St Thomas Aquinas (1225–1274) enthused about the quest to understand 'God's own knowledge, which is the single and simple vision of everything'.[3] Aquinas's remarkable achievements involved combining the very best sacred and secular forms of knowledge that

2   C. S. Lewis (1994) *The Discarded Image: An Introduction to Medieval and Renaissance Literature* Canto, p. 10–11

3   Aquinas *Summa Theologiae* Ia. I, article 3

were available in his day. He used the science and philosophy of Aristotle to help him to explore the implications of the Bible and the writings of the Church Fathers. He believed that Christian teaching could reveal a framework for all truth, and that other disciplines could join together in filling in the details. In later centuries, the Renaissance enquiry into all truth continued to develop this tradition. Pico della Mirandola used a theological structure when he brought together ideas about the beauty of the cosmos, the potential of human beings, rationality, virtue, mathematics, the elements, and other subjects.

The Renaissance was, undoubtedly, a golden age in the history of western civilisation. But my task in this book is not to try to turn back the clock to those times, or to replace the ideas in our minds with theirs. Five centuries have gone by, bringing a wealth of new discoveries for us to rejoice in. Scientific investigation has vastly increased our understanding of the universe, its size, its history, its inner workings, and the evolution of life on earth. We have also learned many things about human community, finding out how to give more freedom to individuals, abolishing slavery, developing democracy, opening up equal opportunities for women, and recognising the potential for goodness in same-sex relationships.

I will seek to show how such valuable developments can enlarge and illuminate the theological vision which I am describing, rather than conflicting with it. I think that they represent positive and healthy progress within a tradition which still makes the most sense when understood from a Christian perspective, as I shall explain. But, of course, the centuries since the Renaissance have brought many conflicts and stories about conflicts, especially relating to the interactions of science and religion. Along the way, this book will re-examine that history, and seek to correct some misunderstandings of it.

Looking back over history, I would like to suggest that there are two big pictures of reality which have been especially influential in western thought over the last thousand years. I will call the first picture the *hierarchical cosmos*, and the second the *mechanical cosmos*. You may not know these names, but you will quickly recognise that you live in a society which has been shaped by the two views of reality that they present. Both pictures have clear interactions with theology, although the mechanical picture provides a way of moving away from religion for those who wish to. They have both been immensely valuable in the intellectual history of the west, and they have also had great political significance. The hierarchical picture of the cosmos is associated with the powerful alliance between the Church and the aristocracy which began to form three centuries after the time of Jesus Christ. And the mechanical picture of the cosmos is associated with rebellions against that power in the modern world. From my perspective, both pictures are deeply insightful, but also have significant limitations. Both pictures offer a place for God, but offer us a view of God which includes some serious distortions. Discussing those two pictures of reality will help to clarify the ways in which I am now seeking to move on to a rather different idea.

When I have explained the strengths and weaknesses of both, I will introduce a third possible picture, the *social cosmos*. It is a view of reality which I believe is closer to the teachings of Jesus Christ. It will enable a Renaissance vision to be re-established for the 21st century, supporting a Theology of Everything that takes all of our experiences and discoveries seriously.

THE FIRST OLD PICTURE:
THE HIERARCHICAL COSMOS

I have already said some appreciative things about St Thomas Aquinas and the medieval interest in the unity of all truth. And I shall say some further admiring things in the second chapter about the beauty of medieval cathedrals. I shall even provide evidence in the third chapter that medieval people were far less ignorant and irrational than later eras have suggested. However, I do not wish I was living in the Middle Ages, or even the Renaissance, and this book is not an attempt to go back there. The unified picture of the cosmos which flourished in the Middle Ages and the Renaissance presented an inspiring vision of humanity's place in a meaningful cosmos. But it contained a fatal flaw which has led to its downfall: it was far too strongly linked to a rigid and dictatorial social system.

Medieval thinkers loved hierarchies, and it is worth noting that the term 'hierarchy' comes from the Greek words for 'priest' and for 'authority'. The unifying force in the spiritual, political and intellectual life of western Europe in the Middle Ages was the Roman Catholic Church, which remains the classic example of a social hierarchy. At the top is the Pope, who in 1302 declared that 'it is absolutely necessary for salvation that every human creature be subject to the Roman Pontiff.' Below him, the chain of command includes cardinals, then other arch-bishops and bishops, then parish priests. It is a patriarchal hierarchy, so all of these leaders are male. Finally, at the bottom, are the ordinary lay-people, who are commanded to obey the church's teachings and to confess their sins to its leaders.

In parallel with the Church hierarchy, medieval society had an aris-tocratic hierarchy based around the ownership of land, which was the main source of income in an agricultural age. Each country had a king (or when necessary a queen), ruling over various ranks of nobility, such as dukes, earls, knights, and other land-owning gentry. Finally, at the bottom, showing due deference to their lords of the manor, were the peasants, working in their masters' fields and generating the wealth enjoyed by their superiors.

The two hierarchies were closely connected. Popes and archbishops would crown kings and emperors. Monarchs were involved in the appointment of bishops, and minor aristocrats were patrons of local churches (in which they could install their younger sons as priests). Senior clergy lived in great palaces with many servants, and were highly influential political figures. This was a social, political and ecclesiastical alliance which flourished for well over a thousand years, and which gave great stability to western European society. It began to form in the fourth century, when the Roman Empire stopped perse-cuting Christians and enshrined Christianity as its established religion. This alliance of Church and state survived the fall of Rome, and held together European civilisation for many centuries.

In addition to these two hierarchies of powerful men, there was believed to be a celestial chain of command also, high up in the heavens: a hierarchy of angelic beings ruling over the cosmos. At the top were the Seraphim, Cherubim and Thrones, followed by the Dominions, Powers and Authorities, followed by the Principalities, Archangels and Angels. And there was a hierarchy of the souls of the dead, rising up through the levels of purgatory towards the glories of heaven, where Mary was enthroned among the saints as Queen.

Above the heavenly choirs of angels and exalted souls was, of course, God. He was the source of all power in heaven and earth, depicted as the ultimate imperial dignitary. He ruled over the angelic, ecclesiastical and aristocratic hierarchies, which communicated his authority across the whole of creation and down to all individual human beings. In this fixed and hierarchical system, all people on earth knew their appointed places and social ranks, whether they were dukes or servants or farm labourers. They were each born into a particular place in society, and believed that it was God who had decided their status. All knew their roles and the contributions which they were called to make to society. They knew where they belonged in the world and how they related to each other. They understood the meaning of their lives, and were brought up to serve God and to honour his appointed representatives. Similar hierarchical systems are found in other historic cultures and religions around the world, sometimes regarding kings and emperors as divine figures, and sometimes believing that people's positions in society are determined by their actions in their previous lives.

The natural world was hierarchical too: in medieval science, even the physical elements knew their place. The solid objects made of earth sought to return to the earth, falling down to the ground. Water belonged on the surface of the earth, and would find its way to the sea through rivers. Air belonged above the earth, and fire would also seek to go upwards, through flames which pointed to the sky. Above everything else were the spheres of the heavens, made of celestial bodies moving in eternal circles. Everything and everyone had an appointed place.

The traditional aristocratic and ecclesiastical hierarchy of western Europe held itself tightly together for many centuries, giving order and structure to the lives of people and nations. It offered an all-embracing, coherent understanding of reality, providing fertile ground for the cultural genius of the Renaissance. It was an inspiring vision of an ordered and purposeful cosmos, within which human lives and relationships were seen as important and meaningful. But its great weakness was that it enshrined an inequality of power which could be very cruel. It has therefore faced a barrage of opposition over the last five centuries, articulated by philosophical and theological rebellions, supported by social and economic transformations, and culminating in political revolutions. Famous milestones in its decline include the Reformation in the 16th century (at which the Protestants rejected the universal leadership of the Pope), the American Declaration of Independence of 1776 (which rejected the authority of the King of Great Britain), and the French Revolution (which led many aristocrats and clergy to their deaths at the guillotine from its beginnings in 1789). The vast social and economic upheavals of the Industrial Revolution of the 18th and 19th centuries greatly accelerated the decline of the old system.

The hierarchical picture of the cosmos has long since lost most of its traditional authority, but its influence has declined gradually rather than being conclusively replaced. Many aspects of its hold on people's imaginations have lingered on for a surprisingly long time. The leisure activities of today's world show that we are still fascinated by the glamour and the security of the old hierarchical cosmos. Disney enthusiastically presents a medieval fantasy world of magic castles and princesses on screens and in theme parks. Millions have watched *Downton Abbey*, which shows the final decline of a remnant of the old social order with affectionate nostalgia. The audience does not just dream of being the Earl or Countess of Grantham, but also wonders whether faithfully serving below stairs in a beautiful palace might be more rewarding than most of the short-term opportunities we have in today's grey offices and warehouses. The old hierarchical cosmos both repels and fascinates us.

The repulsion comes, of course, from its lack of freedom, its enforcement of arbitrary privileges, its sexism, and from the opportunities it gave for cruelty, oppression and uncaring incompetence. I wish to claim in this book that good theology is inherently life-affirming and peaceful, but it would be hard for me to do that if I were to advocate a return to a love of hierarchies. Power can corrupt people, and the history of Christian aristocratic leadership includes some who have claimed a God-given right to behave appallingly badly: being racist, sexist, tyrannically cruel, or simply completely indifferent to the sufferings of the poor. Similar problems are found in other historic faiths and cultures. As a result, the old hierarchical picture of the cosmos has been undermined by centuries of resentment, rebellion and revolution, which have eventually broken apart the old system.

Elegant trappings of the old order remain, heavily modified by many reforms, such as a British monarch who keeps her opinions to herself while she gracefully signs all the laws presented to her by an elected Parliament. In the Church of England, male and female bishops wear their splendid traditional symbols of authority, but submit to the decisions made by laypeople voting in synods. However, by far the largest and most unreformed continuation of the medieval system remains the male-only hierarchy of the Roman Catholic Church. The Pope no longer governs a large part of Italy or crowns Emperors, but he still rules over the tiny Vatican City State as an independent country, retaining his special historic status as one who is answerable to no earthly power.

Protestantism and atheism both involve rebellions against these old hierarchies, so they have both produced narratives about liberty and progress which have vilified the hierarchical Roman Catholic Church as the great enemy of freedom and independent thought. I shall need to question much of this anti-Catholic propaganda in later chapters while I seek to renew the positive aspects of a Renaissance vision. I think that Catholics have often been much more successful than Protestants and atheists at celebrating the harmony of all truth, the rationality of theology and the significance of beauty. I shall also want to recover that deep awareness that human beings and relationships are among the most significant features of the cosmos. But I do think that hierarchies have serious limitations, and that Protestant theology and secularism have some very important things to say about human freedom.

Hierarchies are natural, and provide a limited but effective social structure among various creatures. The little flock of chickens in my garden has a pecking order, in which each hen knows her position in the queue for food. After a few fights to establish their rankings, and the occasional confrontation to maintain them, they are able to coexist in an orderly fashion. Human beings similarly very naturally form hierarchies, as seen in the different levels of management in organisations from companies to schools. Armed forces rely on hierarchies, within which Generals can plan strategies and Sergeant Majors can keep the troops in order. And, even though our old aristocratic hierarchy has lost most of its power, democratic societies have generated a new set of imbalances of wealth and influence among their citizens. Europe is no longer ruled by inter-married royal families, but a new (and rather more hidden) global elite of billionaires have quietly gained enormous power.

All of this is as natural as the behaviour of my chickens, and seems to me for now to be an inevitable tendency in human society. However, I see it as something connected with our more primitive animal instincts rather than with our highest spiritual ideals. I regard our social hierarchies as an expression of the ways in which we seek territory, power and status, rather than as something which is of great transcendent significance. Above all, a Christian theologian must point out that Jesus did not praise the hierarchies of his day, but seemed to spend rather a lot of time trying to undermine them.

Jesus washed his disciples' feet, an unpleasant task normally performed by a servant, and told them to follow his example[4]. He said that the last would be first and the first would be last,[5] and that the meek would inherit the earth.[6] He said that those who humble themselves would be exalted, and those who exalt themselves would be humbled.[7] He said that anyone who wanted to become great would need to become the slave of all.[8] And he said that it was easier for a camel to pass through the eye of a needle than for a rich man to enter the kingdom of heaven.[9] He was frequently very affirming and welcoming

4   John 13.1–12
5   Matthew 19.30
6   Matthew 5.5
7   Luke 14.11
8   Mark 10.44
9   Matthew 19.23–24

to people of low status, and very critical of those in power. He criticised religious leaders whose attention was focussed on enjoying being greeted with respect, and poured scorn on those who loved having special titles and seats of honour at banquets.[10]

In all the centuries when the Christian Church has amassed great wealth, political power, and has emphasised the status and dignity of its leaders, it has lost touch with some of the values of its founder. I admire Pope Francis for choosing to live in humble accommodation instead of the Vatican's traditional palatial Papal Apartments. And I think that all church leaders have more authenticity and credibility when they are not seeking after social status or unfair amounts of political influence. I also think that good theology should seek to explore the varied experiences of all people, rather than seeming to suggest that God is only encountered through the hierarchies and ceremonies of the Church.

One of the traditional attractions of the hierarchical picture of the cosmos for theologians is that it gives a very obvious position for God at the top of all the chains of command. It is a very clear picture, but it may offer us a very distorted view of God. The character of God, in good Christian theology, is meant to be glimpsed primarily through the character of Jesus Christ, who first came as a humble servant and whose life was full of love for all people. However, the hierarchical picture of the cosmos can make God seem like an exalted form of a human emperor, and perhaps as one who has the kinds of faults and insecurities that human dictators often have. The hierarchical God may appear to be one who is forever demanding homage in order to maintain his honour and dignity in the eyes of his people, or who is far too distant to have any connection with anyone other than important kings and archbishops. And this perception of divine distance gets even worse while the status of kings and archbishops fades away in the modern world. Without the earthly hierarchies leading the way up to the heavenly ones, the old connections disappear. A traditional description of God can make him sound like a relic of a former age, enthroned on high in dusty isolation. And so the old account of the universe loses its sense of interconnectedness and meaning.

10   Matthew 23.1–12

This Theology of Everything will therefore seek to learn from the philosophical strengths of medieval and Renaissance thought, but it will reject the hierarchical system which it enshrines, and will try to correct the ways in which its picture of God may now mislead us. But the hierarchical picture is not the only view of God which the western world has produced. The big picture which gradually replaced the hierarchical cosmos deals with some of its problems, but has introduced another familiar set of distortions to our view of life.

THE SECOND OLD PICTURE:
THE MECHANICAL COSMOS

More than anything else, it was the Industrial Revolution which destroyed the medieval alliance of theology, aristocracy and ecclesiastical power. Since the late 18th century, human life has been transformed by the successes of science, technology, engineering and global commerce. The old hierarchical social order of land-owning aristocrats and farm labourers has been broken apart, and a whole new middle class of ambitious entrepreneurs, industrialists, merchants, bankers, stock-brokers, academics, politicians and assorted professionals has gained power. In this industrialised era, we have been extraordinarily successful in mechanising our lives, and now inhabit environments manufactured with steel, concrete, plastic, tarmac, and all kinds of electrical circuitry and powerful machinery. Engineering has reshaped our lives, heated our homes, captured our imaginations and directed our philosophies. Computers relay the latest prices of stocks and commodities around the world in an instant. The world of machinery now seems so precise, so undeniably powerful and so demonstrably true that it has taken over our view of reality. Where medieval Christians projected their social hierarchies out onto the skies as ranks of angels and patron saints, the following era has done the same with its industrial triumphs. We have come to see the universe as an enormous piece of technology.

The modern world has long been inspired by, or haunted by, the belief that the entire cosmos is like a giant machine. Our civilisation no longer shares the belief that reality is shaped around God, human beings and relationships, but has come to see it more and more as an enormous and impersonal piece of engineering. This view of a mechanical universe has been encouraged by a cascade of scientific discoveries, uncovering fundamental laws of physics and fuelling our technological progress. These discoveries notably include the work of Isaac Newton (1642–1727) on gravity and motion, and James Clerk Maxwell (1831–1879) on electromagnetism. Such great achievements in the field of classical physics are so impressive that they have seemed to offer a complete account of the whole of reality in terms of matter, forces and motion, as if it were a giant steam engine. It has been widely believed that all future events are completely determined by the current positions and trajectories of all the objects in the universe, squeezing out any sense of human free will. Every atom inexorably follows the laws of physics, like cogs turning predictably in a giant clockwork mechanism. And so it has seemed that the whole of reality is impersonal and industrial.

The clockwork view of the cosmos attributes no significance to any human relationships or hierarchies, so this worldview has been enthusiastically embraced by many of those campaigning against old aristocratic social structures. One person can be seen as being much like any another in a mechanistic worldview: an assemblage of skin, bone, brain cells and other components, rather than as a member of a divinely-ordained hierarchy. There need be nothing special about kings or bishops in a mechanical cosmos, and the whole of humanity can be regarded as completely equal in its lack of any cosmic significance. The revolution can begin. The publication of Darwin's discovery of evolution in 1859 (which I shall discuss in chapter 4) reinforced the radical new sense that people's place in the world was determined by chance and competition rather than through any great cosmic plan.

The mechanised view of the cosmos took hold of western imagination as industrialisation transformed people's lives. Workers moved from agricultural villages into fast-growing cities, transported by steam trains and then by electric trams, informed by telegraph and then by radio, in newly-engineered environments surrounded by industrial power. In the first half of the 20th century, unprecedented numbers were conscripted into vast armies, serving as obedient little gearwheels within the colossal machinery of industrialised warfare and bureau-cratically-planned genocide.

When the cosmos is seen as a giant clockwork mechanism, it can easily appear to be an impersonal and meaningless space, within which our tiny human feelings and occupations have no significance. Reality seems to be primarily about atoms and their movements, and the fundamental truths about the universe seem to consist primarily of a set of facts about the properties of matter. As a result, we have together become very confident about the significance of our scientific measurements of the mighty machine around us. And we have together become much less confident about the significance of our awareness of beauty, meaning, goodness, consciousness, wonder and love. These experiences may now seem like mere quirks of human personality, the arbitrary effects of various electrical connections in our brains.

The mechanised view of nature starts with an awareness of the consistency and reliability of scientific measurements, and then leaps dubiously to the conclusion that reality consists only of those things that can be measured in laboratories. It is therefore very different from this Theology of Everything, which will affirm the significance of all our experiences. But it is deeply embedded in much modern western thought, in ways that I will need to keep on unpicking throughout this book. It has been given various different labels by its admirers and critics. Alister McGrath has described this model of the cosmos as the 'Mechanical Universe'[11]. Others write about 'naturalism', to define the idea that nothing exists beyond nature and its various laws. And it is associated with 'scientism', which is the idea that science provides the only valid source of truth. More informally, various writers have enjoyed using the phrase 'nothing buttery' to describe the idea that reality consists of 'nothing but' atoms behaving in a mechanistic way.[12] It is worth noting that science itself does not imply scientism, and a great many scientists are not enthusiasts for 'nothing buttery', as I shall describe in chapters 3 and 4. However, the mechanical universe is a very influential image.

11   Alister M McGrath (2002) *The Re-enchantment of Nature* Hodder & Stoughton, p. 101
12   See Rodney D Holder (2008) *Nothing But Atoms and Molecules?*
      Faraday Institute for Science and Religion

A clockwork view of the cosmos often leads to 'reductionism', the idea that the full truth about the universe can be found by taking it to pieces and by explaining it in terms of its most basic cogs and wheels. Reductionism, for example, understands consciousness as a property of the brain, and understands the brain in terms of the molecules that form brain cells, and those molecules in terms the atoms they are made of, and those atoms in terms of sub-atomic particles. But reductionism misses the ways in which the phenomena we experience are far greater than the sum of the parts which make them possible. Consider, for example, the works of Shakespeare, and the experiences which his dramas explored, and the place of his stories in our shared history. They add up to something that goes far beyond the properties of the atoms which made up Shakespeare's brain and his quill pen.

Belief in God has continued for many within this mechanical view of the cosmos, but it has seemed increasingly difficult and controversial. The only place which the picture easily offers for God is the role of the designer. He becomes the ancient watchmaker, the engineer who invented the machine and constructed all of its wondrous parts long ago. He also becomes the law-giver, the one who established the laws of physics which govern matter and the moral laws which human beings are called to obey. People can still look admiringly at nature and regard it as his handiwork. But there can now seem to be no continuing role for God, because any suggestion of a later involvement in the cosmos would seem like a breach of his own laws.

Religious enthusiasts now therefore often find themselves forced into a corner full of endless arguments about whether or not God 'intervenes', or whether or not there are any gaps in the scientific account of the universe which might suggest the need for some occasional maintenance visits by the manufacturer. Some feel that they must resist discoveries about evolution and assert the need for God's direct involvement as the 'intelligent designer'. But the more we discover about the vast size and great age of the universe, and the more complete our understanding of evolution becomes, the more distant, detached, long-departed and thoroughly optional any such designer may appear to be.

We might admire the Great Architect of creation, in the same way that we might admire the builders of Stonehenge, but it becomes harder to expect to feel any kind of present connection with him. In a mechanical cosmos, spirituality dwindles and religion goes cold. The result, therefore, is one of the most significant aspects of the fragmentation of our understanding of reality. In our technological world, there is a great divorce between spirituality and science in most people's minds. In this picture of the universe, the divine is pushed into the remote past and the far distance, leaving us feeling that we are alone in an impersonal and meaningless cosmos. And, without a shared faith to establish the transcendent significance of goodness, love, beauty and the meaningfulness of life, such ideas can become seen as subjective, arbitrary, irrational and private. We still pursue them, but in a much more fragmented way, as individuals or through gatherings of like-minded eccentrics.

The emotional difference between the hierarchical and mechanical views of the cosmos can be seen vividly in a comparison of London's two most famous art galleries. Traditional art is found in the National Gallery, a neoclassical building whose pillars and porticoes reside firmly within the western understanding of beauty inaugurated by the ancient Greeks. The paintings inside engage with widely-shared, traditional understandings of aesthetics. There are landscapes and flowers, and there are depictions of well-known stories from Greek mythology, from the Bible, from the lives of the saints, and from important historical figures. Important leaders and wealthy patrons may appear as themselves or in the guise of saints and heroes. The gallery is a grand and imposing building communicating a tradition of greatness, but it offers warm and intimate spaces within which visitors find familiar shared stories. The paintings contain a wealth of imagery which anyone can easily appreciate and can recognise as being beautiful. They represent traditions of western art which are awe-inspiring, but which offer a shared narrative within which the individual human being is invited to feel at home. The gallery speaks of the power of tradition, but in a way which is very recognisable and accessible.

On the other side of the Thames, the Tate Modern is a bold rede-velopment of a derelict power station, a vast industrial building that conveys a sense of technological muscle rather than beauty. It contains a colossal turbine hall, framed with vast steel girders, where the gen-erators supplying central London's electricity used to turn. It would be hard to imagine a more dramatic symbol of the mechanical cosmos. With this industrial space, the art is modern, quirky, challenging, and often grotesque, rather than traditionally beautiful. Visitors wander among ingenious installations of pipes or planks, or puzzle over abstract collections of geometric shapes and splashes of colour. Within this mechanical environment, there is no longer a shared understanding of beauty which the art can engage with harmoniously, and therefore many people find it baffling, alienating, and ugly. Some of it succeeds in being popular in its rejection of stuffy old hierarchies, but its opposition to familiar imagery can make much of it seem obscure, self-indulgent and elitist. It is the art that results from the collapse of confidence in the shared narratives and views of aesthetics that developed within the hierarchical cosmos. It celebrates the brave creativity of individuals who dare to express themselves within a meaningless world, and who no longer defer to any shared understandings of meaning. Their work resides within a giant industrial machine. And the machine itself is an exciting expression of human technological triumph, but also an impersonal environment on a very inhuman scale.

Since the Industrial Revolution, we have gained great power over the natural world, at the same time as losing our civilisation's shared sense of the God-given significance of human beings. We have arrived at what C. S. Lewis called the 'empty universe'.[13] We are very successful in the ways that we excavate, process, manufacture, trade, consume and discard vast quantities of stuff, but very unsure as a society about what any of it might mean. We objectify nature, rather than showing it love or regarding it as the bearer of a sacred message. The universe provides us with a fantastic kit of parts, which we have dismantled and rebuilt in all kinds of profitable ways. We can change the arrange-ments of atoms, forming oil into plastics and synthesising medicines,

13   The title of an essay written in 1952

pesticides and fertilisers. We can extract metal from rocks and make it into aeroplanes. We can build rockets and computers and skyscrapers. We can even unleash the colossal nuclear energies that hold together the matter at the heart of atoms, harnessing it to power our cities or even to obliterate them. But we no longer have a shared way of talking about what, if anything, our lives mean. Much of modern philosophy, art and literature is haunted by the fear that our lives have no purpose beyond anything we might invent for ourselves. Every person may seem to be alone with their arbitrary attempts to construct meaning in the midst of a meaningless machine.

But there are actually some very good reasons for now regarding the clockwork cosmos as an expression of short-sighted greed, political opportunism, obsolete science and decaying theology. I hope that my account of a mechanised universe has annoyed you, because we can do much, much better than this. If you are a scientist who knows that your research is full of beauty and wonder, or a spiritual person who knows that your faith relates to much more than a long-departed engineer, or a lover of nature who knows that our relationship with the world has gone badly toxic, then I hope you will find that we have much in common. Throughout the rest of this book, I intend to argue against the image of reality as a machine, and to show that a much more enlightening alliance of new science, wise theology and compassionate living is possible. The result will be a view of the cosmos which is not mechanical, nor hierarchical, but joyfully social. Theology will offer a framework, and science will help to fill in some of the details. And so I will now let some newer and better science have the first word.

QUANTUM MECHANICS MELTS THE CLOCK

The truth is that the universe is actually a lot more weird, surprising and genuinely personal than the clockwork image suggests. As physicist and theologian Rodney Holder writes, 'the old mechanistic universe is dead and modern physics has replaced it with something far more supple and conducive to a spiritual outlook.'[14] Remarkably, physicists

14   Rodney D Holder (2008) *Nothing But Atoms and Molecules?*
     Faraday Institute for Science and Religion, p. 132

discovered the evidence which disproves the idea of a mechanical cosmos nearly a century ago, but most people have still not noticed. The clockwork idea took hold of our cultural imagination at a time when people were still making some attempt to share a joined-up understanding of reality, and it helped to fuel a social revolution. Today, however, physicists are mostly left to do their own thing and to discuss equations and data with their colleagues in a way that few other people can understand.

Quantum mechanics is a revolutionary breakthrough in physics which began in the early 20th century, as a result of studying the behaviour of matter in its smallest forms. It examines the phenomena exhibited by the tiniest of sub-atomic particles, the entities which people always expected to function as the smallest cogs in the machine. It turns out that they were completely wrong. Down at that level, things really do not work like impersonal machinery at all. Quantum physics shows that matter follows probabilities rather than fixed laws. And, far from just continuing without us in its own inexorable way, matter seems to respond to a vital role played by conscious observers. Down at its simplest level, this seems to be a world of relationships rather than clockwork.

Take, for example, an electron. Electrons are tiny particles which form the outer shell of atoms and which enable those atoms to join up with others to make molecules. They also whizz up and down wires in the form of electricity. But, sometimes an electron might be travelling on its own through space. Classical physics would tell us to picture it as a miniature snooker ball, and to think about it occasionally bouncing off other miniature snooker balls, following the sort of completely predictable trajectory that a good snooker player would recognise. However, things are much more surprising down in the land of the very small.

The newer physics tells us that we have to think of the electron not usually as a particle but as a wave of probability. Amazingly, the electron does not normally exist in any definite position. Instead, there are some places where it would be more likely to be found if we were to look for it, and some other nearby places where it is less likely to be, and a map of these places would be made up of moving stripes, like the waves on the sea. When the electron wave meets an obstacle, it behaves like waves on the sea meeting a rock. New probability waves ripple away in all directions and overlap with each other. The map of the places where the electron might be gets more spread out and more complex. And the situation is not just that the position of the electron is hidden; it really is that the electron does not actually exist in any one specific place.

One of the leading interpretations of quantum mechanics says that the electron will continue in this highly ambiguous way until *someone* somehow looks for it and forces it to commit itself to being in one exact place. This is called collapsing the wave function. And it happens when a scientist deploys some kind of detecting device, or when the electron interacts with the wider world in way that we can notice. Even then, according to the Uncertainty Principle developed by Werner Heisenberg in 1927, the electron can never have both a precise position and a precise momentum at the same time.

Heisenberg criticised the 'naïve materialistic way of thinking that still prevailed in Europe'. Rather than being a clockwork mechanism following inexorable laws, the world revealed by twentieth century physics is a much more flexible environment made up of probabilities and relationships. The future is not determined by the present positions and movements of all the particles in the universe, because those values have no precise existence. Tomorrow is wide open with possibilities. And Heisenberg noted that the new physics dissolves the rigid framework of the nineteenth century, such as its idea that matter is the primary reality.[15] Far from being an impersonal machine where we are just another set of cogs, the role of the conscious observer now appears to many to be central to the functioning of the universe. Quantum mechanics is consistent with my claim that the cosmos is primarily concerned with consciousness and relationships.

Today's physics, unknown to most people, actually suggests that the behaviour of the cosmos depends on us looking at it. It relies on interacting with observers. This is a weird and wonderful idea which has never been fully assimilated in the popular understanding of the

15   Werner Heisenberg (2000) *Physics and Philosophy* Penguin Classics, p. 141, 137–138

world. The mechanical cosmos appeared to be a world reducible to precise and objective measurements, within which our own experiences were of no significance. But reductionism has, remarkably, uncovered the opposite. Matter at its most basic is not like a tiny collection of cogs and wheels doing its own impersonal thing: it actually seems to depend on the involvement of consciousness.

The role of the observer is so significant in quantum mechanics that some physicists have suggested that the universe itself can only come into being because we are here to observe it.[16] It is the presence of intelligent, conscious observers that collapses all the various wave functions and enables the universe to settle into its visible state and to be what it is. Far from being passive observers of the inexorable workings of a giant and impersonal machine, our interactions with the universe are actually of huge importance.

I will therefore argue in this book that the universe should be understood as something which is here to be observed and enjoyed by living creatures. It is not an impersonal collection of mechanisms, but it is something which gives rise to the presence of intelligent observers and which invites their participation. We should think of the cosmos primarily as interactive and social, not as mechanical. As the Theology of Everything suggests, it is a place where we belong. It is the setting for the development of consciousness, interaction, community and love.

A TRINITARIAN PICTURE: THE SOCIAL COSMOS

I have described two images of reality which have been extremely influential in western thought. Each of them offers a place for God, but each seems to me to have limitations. In a hierarchical cosmos, the image of God is that of the supreme Emperor, enthroned at the top of all hierarchies, with his commands communicated downwards through the ranks of his servants. In a mechanical cosmos, the image of God is that of the watchmaker, the inventor who constructed the machine at the dawn of time. Both images communicate something of the greatness and the rationality of God, but they each have significant

16   See John D Barrow and Frank J Tipler (1986) *The Anthropic Cosmological Principle* Oxford University Press, p. 22

limitations. The first says too much about relationships of power, and not enough about love. The second completely marginalises any sense of relationship. The first makes God seem very detached, now that all of the supporting hierarchies have dwindled away. And the second makes God seem very uninvolved, now that we understand the universe to be so very old. I have described them in detail here mainly in order to explain that they are *not* what I am advocating in this book.

Instead, I will set out to describe the *social cosmos*, claiming that the universe should be recognised as the setting for the development of consciousness and relationships. Its most complex and remarkable features known to us are the lives of human beings, and the ways in which we can be drawn into loving relationships with each other and with God. The universe is a purposeful, life-giving environment, shaped as a space within which intelligent, conscious beings can evolve. It is a social environment, within which we can learn to build loving relationships and to develop civilised communities. It is a beautiful environment, attracting us to each other and kindling our sense of spirituality and wonder. It is shaped by the love of God, who seeks to enable people to flourish in relationships with each other and with him.

The hierarchical picture of the cosmos has a place for the supreme emperor, and the mechanical picture of the cosmos has a place for the great watchmaker. But a social picture of the cosmos connects with an image of God which is much more authentically Christian than either: the understanding of God as Trinity. In genuinely Christian theology, God is not simply a great monarch ruling alone, or a self-contained isolated genius. Instead, the very nature of God involves the dynamism of being three interacting persons, a network of loving relationships. God is a unity, but God exists as the three equal persons of the Father, the Son and Holy Spirit, in relationship with each other. And the love of these three persons overflows into the creation of a universe, through which new conscious beings arise and can be drawn into this divine network of love.

Much of the best theology of the last hundred years has been rediscovering the significance of the Trinity. Protestant theologians Karl

Barth (1886–1968) and Jürgen Moltmann (born 1926), Catholic theologian Karl Rahner (1904–1984), and Orthodox theologian John Zizioulas (born 1931) are eminent and varied examples of those who have worked in this field. Much recent Trinitarian theology has rediscovered a social theme, exploring ideas of love, vulnerability, otherness and mutuality more deeply than might be expected from the hierarchical and mechanical images of the cosmos. The approach emphasises the importance of freely chosen and equal relationships, rather than the imposition of absolute power from on high or the inexorable turning of wheels. Feminist theologian Elizabeth A. Johnson describes a social understanding of the Trinity as a 'profound critique... of patriarchal domination in church and society.' She writes:

> The Trinity as pure relationality, moreover, epitomises the connectedness of all that exists in the universe. Relation encompasses and constitutes the web of reality and, when rightly ordered, forms the matrix for the flourishing of all creatures, both human beings and the earth.[17]

That is the view of God which I will explore in this book. Above all, I am suggesting that good theology gives us a way of talking about the whole shape of reality and about every area of human experience, and provides a way of inspiring us to seek the good of all. It does not simply describe an exalted emperor or a long-departed engineer, and it should no longer be seen as a mandate for the imposition of power. We can rediscover both of the aspects of the Renaissance view of God and people which I described at the start: firstly, that all of our experiences have something to tell us about reality and, secondly, that theology can offer a framework for understanding all of those experiences and nurturing all that is good. Since the collapse of our traditional hierarchies, and since the development of the mechanical view of the cosmos, language about God has often sounded as if it were referring to a solitary and rather implausible entity in the far distance, detached from our ordinary view of the world. Instead, I am suggesting that a belief in a

---

17   Elizabeth A Johnson (1992) *She Who Is: The Mystery of God in Feminist Theological Discourse* The Crossroad Publishing Company, p. 222–3

God offers the best way of talking about everything: the whole universe and all of our different experiences of it.

The remaining six chapters of this book will therefore go on a wide-ranging tour of human knowledge and experience. In Chapter Two, I will discuss the beauty of nature, its impact on scientists and poets, and its spiritual significance. In Chapter Three, I will show how the scientific structures of the universe can be understood within a belief in the faithfulness and creativity of God, rather than as features of an impersonal machine. In Chapter Four, I will discuss evolution and show how both theology and science give a much more dynamic and developing account of the universe than the two static pictures of the hierarchy and the machine. I will also say more about the ways in which science suggests that human beings do have a significant place in the cosmos. In Chapter Five, I will therefore discuss our experiences of the meaningfulness of life. Then, in Chapter Six, I will describe how genuine freedom allows the existence of evil as well as goodness, and show how Jesus overcame evil with love. Finally, Chapter Seven will draw both on the teachings of Jesus and on our discoveries about the history of the cosmos in order to discuss the future of the universe and the possibility of a life with God and each other that goes beyond death.

SUGGESTIONS FOR FURTHER READING

Alister McGrath's *The Re-enchantment of Nature* (Hodder & Stoughton, 2002) explores various relevant themes, including a useful chapter on the mechanical view of the universe.

There is remarkably little which explores well the consequences of quantum physics for Christian theology. The chapter on *Theology and the New Physics* by Laurence Osborn in *God, Humanity and the Cosmos* edited by Christopher Southgate (T & T Clark, 2011) is a good place to start. Explorations of possible parallels with eastern mysticism, notably Fritjof Capra's *Tao of Physics* (Wildwood House, 1975) have so far received much more attention.

As I have said, much modern theology has been exploring the significance of the doctrine of the Trinity. Jürgen Moltmann's *The Trinity and the Kingdom of God* (SCM, 2000) is very relevant to the themes I am presenting here.

My favourite book exploring our sense of wonder is *This Sunrise of Wonder* by Michael Mayne (Darton, Longman and Todd, 2008).

Chapter Two
The Beauty of the Universe

INTRODUCTION

Our beautiful cosmos is alive with forces of attraction at all levels. It is not an inert and solid mass, nor a dull scattering of objects drifting away from each other, but it is a complex dance of orbits, interactions and relationships. The fundamental forces of nature set electrons spinning around atomic nuclei, and draw planets and comets along slow ellipses around suns. The stars themselves tug at each other across the light years of space, with forces of gravity that embrace their distant companions in the spiralling arms of unimaginably vast galaxies.

Simple mathematical equations can describe the effects of the laws of physics on inanimate objects, but people feel additional forces on our hearts and minds which go beyond any measurements. Among the most complex phenomena in the cosmos are the relationships and communities formed by living creatures, drawn together by beauty and by empathy and by love. Yet, it is not just other people who attract us. The universe around us also tugs on our hearts, and the beauty of nature is a source of great awe and delight for human beings. It has a central place in the spirituality of many people, who believe that it offers a glimpse of the divine. Christians sing hymns of praise to the Creator of all, decorating elegant churches with freshly gathered flowers. Nature moves the hearts of human beings, including poets, scientists and the many who seek to draw close to God in worship. As I shall describe in this chapter, the Theology of Everything indicates that the beauty we find around us is far more significant than many people now acknowledge.

THE REALITY OF BEAUTY

Every year, about six million visitors go to see Leonardo's *Mona Lisa*. The painting is one of the great artistic treasures of the Italian Renaissance, an icon of a cultural movement which is famous for its works of great beauty. Half a millennium later, Michelangelo's sculptures, Raphael's paintings and Brunelleschi's feats of architecture and engineering still amaze the crowds who come from far away to see them. And the sumptuous choral music of Palestrina is heard all over the world.

Many people today regard our perceptions of beauty simply as an arbitrary set of human responses, but the people of the Renaissance clearly believed that their search for beauty was connecting with an important part of reality itself. They learned all they could from the architecture, art and poetry of the ancient Greeks and Romans, and then added their own creative refinements and joyful embellishments to the developing traditions of western art. In doing so, they felt that they were bringing something very important to light. Following Plato, they regarded beauty as something transcendent and spiritual. They saw it as an ideal which was worth pursuing for its own sake, something greater than us which was good for the human soul.

Because of the mechanical view of the cosmos, our society today is a lot less confident and clear in its thinking about the significance of beauty. As a result, it is hard to imagine the people of the future flocking to see our buildings and our paintings in the way we seek out the dazzling works of the Renaissance. But, although we are less sure about how to talk about beauty together, the pursuit of it still occupies a high proportion of our individual thoughts. The spiritual ideal of beauty lacks the public prominence it had in Renaissance thought, but it is still something which affects us deeply.

Most obviously, the attractiveness of human beings is something that fascinates us and draws us together. Sexual desire is a dominant theme in our songs and our stories, provoking much of the joy, excitement, tragedy and drama of human life. But beauty also comes in many other forms, and together they all provide much of what we find fascinating and meaningful in life. Those who hike up high mountains to admire the view from the top are seeking an encounter with beauty, even if they might not say so in such terms. The same is true of someone who carefully chooses paints, carpets and furnishings to decorate a house, or who kneels in the damp soil to plant a bed of colourful flowers. Others might practise the violin or collect recordings of their favourite singers. Then there are those who enjoy photographing puffins nesting on cliffs high above the sea, or who stand outside on cold dark nights looking at the stars through a telescope. Others might enjoy gazing at the rippling reflections on a lake while fishing, or might take great delight in walking through piles of crisp golden leaves in an autumn forest. A visitor who looks up at the richly decorated vastness of a medieval cathedral is obviously encountering beauty, but so also is someone who takes great care in cleaning and waxing the paintwork of a car. Poets seek the beauty of language, with vivid metaphors and rhythmic words. And beauty is also sought by someone who serves lovingly-prepared food at a table covered with clean linen and decorated with freshly cut flowers.

In these and many other ways, beauty is very important in people's lives. We are attracted to each other's smiles, bodies and words of friendship. We whistle tunes, sing songs and listen to symphonies, finding that music expresses things that we would struggle to say in words alone. And most people have some kind of a love for nature. Even those who could not imagine living away from the excitement and prosperity of cities still tend to crave contact with natural landscapes. The most pleasant areas of cities have parks, tree-lined avenues, gardens, allotments and window-boxes. People feed birds and look after pets. And, when we can get away, we often seek out holidays on mountains and beaches, longing to be refreshed by an encounter with the beauty of nature.

I believe that the philosophers of ancient Greece and of the Renaissance had grasped something important when they understood beauty to be transcendent. They saw it as something which exists even above and beyond us, a true aspect of reality which rewards our attention and elevates our souls. It is something which is worth pursuing for its own sake, a quality which delights our spirits, enhances our lives and leads us closer to the truth about our existence. Beauty is an aspect of reality, a real and important part of the universe around us, and we are greatly privileged to be able to notice it. It is an invitation to look beyond ourselves and to make connections with other people, with nature, and with God. And among the greatest and most meaningful delights of human life is our ability to uncover further elements of the universe's potential for beauty in our own creativity. We have the joy of exploring that potential and enriching each other's lives through pursuits as varied as art, gardening, music, poetry, cookery and architecture.

Beauty has an important place within this Theology of Everything, which suggests that this social cosmos exists to enable interaction and love. The universe's potential for beauty exists as an invitation for us to draw close to each other, and to the divine artist who is the source of all beauty. Christian spirituality therefore has always perceived something of the glory of God through the magnificence and wonder of nature. As poet and priest Gerard Manley Hopkins wrote,

> The world is charged with the grandeur of God.
> It will flame out, like shining from shook foil.[18]

In the Bible, God is described both as the creator of the cosmos and as one who is intimately involved in all of its processes. Psalm 65 says:

> By your strength you established the mountains;
> you are girded with might...
> Those who live at earth's farthest bounds
> are awed by your signs;
> you make the gateways of the morning
> and the evening shout for joy.
> You visit the earth and water it, you greatly enrich it;
> the river of God is full of water;
> you provide the people with grain,
> for so you have prepared it.

As a result, the whole of creation is inspired to respond with music of thankfulness and celebration. Psalm 98 says:

> With trumpets and the sound of the horn
> make a joyful noise before the King, the Lord.
> Let the sea roar, and all that fills it;

18   From a poem entitled *God's Grandeur*

the world and those who live in it.
Let the floods clap their hands;
let the hills sing together for joy at the presence of the Lord.

Human beings have the privilege of being invited into this joyful relationship of adoration and thanksgiving. Large sections of the Old Testament therefore describe the construction of places of worship of fabulous beauty, beginning with a portable tabernacle in the desert and culminating in the great Temple in Jerusalem. Exodus 25 describes God prompting the hearts of the people so that they bring an offering of 'gold, silver, and bronze, blue, purple, and crimson yarns and fine linen, goats' hair, tanned rams' skins, fine leather, acacia wood, oil for the lamps, spices for the anointing oil and for the fragrant incense, onyx stones and gems'. These are used in the construction of the tabernacle, its furnishings and its ceremonial robes of great beauty. 2 Chronicles 5 describes 120 priests playing trumpets at the dedication of the ornately-decorated Temple, accompanied by a choir arrayed in fine linen, with cymbals, harps and lyres.

As I shall discuss later, the Bible emphasises that God is greater than his creation and beyond anything that we might make with our own hands. But it also repeatedly shows how people perceive God through the beauty of creation and make use of that beauty when they relate to him in worship. This is an experience widely shared by Jews, Christians and many others across the millennia.

One of the world's most popular hymns, which began as a Swedish poem and has been translated and adapted across various languages, describes an experience which is recognised by many millions:

> When through the woods and forest glades I wander
> And hear the birds sing sweetly in the trees;
> When I look down from lofty mountain grandeur
> And hear the brook and feel the gentle breeze:
> Then sings my soul, my Saviour God, to Thee;
> How great Thou art, how great Thou art![19]

---

19   Written by Stuart K. Hine in 1949, descending via Russian and German versions from the original Swedish poem written by Carl Gustav Boberg in 1885

This Theology of Everything therefore suggests that the beauty of nature should be taken seriously as an important aspect of reality. It is part of the way that God relates to human beings, and human beings respond to him. Sadly, the mechanical view of the cosmos lacks a sense of the significance of relationships, and has greatly hindered our ability to appreciate the importance of beauty.

BEAUTY AND THE EYE OF THE BEHOLDER

One of the most famous critics of the mechanised view of reality was C S Lewis (1898–1963). He is well-known for his popular books about Christianity, and for his *Narnia* series of children's novels which have delighted millions with their vivid accounts of a magical world overflowing with life and beauty and meaning. Lewis was a Fellow in English Literature in Oxford University, and then Professor of Mediaeval and Renaissance Literature in Cambridge. His immersion in the thought of the Middle Ages and the Renaissance helped him to see the importance of a view of reality in which beauty and goodness are as real and important as atoms and forces.

In a fascinating little book called *The Abolition of Man*, Lewis criticises the philosophy implicit in a school English textbook of his time. The textbook describes two tourists discussing the beauty of a waterfall, and makes this claim: 'When the man said *This is sublime,* he appeared to be making a remark about the waterfall. Actually he was not making a remark about the waterfall, but a remark about his own feelings.'[20] The textbook assumes that language about beauty is simply language about our own idiosyncratic preferences and emotions, rather than language which expresses a connection with something real. But for Lewis, it is a key part of being human that we should learn to perceive beauty and goodness, and to recognise that they are genuine aspects of reality which call for our attention. Without that perception, he suggests that we do great damage to ourselves, abolishing our own humanity. Lewis notes how his approach is in accordance with Greek philosophy, Christianity, Hinduism, Taoism and other beliefs. He writes:

20   C. S. Lewis (2002) 'The Abolition of Man' in *Selected Books* Harper Collins, p. 199

> What is common to them all is something we cannot neglect. It
> is the doctrine of objective value, the belief that certain attitudes
> are really true, and others really false, to the kind of thing the
> universe is and the kind of things we are. Those who know
> the *Tao* can hold that to call children delightful or old men
> venerable is not simply to record a psychological fact about our
> own parental or filial emotions at the moment, but to recognise
> a quality which *demands* a certain response from us whether we
> make it or not.[21]

From Lewis's perspective, our values and perceptions of beauty
are attempts to engage with something which is just as real as the
laws of physics. But the modern world has widely come to agree
with the textbook he criticises, and to say that 'beauty is in the eye
of the beholder'. As a result, beauty is something we may be rather
unsure about, or which we may disagree with other people about. On
the one hand, there are some people who will have no hesitation in
stressing the importance of beauty in human life and society. They will
enthusiastically agree that music, poetry and art are among the most
meaningful human endeavours, and that gardening, cooking, wine
tasting and walking in the countryside are all examples of the kinds
of things that actually make life worth living. They will then affirm
that this experience of life tells us something important about reality.
On the other hand, there are others who may be very surprised that
I have put beauty near the beginning of a book which is supposed to
be about everything. It is not that they do not appreciate music and
poetry, just that they assume that their enjoyment is a matter of arbitrary individual preference. They may see it as an enjoyable quirk or
a fortunate accident, rather than as a significant aspect of the truth
about the universe.

That second group is influenced by the philosophy of the mechanical cosmos, and the ideas expressed in the textbook which Lewis
criticises. They would agree with the words of David Hume, a philosopher of the 18th century Enlightenment, who said that 'beauty is
no quality in things themselves: it exists merely in the mind which

21   C. S. Lewis (2002) 'The Abolition of Man' in *Selected Books* Harper Collins, p. 405

contemplates them.'[22] It is a very widespread view, and one which has done much to influence modern society. Our life together now proceeds mostly on the assumption that beauty is something purely subjective which we may wish to pursue as individuals and as consumers, rather than as something real and objective which we should all cherish together. Democratically elected governments are usually expected to pursue measurable economic goals rather than aesthetics, only rarely giving their attention to national parks or art galleries. We expect our politicians to help us to become richer so that we can then individually spend our money on our own private choices of gardens, holidays, romantic dinners and music collections. We do not expect political parties to issue manifesto commitments to the task of making our life together more beautiful.

If Hume's approach is correct, then it means that our statements about beauty are just ways of declaring our own arbitrary tastes, and they do not give an account of a property of an object in itself. So if I tell you that a mountain is majestic, or a cottage is welcoming, or a symphony is moving, or that the Milky Way is glorious, then I am just telling you about my own tastes in landscapes, buildings, music and galaxies. I am describing my own emotional responses rather than anything which could be claimed to be objectively true about those things. I may have feelings of wonder when watching the sun set or feelings of delight when listening to Mozart, but those are phenomena which are localised in my own brain. Others, the theory goes, might think and feel something completely different, and their opinion would be just as valid. And so the judgement that flowerbeds are more beautiful than concrete slabs is, many would say, just some preference which many human beings happen to have.

To me, this emphasis on individualism is another example of the kind of habitual fragmentation which misses the full wonder of the cosmos. I want to suggest that beauty is a genuine aspect of reality, something which is important and objective and which we are meant to notice. Indeed, I think that we will not understand the whole truth about reality unless we pay attention to its beauty. I cannot prove this

22   D. Hume, 'Of the Standard of Taste', in *Essays Moral, Political and Literary*, I.XXIII.8

assertion by breaking beauty into measurable parts, because I think that the beauty of the cosmos is something which is greater than any ingredients we can master. It is something beyond us which commands our attention, something which we are very privileged to be able to perceive.

But many would disagree with me. Alongside those who see words about beauty simply as arbitrary individual preferences, there are many who see our aesthetic judgements as arbitrary social constructs. They point out that different views of beauty are found in different societies and in different times. Fashions change from year to year, and traditions of art and music differ greatly between different cultures. And the computer-enhanced photographs of today's undernourished models are not the same as the more voluptuous ideals of beauty shown, for example, in Renaissance paintings.

This is a significant argument, but I think it is much weaker than it first seems. I agree that tastes in beauty and judgements about aesthetics may vary from person to person and from time to time. But rare is the person from any time or place who would genuinely prefer a view of rusting iron girders to a panorama of hillsides, oak trees and daffodils. Of course, it is true that fashions may shift from year to year, but that has more to do with our continual exploration of beauty and the playful ways in which each new style responds to its predecessors. And, while there may be aspects of the art of other cultures which we do not fully understand, there are usually good things we could learn to appreciate if we tried.

Styles, preferences and visual languages may indeed vary from place to place and age to age, but the great art galleries, museums, palaces, cathedrals, concert halls and theatres of the world attract crowds of visitors from all around the globe. Japanese visitors to London have no difficulty in appreciating Westminster Abbey, just as Canadian tourists can marvel at the Angkor Wat temple in Cambodia. People from all cultures can identify great beauty when they see it. Despite their many different beliefs, these people all recognise at least a glimpse of something wonderful which demands their attention, something which inspires and refreshes. The greatest music can captivate us and startle us, seeming to transport our consciousness to another realm. The writings of Shakespeare, the architecture of the Taj Mahal, the music of Bach and the paintings of Botticelli all have a greatness which seems to transcend time and culture, and to point to something universal and captivating. They point to something which is part of the fabric of reality.

It is a great joy that human creativity often taps into this powerful aspect of reality. In architecture, design, art, literature, fashion, drama and music, human beings can make use of the universe's potential for beauty. Just as an engineer might make use of mechanical forces or electrical energy, so an artist, poet or musician may draw on the presence of beauty. Leonardo, of course, knew how to do both. Beauty is something which we are privileged to be able to perceive and to express. It is something wonderful which is just as real as any energy that could be quantified by a physicist. And it is something sophisticated and complex which is far greater than the sum of any measurable ingredients.

Human history has produced many examples of the wonders that can be produced when people share a vision of beauty as a transcendent reality, something which goes far beyond individual whims. That kind of shared vision has often been especially strong when it has a religious basis, as found in the Renaissance, and as seen in many of the great classics of European architecture, music and art. Around the world, it is usually the case that churches, mosques, shrines and temples are prominent amongst our most admired buildings. Religious doctrines may vary considerably, but it usually the case that spirituality is associated with some kind of encounter with beauty. Churches have often been great patrons of the arts, as they were in the Renaissance, funding the work of Leonardo, Michelangelo and many others. Religious people cherish the experience of wonder and the awareness of transcendence that can be gained when we are in the presence of sights and sounds which captivate us. Soaring architecture, stained glass, gentle candlelight, elegant calligraphy, colourful mosaics, embroidered robes, peaceful chanting, rousing hymns, jubilant dancing, fragrant incense and much-loved poetry are all ingredients in the religious enjoyment of the ways that beauty can elevate the human soul. And individual

religious traditions have often developed their creativity and appreciation of beauty to an astonishingly high degree. Those who do not share
a particular faith are often still filled with awe by its artistic excellence.

However, in a diverse society which lacks a shared religious vision,
the process of learning to value beauty together is far less straightforward. But I still think that the appreciation of beauty is a skill which can
be developed together, just like the understanding of mathematics or
science. It involves a gradual process of gaining insights into an aspect
of reality. Good taste is something which we can learn from people
who appreciate beauty more deeply.

It is unfortunate that many people today would avoid this task by
politely insisting that tastes vary and that anyone's opinion of beauty
is just as true and valid as anyone else's. This politeness sounds very
democratic, egalitarian and inclusive, and it avoids a few arguments,
but it abandons the shared pursuit of something important. It leads to a
dumbing down of our shared understanding of aesthetics. And it leads
our society as a whole to see the more sophisticated forms of beauty as
being frivolous luxuries, expressions of snobbery or relics of the past.

It is, sadly, difficult to imagine today's cities investing the time,
money and creativity necessary to produce something as wondrous as
a medieval cathedral. When we cannot agree to value beauty together,
then the unifying project that we tend to fall back on is the shared
quest for financial efficiency. This has often been disastrous for modern
architecture, which has blighted many cities with intelligently designed,
efficient, economical buildings that are depressingly hideous or devoid
of all character. The modernist architects who stacked up logical, prac-
tical concrete boxes held a mechanical view of the cosmos, and did not
understand the needs of our souls. We are not cogs in a giant machine.
We flourish more in homes and offices which have elegant proportions
and creatively designed characters, surrounded by gardens and trees.
We are inspired to live life to the full much more by beauty than by
utility and efficiency.

Sadly, without any shared pursuit of high ideals in aesthetics, our
visual environment tends to be left to those who are trying to sell us
their products. Pictures and video clips surround us in our multimedia

world. But the commercial pressure is always to mass-produce imagery which can appeal instantly to as many people as possible. In the absence of a shared and patient exploration of the highest forms of beauty, our world becomes saturated with visual stimuli produced by advertisers who are simply hoping to grab the crowd's attention for a second or two.

We have therefore ended up in a very strange situation. As individual consumers, many people are happy to spend a significant proportion of any surplus income on visits to beaches, mountains or historic buildings, or on improving the appearances of their own homes. We are confident in engaging in financial transactions which involve buying and selling experiences of beauty. But we struggle to take seriously the idea that beauty is some kind of public good, an aspect of the flourishing of human society which we could meaningfully discuss together. Today's civilisation often fails to notice the real transcendent significance of the beauty of creation, while frequently defacing the world with mass-produced ugliness.

SCIENCE AND THE BEAUTY OF NATURE

Despite our inability to talk about the importance of beauty, it is not difficult to find widespread and varied examples of its impact. There are some fascinating common factors which can be found in many of the most profound and life-changing experiences of a wide variety of people. When poets, scientists and priests talk about why they do what they do, they will often mention that they have been greatly inspired in some way by a sense of wonder at the beauty of nature. They will describe that inspiration in very different terms, and they may greatly misunderstand each other's words. But here is something vitally important about the human experience of life which is shared among people with a vast range of different beliefs. Environmentalist Michael McCarthy writes:

> There can be occasions when we suddenly and involuntarily
> find ourselves loving the natural world with a startling
> intensity, in a burst of emotion which we may not fully

understand, and the only word that seems to me to be
appropriate for this feeling is *joy*.[23]

And a response of wonder at the beauty of nature is widely reported
by atheist scientists. Richard Dawkins writes:

> The feeling of awed wonder that science can give us is one of
> the highest experiences of which the human psyche is capable.
> It is a deep aesthetic passion to rank with the finest that music
> and poetry can deliver. It is truly one of the things which make
> life worth living.[24]

Although many others find science intimidating and even ugly, scientists themselves are usually exploring an experience of wonder which
would be widely recognised and cherished by non-scientists. They
do what they do because they find it beautiful. They uncover hidden
marvels using telescopes and microscopes, and they find an inspiring
elegance in the symmetries and harmonies of the equations of physics.

It is easy for all of us to appreciate photographs of galaxies or to
enjoy documentaries about tropical fish, and to recognise that astronomers and zoologists are studying something beautiful. It is perhaps
harder for many people to appreciate that mathematicians and theoretical physicists are having a similar experience, but that is exactly how
they describe it. A page of algebraic symbols and squiggles may seem
incomprehensibly ugly to many, but those who understand this mathematical language find that it is the gateway to a world of delights. What
fascinates me most is the way that people studying the fundamental
equations of physics often describe their work as the pursuit of beauty.

Paul Dirac (1902–1984) was a Nobel Prize-winner whose achievements included predicting the existence of antimatter. He wrote: 'It
seems to be one of the fundamental features of nature that fundamental
physical laws are described in terms of a mathematical theory of great
beauty.'[25] Remarkably, he insisted that experience had shown him that

---

23 Michael McCarthy (2015) *The Moth Snowstorm: Nature and Joy* John Murray, p. 32
24 R Dawkins (1998) *Unweaving the Rainbow* Penguin, p. xii
25 P A M Dirac (1963) 'The Evolution of the Physicist's Picture of Nature'
    in *Scientific American*, volume 209 number 5, p. 45–53

'it is more important to have beauty in one's equations than to have them fit experiment.' Experimental data can be wrongly analysed, he suggested, but finding beauty tends to be a stronger sign of being on the right path. Another Nobel Prize-winning physicist, Frank Wilczek, has recently written a book posing the question 'Is the world a work of art?' He writes this about the equations which describe electromagnetism:

> Beauty as an experience: The Maxwell equations can be written pictorially, in terms of flows. When so presented, they depict a sort of dance. I often visualise them in that way, as a dance of concepts through space and time, which is a joy. Even at first sight the Maxwell equations give an impression of beauty and balance. Like the impact of more conventional works of art, that impression is easier to experience than to explain. Paradoxically, there's a word to describe beauty that can't be described in words – 'ineffable.' Having experienced the ineffable beauty of Maxwell's equations, one would be disappointed if they were wrong. As Einstein said in a similar context, when asked whether his general theory of relativity might be proved wrong, 'Then I would feel sorry for the good Lord.'[26]

Science does not officially analyse beauty, but scientists themselves are frequently motivated by the beauty that they find in nature at all scales, from the sub-atomic to the galactic. And this discovery of beauty in realms far beyond normal human experience fascinates me. We human beings evolved our brains when we were hunters using primitive tools. It is not surprising that we might have developed the sense of curiosity which would lead us to explore a bit more of the forest, or the visual ability to recognise different kinds of fruits. But why did we evolve the ability to appreciate forms of beauty that would not be discovered until people started using telescopes and microscopes thousands of years later? Why did primitive human beings develop the capacity that we can now use to enjoy the vast spiral arms of the Andromeda Galaxy, or the microscopic intricacies of living cells, or the equations of electromagnetism? And why is the universe so beautiful in this way at all of those levels?

26   Frank Wilczek (2015) *A Beautiful Question: Finding Nature's Deep Design* Allen Lane

Scientists have the amazing privilege of uncovering more and more of the beauty of the universe. And everything they find seems to me to suggest that there is something very important about that beauty in itself, and about our perception of it. Just as quantum mechanics suggests that the universe expects the involvement of observers, so the beauty of the universe at so many levels suggests that it is meant to be seen and to be enjoyed. This is, I think, the fundamental truth behind modern physics, the idea which unites all of its discoveries. The deepest truth behind all science is that the universe is life-giving and relational. It is a social environment, intended for the development of consciousness, beauty, attraction and community. It is a place of communication and love.

SPIRITUALITY AND THE VOICE OF BEAUTY

In a fascinating passage, Dawkins acknowledges the similarities between his experiences of wonder at the beauty of nature and the experiences which lead others towards a spiritual view of life. He recalls his school chaplain's moving account of the boyhood experience which later inspired him to become a priest:

> The boy lay prone in the grass, his chin resting on his hands. He suddenly found himself overwhelmed by a heightened awareness of the tangled stems and roots, a forest in microcosm, a transfigured world of ants and beetles… Suddenly the micro-forest of the turf seemed to swell and become one with the universe, and with the rapt mind of the boy contemplating it.[27]

Dawkins rejects the religious beliefs of his chaplain, but he notes the account's similarity to the kinds of childhood experiences which inspired him to explore science as an atheist. He writes:

> In another time and place, that boy could have been me under the stars, dazzled by Orion, Cassiopeia and Ursa Major, tearful with the unheard music of the Milky Way, heady with the night scents of frangipani and trumpet flowers in an African garden.[28]

27 R Dawkins (2006) *The God Delusion* Transworld Publishers, p. 31
28 R Dawkins (2006) *The God Delusion* Transworld Publishers, p. 31–32

I soon part company with Dawkins' arguments about God, but here I am fascinated by his description of his response to the beauty of the natural world. He admits that it is hard to say why the same emotion should have led his chaplain in one direction and him in the other. But he reports that 'a quasi-mystical response to nature and the universe is common among scientists and rationalists.' I am captivated by his two accounts, because they have elements in common with the experiences which developed my interest in astronomy and then, to my surprise, led me to lose my childhood faith in atheism. There is a shared experience of wonder here, part of our humanity, part of the way that we have encountered the reality we all inhabit. It is hard to analyse and impossible to quantify, but it is real.

I find it very moving to read about the life-enriching experiences which have filled Dawkins and many other scientists with wonder and curiosity about the details of the natural world. I like the way that he describes how the detailed scientific study of the world around us can be filled with a sense of beauty and wonder. I think that it enriches our shared civilisation when people talk about such life-changing encounters with the glories of nature. And so I first of all want to affirm such experiences as important insights into human life and our relationship with the cosmos.

But, while Dawkins then disappears enthusiastically into the reductionist world of cataloguing the inner workings of nature, it seems to me that there is more to be said about our encounter with the beauty of nature as a whole. To me, Dawkins' experience does provide a tremendous motivation to be a scientist, but it also points beyond the project of taking nature to pieces.

Although Dawkins and his chaplain have both felt something very similar, and it is something which many others could identify with to some degree, people differ greatly in how they interpret such experiences. In many cases, they are very unsure what to say or to think about them. The mechanical view of the cosmos has left traditional Christian teachings about creation sounding dead and hollow to many. William Bloom, a writer on New Age spirituality, describes the sense of a spiritual connection with nature which people often feel, but he notes that many of them feel no connection with traditional religious language. Some people find the concept of God meaningful, while 'for others it is provocative and describes a superstitious and naïve idea about a man in the sky who creates and decides everything'. Bloom finds that he can reach a wider audience by suggesting that 'spirituality is about connecting with the wonder and energy of nature, cosmos and existence.'[29]

I will have more to say about God and the beauty of the world, but would like first to note that Bloom's description of a sense of dynamic connection is very helpful. It seems to me that it is important for us to consider whether or not we think that some form of *communication* is taking place when the beauty of nature kindles this sense of wonder in our hearts.

In our relationships with each other, we are familiar with ways of using beauty as a form of communication. We might play music or write poetry to express our feelings to one another. Or we might dress up to go out for a dinner in celebration of a birthday. But what about those experiences of wonder at the beauty of the natural world? Are these feelings simply arbitrary aspects of our own nature, or are we in some sense *meant* to feel this way? Is the universe itself, or a divine presence which permeates it, *wanting* to give us these kinds of experiences? Does the life-changing impact which beauty can have on our consciousness tell us something about the human spirit, about our relationship with the cosmos, and about a purpose behind the universe?

A confident atheist might say that beauty has no kind of greater significance, and contains no form of communication. Our perception of beauty happens to have evolved as a delightful quirk of human nature, and we can enjoy it perfectly well without speculating about any kind of higher meaning. Others may say that it is pointless to ask these questions, because we could never be sure of the answers. It is certainly true that this discussion is going beyond the forms of knowledge which can be found by classifying insects or sequencing DNA. We will not be able to find answers by taking nature to pieces. But I think that these challenges are worth facing because of the importance of this dimension of human experience.

29 William Bloom *The Power of Modern Spirituality* Piatkus, 2011, p. 32–34

If there is an intention behind the beauty of nature, and if it is in some way an act of communication, then there is some kind of deep connection between us and the universe as a whole. That connection suggests that we find ourselves in a cosmos which contains some kind of higher purpose, a purpose which is meant to involve us. We are in a world which has the capacity to inspire us and to fascinate us, and which invites us to observe it and to enjoy it. It can elevate our souls, motivating us to develop as people who respond to its beauty in humble wonder and joyful curiosity. It calls us to venture out with compasses, microscopes and paintbrushes. If there is an intention behind the beauty of nature, then Pico della Mirandola was correct in writing about the *Dignity of Man*. It means that the human race has the spiritual capacity to respond to a noble calling which comes from the heart of all reality.

A poet who describes this experience particularly well is Wordsworth. His writing is part of the Romantic movement, which reacted against the cold logic of the Enlightenment and its clockwork view of the cosmos. Wordsworth's delight in the beauty of nature reaches its peak in a sense of a divine presence which flows through the world around him and engages with the highest faculties of his own soul. He writes:

> I have felt
> A presence that disturbs me with the joy
> Of elevated thoughts; a sense sublime
> Of something far more deeply interfused,
> Whose dwelling is the light of setting suns,
> And the round ocean, and the living air,
> And the blue sky, and in the mind of man,
> A motion and a spirit, that impels
> All thinking things, all objects of all thought,
> And rolls through all things. Therefore I am still
> A lover of the meadows and the woods,
> And mountains; and of all that we behold
> From this green earth.[30]

I love Wordsworth's poem now, but there was a time when it would have meant very little to me. My sense of wonder came alive

---

30 From *Lines Written a Few Miles above Tintern Abbey*, 1798

during my teenage years. Living in London, travelling to school by underground train, and spending much of my spare time programming our home computer, it took me a while to notice the world outside my man-made technological enclosure. However, I happened to develop an interest in astronomy, and came to spend an increasing amount of time in the garden after dark looking up at the stars. I was a very anxious person at the time, with the usual quota of teenage insecurities, and I began to find it very comforting to look at the stars and planets, to contemplate the immensity of space, and to know that all this grandeur would continue even if I messed up my life and failed in my various ambitions. It was good simply to relax in the presence of something so much greater and more enduring than me.

One night in my final year at secondary school, I was escaping my worries about my approaching exams by lying on the garden bench and looking up at the night sky. I was gazing up at the bright constellations in the vast universe and wondering what it all meant. But I then had an extraordinary, overwhelming and almost indescribable experience. My perceptions of everything shifted. I became very aware that everything around me, every blade of grass and every atom, was infinitely precious and beautiful beyond words. At the same time, I felt a clearer sense than ever of the scale of the universe: an unimaginable expanse full of so much wonder. And through all this, I felt a sudden awareness of a purposeful, loving intelligence present all around me, an energy which made the stars shine and the trees grow. I could see that there was something vast and wonderful going on in and through the universe, which somehow I was meant to be part of.

Using the only concept which seemed remotely adequate, I felt to my surprise that I had encountered God. But God was not the angry bearded gentleman I had pictured from the tedious Religious Education lessons at school. I felt deeply grateful for simply existing and being able to have such an experience. I cried tears of sorrow for the years of arrogance and moodiness in which I had never noticed the glories which surrounded me. I was filled with new feelings of thankfulness, delight and awe-struck amazement.

As a newly-lapsed atheist and a very shy teenage boy, I was far too embarrassed to talk to anyone about this experience. It was not something I could reproduce on demand, and I was very unsure what to do about it. It did not seem to point towards any one particular religion. It was a long time before I told anyone what had happened to me. But glimpses of the same vision recurred and continued to surprise me, flowing more and more into my everyday experience. At that time, I found that I started to see colours far more vividly than ever before. I could be hurrying along deep in thought and suddenly be startled by the blue of the sky or the green of the trees. Ordinary experiences began to seem richer and more meaningful. I once spent a long time simply looking at a plate of salad, captivated by the intricate structure of each lettuce leaf, then eating it slowly and savouring every crisp texture and every burst of flavour.

But in and through all this was a sense that someone was trying to tell me something, a sense that I was being gently but insistently tugged in a new direction. My sense of wonder at the natural world continued to grow and inspired my studies of science. But, above all, I also knew that my life needed somehow to be in harmony with this universal divine presence which I had sensed. And I slowly began to find it increasingly meaningful and rewarding to look for ways of expressing my gratitude for all that I had been given. It began to mean much more to me to look for ways to enrich the lives of others rather than simply worrying about myself.

Those were, for me, a private set of very intense experiences. But the history of human beliefs and cultures, although very varied, seems to suggest that such experiences have been widespread and powerful. Many civilisations, in widely separated times and places, have developed a sense that the cosmos is somehow sacred, and is closely connected with divinity. In many different ways, people have adopted an attitude of reverence towards nature, believing that the relationship between us and the world is important. They have emphasised the importance of attentiveness to nature, believing that the universe has significant things to tell us.

Hindus, for example, see the whole realm of nature as a set of manifestations of divinity. They may worship in sacred mountains and rivers, or seek to treat living creatures with reverence. Similarly, the spirituality of Native American tribes emphasises their relationship to the land, with a strong sense of the sacredness of the earth. But even atheists and sceptical agnostics may still find themselves resorting to language which suggests a spiritual experience of revelation. The astronomer Carl Sagan, for example, said: 'The sky calls to us. If we do not destroy ourselves, we will one day venture to the stars.'[31] An extraordinary range of people have felt that the universe was offering them some kind of invitation or message, a call to explore their place within it. Throughout history, human beings have responded to the beauty of the cosmos with a profound sense of wonder. To many, the cosmos itself almost seems to have a voice, an insistent and joyful declaration that somehow works without audible words.

Three millennia ago, the Jewish writer of Psalm 19 sang these words about the beauty of the starry skies:

> The heavens are telling the glory of God;
> and the firmament proclaims his handiwork.
> Day to day pours forth speech,
> and night to night declares knowledge.
> There is no speech, nor are there words;
> their voice is not heard;
> yet their voice goes out through all the earth,
> and their words to the end of the world.

The Theology of Everything can help us explore our awareness that there is something real and important going on in our encounters with beauty. When an astronomer suggests that the stars are calling us to explore them, or a hiker finds that the view from a mountaintop puts her anxieties into perspective, or a visitor to a great cathedral feels inspired to be more patient with his irritating colleague, something important is happening. There is an act of wordless communication which has an effect on us. It is not something which we have ever been

---

31 From the beginning of part 7 of his TV series *Cosmos*, 1980

able to quantify or take to pieces or measure in a laboratory. The beauty of nature has a significance which comes from being far greater than the sum of its atomic ingredients, which sadly means that we have found it harder to talk about in a scientific age.

I believe that beauty is an important aspect of the whole nature of reality. And I regard the beauty of the cosmos, and of every leaf and every galaxy, as a glimpse of the glory of God, a revelation of the divine energy which sustains every moment of the universe's existence. Above all, I would suggest that the beauty of nature is a form of communication. It is an invitation to a relationship of love. People who take care over their appearance and seek to look attractive do so because they want others to notice them and to respond to them. An artist who paints a picture wants it to have an effect on other people. A composer who writes a symphony feels emotions which he knows he can evoke in others through his music. They are all seeking to communicate and they are all seeking a response. The fact that our universe is charged with so much beauty, from snowflakes to galaxies is, I believe, a channel of communication. It is a sign of love from one who longs for us to know him, and to flourish in living lives of wisdom and love. Beauty, like all the aspects of reality I shall describe, exists because the universe is intended to be the setting for relationships among its inhabitants, and relationships between them and God.

But this revelation is not overwhelming and it is not unavoidable. It is far from being so loud and so insistent that we cannot ignore it. We have been given space to be ourselves, to make our own choices. Beauty is only an invitation, a set of clues which we may choose to follow in our own way if we wish. If we do respond, then we may come to regard it as an invitation to a freely chosen relationship of love.

The beauty of the universe has inspired in me, as in many others, a feeling of deep gratitude as well as wonder. That invitation to a relationship calls forth in us a response which is relational, a joyful sense of thankfulness for what we have been given. It brings the feeling that there is one to whom we can express our thanks, to whom we can respond in wonder and adoration. Such a response does not imply that God is an insecure tyrant who wants us to keep massaging his ego. Instead it sees God as the glory above all glory, the wonder above all wonders, the source of all that exists, the one from whom all the beauty of nature blazes. If the appropriate response to the circling planets or to the mighty waves crashing on the ancient cliffs is one of wonder and delight and awe, then this is even more true of the divine presence which we may sense through nature. It is a liberating and joyful experience to realise that life is a gift which far surpasses any of our own achievements, and to explore the meaning of that gift by responding in love and thanksgiving.

GOD AND NATURE IN CHRISTIAN SPIRITUALITY

Sadly, the mechanical view of the cosmos has distorted many people's perceptions of Christian spirituality, and has left many Christians feeling unsure of how to talk about nature. A clockwork universe suggests to many atheists that beauty is simply in the eye of the beholder, without having any divine significance. The situation only partially improves when people talk about beauty as a feature of the design of the cosmic machine. Their acknowledgement of the reality of beauty is a step forward, but it still resembles the way that people admire the paintings of a dead artist, rather than sounding like a present encounter with God. However, I am suggesting that both views are incomplete. Beauty is not just about the individual opinions of a sight-seer, and nor is it just a fixed quality of excellence in things in themselves. It is something dynamic and relational, involving both sides. It is interactive and engaging, an act of communication which evokes a response. God speaks to us in the present through the beauty of the world.

In a mechanical view of the cosmos, the response of a religious person to the beauty of nature is an appreciation of the skill shown by the Great Architect when constructing it long ago. But this admiration may be tempered when a sceptic points out various areas of ugliness in creation. There was a famous difference of opinion between the philosophers Leibnitz and Voltaire in the 18th century, after Leibnitz foolishly declared that this was the 'best of all possible worlds'. Voltaire responded with angry satire in his 1759 novel Candide, drawing attention to earthquakes, wars, sickness and cruelty.

But I am not suggesting that the world is a finished work of perfection. Beauty is a voice through which God seeks to inspire us to live with wonder and compassion. It is part of the way in which God calls his unfinished creation to grow towards what it is meant to become. It is a dynamic part of the relationships of love which can grow to connect individuals, the world and God. In chapters four to seven, I shall discuss ways in which both science and theology can give insights into the cosmos as something that has been developing and is still developing, rather than as something allegedly perfect. And there will be much to say in those chapters about the dramatic stories of goodness, evil, reconciliation and love.

Good theology can value the beauty of the world as part of the way in which God draws us into loving relationships and inspires us to live with compassion and wisdom. However, the distorting effects of the mechanical idea of the cosmos mean that many people now notice little of beauty in the Christian view of God as creator. And they often blame Christianity for contributing to the modern western worldview which has objectified nature and permitted enormous damage to the environment. Many who feel a sense of spiritual encounter through nature have long since abandoned Christianity for forms of New Age or Pagan spirituality, or for their own individual and private beliefs.

Nevertheless, there have been many lively renewals of interest in forms of Christian spirituality which connect more deeply with a love for nature. Celtic Christianity is one example, celebrating the faith of the people who lived in the wild and rugged landscapes of the north-west fringes of Europe in the first millennium. The Iona Community thrives today on the isolated Scottish island where St Columba founded a monastery in 563, and has been widely influential in its work for social justice, ecumenism, and the environment. Its songs and liturgies have encouraged the renewal of Christian worship using Celtic imagery from the natural world.

Perhaps the best known example of Celtic spirituality is St Patrick's Breastplate, a prayer attributed to the 5th century patron saint of Ireland. It is a long prayer which links the Trinity and the life of

Jesus Christ to the encounter with God in nature and daily life. Four verses in the 19th century English hymn based on it are as follows:

> I bind unto myself today
> the strong Name of the Trinity,
> by invocation of the same,
> the Three in One, and One in Three.
>
> I bind unto myself today
> The virtues of the star-lit heaven,
> The glorious sun's life-giving ray,
> The whiteness of the moon at even,
> The flashing of the lightning free,
> The whirling wind's tempestuous shocks,
> The stable earth, the deep salt sea,
> Around the old eternal rocks.
>
> I bind unto myself today
> The power of God to hold and lead,
> His eye to watch, his might to stay,
> His ear to hearken to my need;
> The wisdom of my God to teach,
> His hand to guide, his shield to ward;
> The word of God to give me speech,
> His heavenly host to be my guard.
>
> Christ be with me, Christ within me,
> Christ behind me, Christ before me,
> Christ beside me, Christ to win me,
> Christ to comfort and restore me,
> Christ beneath me, Christ above me,
> Christ in quiet, Christ in danger,
> Christ in hearts of all that love me,
> Christ in mouth of friend and stranger.

Good theology has always affirmed, as Patrick did, the presence of God both alongside us and above us. It says that God is *transcendent*, meaning that he is beyond the cosmos, and also that he is *immanent*, meaning that the divine presence is all around us and is intimately close to us. God is not merely a Great Architect who laid the foundations of the universe 13.8 billion years ago, but is the one who holds it in existence, actively supporting its being and sustaining all of its processes. God is known in the sun's rays and in the deep salt sea. God is there for us to encounter in and through the beauty of the world in the present moment, and yet God is also far beyond us.

Both of these ideas are affirmed in the Bible. 2 Chronicles 2.6 describes the transcendence of God, saying that 'the highest heaven cannot contain him.' But in Acts 17.28, St Paul describes the immanence of God, affirming the insights of a poem that says 'in him we live and move and have our being.' It is an image that suggests that the universe dwells within God, who constantly supports our existence.

Aquinas wrote that 'the being of every creature depends on God, so that not for a moment could it subsist, but would fall into nothingness were it not kept in being by the operation of the Divine power.'[32] More recently, Schleiermacher (1768–1834) placed the same idea at the heart of his theological writing, contributing another insight to the Romantic movement's exploration of the emotional dimensions of human experience. Schleiermacher emphasised that the Christian idea of creation was not meant simply as a statement of an ancient event, but that it described a deeply-felt human experience in the present. We can become aware that we are frail and finite creatures whose existence moment by moment rests entirely on God's loving action in sustaining the cosmos.

Of all the creatures in the world, we human beings have the greatest capacity to understand that dependence. But we appreciate it more when we are aware of our place within nature, and when we have the humility to notice the wonder of the created world around us. The *Canticle of the Sun* by St Francis of Assisi (1181/1182–1226) rejoices in the web of relationships which make life possible, echoing the Psalms in calling upon all creation to praise God.

> Be praised, my Lord, through all your creatures,
> especially through my lord Brother Sun,
> who brings the day; and you give light through him.

---

32   Aquinas *Summa Theologiae* 1a Q104 A1

And he is beautiful and radiant in all his splendour!
Of you, Most High, he bears the likeness.

Be praised, my Lord, through Sister Moon and the stars;
in the heavens you have made them bright,
precious and beautiful.

Be praised, my Lord, through Brothers Wind and Air,
and clouds and storms, and all the weather,
through which you give your creatures sustenance.

Be praised, my Lord, through Sister Water;
she is very useful, and humble,
and precious, and pure.

Be praised, my Lord, through Brother Fire,
through whom you brighten the night.
He is beautiful and cheerful, and powerful and strong.

Be praised, my Lord, through our sister Mother Earth,
who feeds us and rules us,
and produces various fruits
with coloured flowers and herbs.

Christians have mostly been very enthusiastic about using this created beauty to enhance our present experience of wonder. The builders of the great medieval cathedrals and churches shared St Francis' belief that the dazzling radiance of the sun resembled the glory of God more than any other part of nature. And so they built flying buttresses and vast pointed archways in order to provide huge windows in their places of worship, and to flood these awesome spaces with the sunlight that came streaming through the colours of the stained glass. The artists, architects and musicians of the Renaissance continued to explore the world's potential for beauty, believing that through it they were glimpsing something of the beauty of God. Structural engineering, art and spirituality were all combined in one united and wondrous vision. And those who came to worship felt that they were experiencing something of the wonder of God through such beauty, even though the fullness of that divine presence remained far above them.

Christians have often found the philosophy of Plato very helpful in articulating the idea that God, like the sun, is experienced by us here and now and yet also remains far beyond us. We can see the world in the light of his beauty, even while still unable to stare at him directly. For Plato, the beauty and truth and goodness that we experience in this world are just faint shadows of far greater eternal forms that exist in a higher divine realm. A sixth-century Neoplatonist theologian applies this approach to God, presenting 'the Beautiful' as one of the divine names:

> Beauty 'bids' all things to itself (whence it is called 'beauty') and gathers everything into itself... It is the superabundant source in itself of the beauty of every beautiful thing... From this beauty comes the existence of everything, each being exhibiting its own way of beauty. For beauty is the cause of harmony, of sympathy, of community. Beauty unites all things and is the source of all things.[33]

This understanding of the transcendent importance of beauty helps to articulate a very widespread human experience. We, from time to time, and usually completely unexpectedly, may find ourselves completely filled with wonder by an experience of the beauty of nature, or of human love, or of some sudden new insight into the truth. Such experiences can feel more real and more important than anything else, and yet they can also seem to slip through our fingers, being impossible to reproduce on demand. But they inspire us to keep on searching, sensing that we are on a journey towards a greater beauty, a deeper love and a fuller truth than we are currently able to experience. It is a theme often found in the writings of C. S Lewis, who said:

> We do not want merely to *see* beauty, though, God knows, even that is bounty enough. We want something else which can hardly be put into words – to be united with the beauty we see, to pass into it, to receive it into ourselves, to bathe in it, to become part of it.[34]

33   Pseudo-Dionysius the Areopagite *The Divine Names* chapter 4, 701D, 704A
34   C. S. Lewis (2001) *The Weight of Glory* HarperSanFrancisco, p. 42

This spiritual longing for divine beauty is something that can easily be diverted for a while by our more primitive instincts to seek possessions and power. With regret, St Augustine prayed: 'Late have I loved you, beauty so old and so new: late have I loved you.'[35] He and many others have found that the relationships between people, God and the beauty of the world are frequently distorted by greed and arrogance. Many people, often for a long time, make the mistake of seeking to control and master the beauty of the world, dreaming in vain that great pleasure will come from the ownership of jewels or yachts or palaces. But beauty is meant to inspire deep relationships, rather than greed. And the full delight of the glory of God is far more often found through love, humility and a childlike sense of wonder than through worldly triumphs. There are people who own almost nothing who can see more beauty in one fallen leaf on a crisp autumn morning than many rich people can see in all their gilded mansions.

Nature is more than a machine to be exploited, or a treasure to be owned. Its beauty is there to call us into a relationship of love with God, with each other, and to inspire us to care for the world around us.

SPIRITUALITY AND THE ENVIRONMENT

However, we have often failed to heed that call, and our technological triumphs have helped us to occupy ourselves simply with exploiting nature. We face today, with more and more urgency, the environmental destruction caused by human beings. Our relationship with the natural world is frequently distorted by our greed, our lack of humble attentiveness to our surroundings, and our lack of wisdom. Instead of responding with gratitude, wonder and reverence towards the beauty which flows through nature, we often either fail to notice it or seek to process it into something we can own or consume. The image of creation as a giant industrial mechanism has enabled the developed world to seize tremendous power over nature, while causing great ugliness, destruction and environmental damage. Things are going badly wrong between us and nature, and this is an economic, social,

35 Saint Augustine *Confessions* X.xxiii

political and spiritual crisis which faces the human race with increasing urgency.

In recent decades, there has been a gradual dawning of awareness among Christians that our view of nature has become dysfunctional. We have more than fulfilled the command given in Genesis 1.28 to 'be fruitful and multiply and fill the earth and subdue it,' and we are now in a very different situation from the time when the woodlands and wildernesses seemed limitless. There is a growing awareness that we have new things to learn about what it means to be God's representatives when we exercise our 'dominion over the fish of the sea and over the birds of the air and over every living thing that moves upon the earth.' Wisdom and compassion are our true calling, rather than rampant irresponsibility.

There are many important measurements that I could quote about the extinction of species, the loss of forests, the depletion of soils, the pollution of oceans and the melting of glaciers. And there are some very pragmatic economic arguments which show that our current misuse of the world's resources is illogical, self-defeating and ultimately harmful to ourselves. But I think that this is not, fundamentally, a problem of measurement, logic and self-interest. It is a problem of *relationship*. We have all heard many statistics, but the deepest problem is that we do not *care* about the world enough. Our connection with nature has become exploitative and toxic. We do not love its beauty enough, or we do not talk about our love for it as something that is deeply important to our humanity. This is, fundamentally, a problem of the heart and the soul. I agree with the diagnosis of Michael McCarthy, who writes:

> It is time for a different, formal defence of nature. We should offer up not just the notion of being sensible and responsible about it, which is sustainable development, nor the notion of its mammoth utilitarian and financial value, which is ecosystem services, but a third way, something different entirely: we should offer up what it means to our spirits; the love of it. We should offer up its joy.[36]

36   Michael McCarthy (2015) *The Moth Snowstorm: Nature and Joy* John Murray, p. 29

Pope Francis, recalling St Francis of Assisi, makes a similar plea for a rediscovery of the spirituality of our relationship with nature:

> Just as happens when we fall in love with someone, whenever he would gaze at the sun, the moon or the smallest of animals, he burst into song, drawing all other creatures into his praise... His response to the world around him was so much more than intellectual appreciation or economic calculus, for to him each and every creature was a sister united to him by bonds of affection. That is why he felt called to care for all that exists... If we approach nature and the environment without this openness to awe and wonder, if we no longer speak the language of fraternity and beauty in our relationship with the world, our attitude will be that of masters, consumers, ruthless exploiters, unable to set limits on their immediate needs. By contrast, if we feel intimately united with all that exists, then sobriety and care will well up spontaneously.[37]

Nature is more than a resource to be managed pragmatically. Its beauty is a revelation of the glory of God, and it is the home within which we are invited to develop relationships of love with each other, with the world, and with God. We have an urgent economic, moral and spiritual need to pay attention to that beauty, and to fall in love with it again.

CONCLUSION

In this chapter, I have described the beauty of the natural world and the impact which it can have on human beings. Profound and life-changing experiences involving a sense of awe at the beauty, grandeur and intricacy of nature seem to be widespread. They are of great importance to people of many different beliefs. The significance of our awareness of the beauty of nature is part of the claim I introduced at the start of the book, the idea that all of our faculties have something important to tell us about reality.

The Theology of Everything describes a cosmos which is social rather than merely mechanical. It therefore affirms the great importance

---

37   Pope Francis (2015) *Laudato Si'* paragraph 11

of beauty as a glimpse of the glory of God and as an invitation to relationships of love. In the remaining chapters of this book, I shall continue to explore how theology can shed light on the connections between beauty and other aspects of reality, including the discoveries of science.

SUGGESTIONS FOR FURTHER READING

A fascinating account of the unified worldview of the Middle Ages and the Renaissance can be found in C. S. Lewis's *The Discarded Image* (Canto, 1994). And, as I have mentioned, the question of the objective reality of beauty comes into his excellent and provocative little book on *The Abolition of Man* (available in the edition of *Selected Books* published by Harper Collins in 2002). For his sense of the beauty of God glimpsed through the world, see *The Weight of Glory* (HarperSanFrancisco, 2001).

The Sixth Tractate of *The First Ennead* by Plotinus (204–270 AD) shows how the philosophy of Neoplatonism describes the transcendent reality of beauty. It is included in the Penguin Classics edition, translated by Stephen MacKenna, published in 1991.

David Bentley Hart's *The Experience of God: Being, Consciousness, Bliss* (Yale University Press, 2013) intersects with the themes of this book in various places, exploring a theological view of the transcendence of beauty on pages 277–285.

Umberto Eco's *On Beauty* (Secker and Warburg, 2004) provides a sumptuously illustrated history of the western idea of beauty.

And for more about a Christian view of beauty, I would recommend *Art and the Beauty of God* by Richard Harries (Continuum, 1993).

It is worth noting the work of Hans Urs von Balthasar (1905–1988), who structured his vast 16 volume Catholic theological epic around the transcendental qualities of beauty, goodness and truth, beginning with seven weighty books on *The Glory of the Lord*. Most people will, however, find this to be a mountain range which they only have time to admire from a distance.

Alister McGrath's *The Re-enchantment of Nature* (Hodder & Stoughton, 2002) is again relevant. And his book *The Open Secret: A New Vision for Natural Theology* (Blackwell, 2008) includes a chapter on beauty.

Chapter Three
Science and Rationality

THE POWER AND THE ISOLATION OF SCIENCE

How can the analytical findings of science fit into a view of reality which places so much emphasis on human relationships? I have talked about the beauty of the universe, which inspires scientists as much as poets. But science itself, we tend to think, deals objectively with cold, hard facts, rather than experiences of wonder. It measures voltages, tests acidities and predicts trajectories. It is rational, logical and mathematical. Non-scientists often therefore assume that science is a rather dull, soulless and potentially irresponsible endeavour. When I told my flute teacher at the age of 18 that I was going away to study physics at Cambridge, his response was to say that he hoped I was not planning to blow up the world. People often associate science with industry and technology, with factories, chimneys, power stations, nuclear missiles and global warming.

The success and power of science are undeniable. Most of us are happy to use mobile phones, the internet, microwave ovens, antibiotics, pacemakers, cars and aeroplanes. We know that there must be something undeniably, objectively, solidly real and true making all this stuff work. So we accept that science must have a genuine grasp of the truth.

The odd thing, therefore, is how few people are actually motivated to study science to a high level. Lots of people find it dull, irrelevant or intimidating at school. Many prefer subjects in the arts and humanities, like English or history or music. And few people actually look to science for answers to the questions that really matter deeply to them. Most people's real concerns are in the areas of relationships, communities, friendships, jobs, desires, ambitions, and questions about how they should live and what they should do. Science and technology are very good at coming up with the tools to enable us to eat well, stay healthy, travel quickly, email each other and build big shiny offices; but no scientist can tell us whether to get married, which jobs to apply for or who we can trust. People do not eagerly queue up outside chemistry laboratories seeking answers to their dilemmas in life.

Therefore, despite the fact that the details of our daily lives are shaped so much by technology, it is considered entirely socially acceptable to be ignorant about the science behind it. Someone who did not know how his microwave worked would be regarded as perfectly normal. However, someone who could not express an informed enthusiasm for at least one kind of music would be seen as very odd. And someone who could not talk about the characters in at least one kind of drama, whether TV soaps, science fiction novels or Shakespeare plays, might be considered cold and inhuman.

A lot of people have no misgivings about being mostly ignorant of science, giving their attention instead to experiences which seem more subjective but more important. In a world transformed by technology, science is not actually what tends to matter to most of us. But, the mechanical view of the cosmos has left us feeling very confused about the status of those things that scientists cannot measure and describe, like beauty, goodness, love, friendship, meaning and purpose. Nevertheless, even when those qualities are not accepted by society as genuine aspects of reality, they still tend to be the things that we actually care most about as individuals.

I would therefore like to suggest that the clockwork view of the universe has greatly confused our understanding of reality and truth. Most people, even when they believe that scientists have the strongest grasp of the facts about the universe, live without paying any detailed attention to science. Most people are happy to use computers while knowing little or nothing about silicon chips. And most people are happy to get on with the business of living in the universe while having only a limited understanding of its physical processes.

The chasm between the arts and the sciences is the most prominent feature of the fragmented landscape of academic life. Those studying literature, music, politics, history, languages, philosophy, religion and art can do so without any reference to science. And so there is a lot of confusion about what science is and how it relates to all the other areas of knowledge and experience.

The people of the Renaissance would be very surprised by the chasm that the mechanical view of the cosmos has opened up between science and other forms of knowledge. The history of science goes all the way back to the ancient world, and for most of that history it has been closely interwoven with the study of philosophy and theology. These overarching disciplines connected the study of nature with the whole of human thought. It was only in the 19th century, through the triumph of the clockwork view of the universe, that science developed into the confidently independent and secular enterprise which we know it as today. For most of its history, the study of nature was called natural philosophy. It was commonly seen as part of the human enquiry into the works of God, and as one aspect of the pursuit of wisdom. It was surprisingly recently that science gained its own specialised academic institutions and began to function independently from the patronage of churches. I shall describe some of that history in this chapter.

When we talk about the practice of science today, we are referring to a vast social enterprise which has taken shape since the 19th century. School chemistry lessons, Bunsen burners, university physics departments, white lab coats, PhDs, Nobel prizes, international conferences and academic journals are all products of the last century or two. Renaissance man would not recognise any of them. The term 'science', in the way we use it now, comes from the 19th century, as does the scientific profession itself.

Before the 19th century, the properties of nature were studied in the social context formed by the hierarchical view of the cosmos. In that time, the only universities were explicitly religious foundations. Natural philosophy was carried out by aristocratic amateurs, clergy and Christian scholars, or by a lucky few who had rich patrons. Theirs was a very settled intellectual system, which proclaimed that God had arranged the whole world, including all the hierarchies of human society. Wealthy land-owning gentlemen in country mansions collected and catalogued butterflies, rejoicing in the ordered structures of the world. They enjoyed the privileges of being born into the upper ranks of a hierarchical society, and they enjoyed the beauty and complexity of the natural world. All was as it was meant to be, they believed, within the fixed and divinely ordained structures of both nature and society. Butterflies were meant to be butterflies, and noblemen were meant to be noblemen.

And so they interpreted the natural world in the context of a long-established set of political and theological ideas. They understood the properties of nature within a framework which connected science to ideas about society, conscience, morality, monarchy, philosophy and spirituality. As I have said, there is much that I would want to modify about that framework, especially its lack of a sense of evolution in nature and flexibility in society, but its interconnectedness is very impressive.

However, the traditional alliance of aristocracy, religion and natural philosophy was torn apart through the social, industrial and intellectual revolutions which peaked in the 19th century. A new set of middle classes gained power and influence, whose ranks included a new group of professionals earning their living as scientists. Science, as the secular enterprise we know it as today, took shape in that context. It was a newly independent enterprise, financed through the fruits of engineering and commerce, producing the innovations which fuelled the fires of capitalism.

The new middle-class professional scientists founded new scientific institutions and fought for their independence from the old aristocratic and religious structures. They encouraged the ways in which the old hierarchical view of the cosmos was giving way to the mechanical view of the cosmos. They were proud to present science as objective, impersonal and unbiased. They were proud to proclaim that it was free from the trappings of outdated political systems and that it was liberated from the superstitions of religious dogma. They were proud to detach science from the wider set of beliefs about reality which had provided a context for natural philosophy.

This confident independence has provided a successful social context for the professionalization of science, but its isolationism has given science its confusing position in our view of reality. And our view of science is coloured by the propaganda produced by those who campaigned for its independence in the 19th century. Theirs was a determined struggle for territory, in which they were keen to show that the new institutions of science needed to be accountable only to scientists, not to any meddling ecclesiastical and aristocratic patrons. And so they retold the history of natural philosophy in order to show that scientists had been persecuted in the past and would be better off on their own. They continued the ways in which radical 18th century Enlightenment philosophers had begun to construct some of the most cherished myths of the modern world, presenting the history of science as a struggle against tyrannical religious forces of superstition and irrationality. In doing so, they distorted our view of history and confused our understanding of philosophy and religion.

I shall need to debunk some of those myths as I seek to get behind the propaganda and the power struggles of those who established the mechanical view of the cosmos and fought against the old hierarchies. I do not wish to turn back the clock to a pre-industrial age, but I do wish to gain a clearer sense for today of how science connects to the rest of our knowledge and experience. Science provides a fascinating set of insights into much of reality, but not all of it, and the clockwork view of the universe is misleadingly incomplete. History shows that the human exploration of nature has usually involved some set of beliefs which go beyond the raw data of scientific discoveries, providing a set of values, a sense of purpose and meaning, a social context, an appreciation of beauty and a sense of wonder. These are the reconnections which we urgently need to make today, and that is the story which I shall explore in this chapter.

THE ANCIENT GREEKS

The story begins with the philosophers of ancient Greece, who laid the foundations of western thought. It has been said that the whole European philosophical tradition 'consists of a series of footnotes to

Plato'.[38] Greek philosophy was all-embracing, a careful enquiry into all truth, and was in eager pursuit of the spiritual wisdom which would nurture the human soul. It spread across the separate territories claimed by today's scientists, philosophers, religious leaders, poets, politicians, geographers and many other specialists.

Plato believed that the cosmos had been formed by a divine craftsman, using principles of mathematics and geometry. He had been inspired by seeing the regular mathematical patterns of the motions of the stars and planets, and he believed that our world got its structure from a divine realm of perfect mathematical forms. Similarly, the Pythagoreans saw signs of a single unified mathematical structure in the cosmos: they found mathematical patterns in the harmonies of music and in the motions of the planets, and believed that the two were connected.

Demonstrating the power of this mathematical approach, the astronomer Ptolemy (c. 90–168 AD) measured astronomical phenomena in detail. He was able to predict the motions of the moon and the planets, even knowing when to expect the next eclipse. And from Aristotle came a detailed enquiry into the mechanics of cause and effect. Since every event is caused by a previous one, Aristotle believed in a divine 'unmoved mover', the one who sets everything else in motion.

These insights established the observation that the universe is full of regular patterns which are open to human investigation, paving the way for modern science. And they also harmonised well with the belief in one God which originated in ancient Israel. The works of the ancient Greeks have therefore been regarded with great interest by Jewish, Christian and Muslim scholars ever since. Especially relevant for Christianity was a Stoic concept called the *Logos* (meaning 'word'), which described a divine, rational principle underlying the whole cosmos, holding all of reality together. This term is mentioned at the beginning of John's Gospel, which declares that Jesus Christ is the human manifestation of this *Logos*. He is, says John, the 'word made flesh', the personal incarnation of the underlying logic of the universe.

38   Alfred North Whitehead, *Process and Reality*, Chap. I, Sect. I

The philosophy of ancient Greece therefore laid the foundations for the intellectual and spiritual life of the western world, encompassing the study of the whole of reality, and nurturing both science and theology in a united way.

FROM THE EARLY CHURCH TO THE RENAISSANCE

Building on this foundation, Christians came to think of the universe as being like a book, an important form of communication in a divine-human relationship. They saw the 'book of nature' as being parallel to the Bible, one of two volumes whose pages revealed the truth about reality. St Augustine (354–430) wrote:

> Some people read a book in order to find God. But the appearance of creation itself is a great book. Look above and below, pay attention and read. God, from whom you want to learn, did not make the letters with ink: he put before your eyes the very things he had made. What louder voice could you seek than that? The sky and the earth call to you: 'God made me.'[39]

As a result, theologians deeply valued observations of the book of nature. At the same time, from the beginning, Christianity developed habits of scholarship involving the careful reading and preservation of texts. Thoughtful study of the Bible, the Church Fathers and the philosophers continued during the first millennium, even during times of famine, invasion and persecution. Monastic communities were outposts of education, and from them grew schools and then the great universities which began to appear from the 11th century onwards. I write these words in a university which was founded in 1209 by Christian scholars. Within such universities, students would study arithmetic, geometry, astronomy, music, grammar, logic and rhetoric, and then proceed to studies in law, medicine or theology. And in the Islamic world, important work was done by Muslim scholars in fields such as mathematics and astronomy between the 8th and the 13th centuries.

The idea that the Middle Ages in Europe were times of ignorance and superstition is part of the propaganda of later centuries. There

39 *Sermones* 68,6

were major technological breakthroughs in areas such as timekeeping, navigation, sailing, the machinery of watermills and windmills, the making of spectacles, and the construction of vast bridges, castles and cathedrals. It was a time of accelerating innovation and economic growth within a society unified by its Christian faith. People of later centuries liked to think that they had invented a new approach to rationality, observation and experiment which set them apart from their stupid predecessors in the 'Dark Ages'. The reality is that we owe a lot to the intellectual vibrancy of those times, but that debt has been concealed by later propaganda.

Those who campaigned to break the power of the churches and the aristocracies in the 18th and 19th centuries had good political reasons for doing so. They had good reasons for wanting liberty, and good reasons for wanting to undermine oppressive social structures. They therefore sought to do damage to the foundations of the entire hierarchical view of the cosmos, by undermining its theological basis. They did not simply attack the political power of the churches, they sought to undermine their intellectual foundations. And so their method involved the very familiar claim that religion is something which has a history of being irrational and opposed to progress. The supporters of the mechanical view of the cosmos developed a strong tradition of propaganda which is deeply woven into our much-loved narratives about the triumphant development of modern western civilisation. Protestants, agnostics and atheists have all rejoiced in the presentation of the Catholic Church as the great archetype of stubborn ignorance and unjustified privilege. The mythology they developed about the irrationality of medieval religion continues to distort our view of the past, and our view of reality. It completely misrepresents the era which founded our first universities.

The most famous piece of propaganda about the stupidity of medieval Catholics is the much-loved story about their belief that the earth was flat. According to this story, they believed in a flat earth until Columbus bravely proved them wrong in 1492. For example, a song by George and Ira Gershwin, written for the 1937 film *Shall We Dance*, includes these lines:

They all laughed at Christopher Columbus
When he said the world was round.

And a play written by Joseph Chiari in 1979 contains this dialogue between Columbus and a hostile senior priest:

Columbus :   The earth is not flat, Father, it's round!
The Prior :   Don't say that!
Columbus :   It's the truth; it's not a mill pond
              strewn with islands, it's a sphere.
The Prior :   Don't, don't say that; it's blasphemy.

The famous idea that Columbus's voyage was opposed by ignorant churchmen seems to have come from a biography written by Washington Irving in 1828. Irving is most famous for writing the story of *Rip Van Winkle*, and his book about Columbus is a creative mixture of research and lively imagination. Irving's story contains a stirring passage where the brave mariner argues the case for a round earth against 'an imposing array of professors, friars and dignitaries of the church', and is 'assailed with citations' from the Bible and the teachings of saints and theologians.[40]

It is a great story about a courageous, rational, free-thinking hero standing alone against the assembled forces of religious ignorance. And it was taken up into a book published in 1874 by John Draper, called *The History of the Conflict between Religion and Science*. From then it became a cherished part of the way that the modern western world understands its daring progress away from medieval Catholic superstition and ignorance. It features in the writings of Andrew Dickson White, who founded Cornell University in New York State in 1865 as a non-religious institution. Above all, it reflects the struggles of that time. Since then, the myth has featured widely in school textbooks, and it has appealed both to atheists and Protestants. It was affirmed recently, for example, in Victor J. Stenger's bestselling book *God, the Failed Hypothesis: How Science Shows That God Does Not Exist*.[41] It is a great story about the 15th century which

40   W Irving (1849) *The Life and Voyages of Columbus* John Murray, p.85–88
41   V J Stenger (2008) *God The Failed Hypothesis* Prometheus Books, p. 48

was told to powerful effect in the 19th century. It just happens to be completely untrue.

In fact, the myth about Columbus has so little connection with reality that it is actually quite funny. There is the small matter that the Atlantic had already been crossed five centuries before by the Vikings. And there is the niggling problem that the continents of North and South America had already been widely settled by people crossing over from Asia about 15,000 years before. So getting to America was not an entirely unprecedented breakthrough in the history of the world. And there is the disappointing fact that Columbus himself got less than a fifth of the way round the globe. But the main trouble with this alleged triumph of science over religious superstition is that it was the Church which was confidently proclaiming that the world was a sphere. The roundness of the Earth was a normal part of the curriculum at the medieval Catholic universities, and was a standard part of the teachings of theologians. A few examples of the influential Christian thinkers who wrote about the spherical Earth are St Augustine (354–430), the Venerable Bede (673–735) and St Thomas Aquinas (1225–1274). And the most famous account of the medieval worldview is the *Divine Comedy* by the poet Dante (1265–1321), which consists entirely of a long description of a cosmos centred on a spherical Earth.

So Columbus got his understanding of the round world from the accepted Catholic scholarship of the day, not in opposition to it. The myth is completely wrong in suggesting that the standard religious view was that he would fall off the edge of the world. His voyage into the unknown was, in fact, encouraged by his faith. But it was also based on his own drastic underestimation of the great distance involved in a westerly route to the Far East, which was why no one else was already going that way. Fortunately, he found the Bahamas roughly where he hoped to find China, and so secured his place in history.

To Columbus belongs the credit for beginning the great phase of the European exploration of the Americas. He tried to sail around the world because Christian scholarship had taught him it was round, and there is no reason to think that he himself was anything other than a devout Catholic. In no way was his voyage a triumph of science over religious superstition. It was part of an exploration of the globe which fitted happily into a set of Christian ideas and values, and a fortunate accident. Nor did his voyage actually do anything to demonstrate the roundness of the earth. The first people to prove this by travelling all the way round it were those who set off with Ferdinand Magellan in 1519, another Catholic crew sent by the Catholic king of Spain.

The great explorers of that time are examples of the intellectual vitality and adventurousness of the people of the Renaissance. They drew on the best of the scientific knowledge of the ancient world and enriched it with new discoveries. Their progress in art, exploration and engineering fitted happily into a unified worldview which was inspired by theology and philosophy. But later propaganda has falsely suggested that their developments in science were fiercely opposed by forces of religious ignorance and superstition.

CATHOLICS AND THE SOLAR SYSTEM: COPERNICUS AND GALILEO

The second great myth about science and religion is that Catholics are violently opposed to astronomy. It has been widely believed that the Catholic Church stubbornly ignored overwhelming evidence, mounting a long and bitter campaign of persecution against anyone who said that the earth was not at the centre of the universe. This view greatly distorts one minor event in history, in which Galileo was forced to stay at home in his seventies after publicly ridiculing his old friend the Pope. If we strip away the anti-religious propaganda from later centuries, then a very different story emerges. It is a story of how a series of Catholic and Protestant scholars transformed our understanding of the structure of the cosmos.

People have been fascinated by astronomy since ancient times. Today's artificial lights distract us from the wonders high above us, but there is plenty that can be seen even with the naked eye. Those who spend a while looking up at the night sky soon notice that the stars rise and set in the same way that the sun does. The constellations appear to be in motion, travelling across the sky every night from one side of the horizon to the other. It seems completely obvious that the stars, the sun and the moon are all turning around the earth in giant circles, while the ground is firmly fixed beneath our feet. For thousands of years, the movements of the stars have been carefully studied, and their motion around us was universally regarded as an established fact.

But among these serenely circling stars, there is a puzzle: the strange motion of what the Greeks named the 'wanderers', the planets. Mercury, Venus, Mars, Jupiter and Saturn are all visible to the naked eye and look like very bright stars, but their movements are surprising. They rise and set each day along with everything else, but they also slowly shift position relative to the stars. Mercury and Venus are always close to the sun, so they are only visible to the naked eye soon after the sun has set or a little before it rises. But Mars, Jupiter and Saturn move independently at different rates. Usually, they are gradually lagging behind the stars, but sometimes they turn around and overtake them for a while.

Ptolemy, the greatest of the ancient Greek astronomers, developed a sophisticated geometrical system which could predict these complicated movements. While each star simply followed a circular path around the earth, he added extra little circles called epicycles to account for the surprising motions of the planets. Each planet did not simply orbit the earth, it looped around a point which was orbiting the earth, accounting for those occasional changes of direction. It was a complex system which worked reasonably well, and it was later adopted by Christian and Islamic astronomers as they worked on calendars for seasons and religious festivals.

The first great breakthrough in our understanding of the planets was made by Nicolaus Copernicus (1473–1543). He worked as a church administrator, one of the canons of a cathedral in Poland. Copernicus discovered that he could simplify the calculations needed for Ptolemy's system if he modified it to place the sun at the centre rather than the earth. He could account for the daily rising and setting of all the celestial bodies by saying that the earth was rotating on its axis. And he could account for the shifting positions of the sun and the planets by saying that the earth was in orbit around the sun, along with Mercury, Venus, Mars, Jupiter and Saturn. This idea nicely explained why Mercury and

Venus stay so close to the sun in our sky, since their orbits are closer to the sun than ours is.

But the balance of the evidence was still against Copernicus's theory. It seemed very obvious that the ground beneath us was not spinning around and hurtling through space. And if the earth really was going on a vast annual journey through space, then each constellation should have appeared to get bigger as the earth got closer to it. When we move towards something, our view of it changes. But not even the tiniest such change in our view of the stars had then been detected. Furthermore, the Copernican System was no more accurate at predicting planetary positions than the Ptolemaic System, and Copernicus still needed to make corrections using another set of complicated and troublesome epicycles. Many astronomers were much more convinced by a later new theory suggested by Tycho Brahe (1546–1601). He suggested that the moon and the sun orbited the earth, while the other planets orbited the sun. It seemed a more obvious match for the evidence then available, all of which suggested that the earth was not moving.

Nevertheless, Copernicus's theory attracted considerable scholarly interest, including the peaceful curiosity of others in positions of leadership in the Catholic Church. Much work was being done on the development of Gregorian Calendar, which was introduced in 1582 by Pope Gregory XIII and is still used by us today. Copernicus's methods of calculation were used by the scholars who worked out that the year is 11 minutes shorter than the 365.25 days previously assumed.

The second great breakthrough was made by Galileo Galilei (1564–1642), who in 1609 became the first person to use a telescope for published astronomical research. Before Galileo, everyone had seen the planet Venus with their eyes as a star-like point of light, but Galileo could now see that it was a sphere lit up by the sun. And he could see how it was being illuminated from varying directions as the months went by. Sometimes Venus is almost between us and the sun, so that it is only partially illuminated from behind, appearing as a thin crescent. At other times it is nearly behind the sun and therefore appears much rounder but smaller. And so Galileo had found the evidence to show that Venus really is in an orbit around the sun, as both Copernicus and Tycho Brahe had suggested.

Galileo therefore became a passionate supporter of the Copernican system. But he still lacked the evidence to make a convincing case for it. He had found clear signs of the orbit of Venus, but his little telescope revealed no proof that anything else was orbiting the sun, let alone the ground beneath his feet. More evidence would be needed to show that Copernicus was right. Any rational evaluation of the facts would see that Tycho Brahe's theory fitted the astronomical observations at least as well.

But Galileo mistakenly thought that the tides of the sea provided the conclusive proof he needed. He thought that the tides were caused by water sloshing around the globe due to its rotation and orbit. In this, he was wrong. People have known since ancient times that the tides are actually linked to the position of the moon.

In his famous argument with the authorities of the Catholic Church, the Church simply insisted that Galileo should present the Copernican system as a hypothesis, not as a proven fact. And they were right to do so, since it was merely one of a number of possible theories which could explain the available evidence. Any reputable university science department or academic journal would take the same approach today in such a situation. If the argument between Galileo and the Catholic Church is assessed impartially according to modern standards of scientific rationality, then it is obvious that it was the Church which was behaving more rationally.

But Galileo fell out with Pope Urban VIII, an old friend to whom he had previously dedicated a book. Urban had encouraged him to write about astronomy, and had even written a poem in Galileo's honour. But problems began in 1632, when Galileo published a book which he presented as a dialogue between fictional supporters of two different views of the cosmos. On the surface, it seemed to be an open debate which humbly allowed equal space for different ideas, so the Church authorities approved its publication. However, Galileo rather unscientifically presented Copernicus's view of the planets as the only alternative to the ancient one, ignoring Tycho Brahe's work. He also ignored Kepler's decisive work on elliptical orbits, which I shall mention next. And he used a comic character called 'Simplicio' to give an obviously weak presentation of the traditional Ptolemaic system, recklessly echoing views which had been expressed by the Pope. Unfortunately, this mockery happened at a time when the Pope was caught up in political conflicts and needed to present himself as a strong and impressive leader.

The result of this sad clash of egos was that Galileo was confined to his comfortable house from the age of 69 and banned from publishing, preventing him from making any further unsubstantiated claims about astronomy. It was other Christian scholars who found the evidence he lacked to support a modified version of the Copernican system. But, in the 18th and 19th centuries, Galileo's story became famous among those who were campaigning against the power of traditional religious and aristocratic hierarchies. In the light of later discoveries, they retold the story as if Galileo himself had found the evidence to prove the Copernican system, and as if his ecclesiastical critics were stubbornly suppressing the truth. Professor Brian Cox, retelling the story in 2014, repeats the familiar assumption that Galileo's observations of Venus provided 'final compelling evidence of a solar system with the Sun at its heart', but that is simply not true.[42] Like most people, Cox misses the vitally important fact that Galileo had found no evidence whatsoever that the earth was in motion around the sun.

If today's scientific establishment had been in operation back then, and Galileo had submitted a paper to a reputable journal, they would have demanded changes before allowing its publication. They would have insisted that he admit that his views were no more than an interesting and unproven hypothesis, which is exactly what the Catholic academic establishment did in Galileo's time. Galileo's situation then was rather like that of someone today insisting that there must be life on other planets. It is an interesting and plausible idea, but such a person would not have the evidence to support it. If he began to be very rude about any leading authorities who disagreed with him, and if he insisted that Stonehenge was obviously an alien artefact which

---

42   Brian Cox (2014) *Human Universe* William Collins, p. 43

proved his theory, then he might not find his scientific career progressing smoothly. Subsequent discoveries might one day prove some genuine evidence, but for now he would be greatly overstating his case.

The familiar Galileo myth tells us very little about Galileo himself, and far more about the views of those people in later centuries who wanted to portray the Catholic Church as the great enemy of scientific truth. They have retold the story in ways which turned Galileo into a great icon for anti-religious propaganda. They have adapted the story to portray the leadership of the Catholic Church as viciously opposed to rationality and to scientific evidence. They have embroidered it, without evidence, with accounts of torture. They have invented the famous image of Galileo, forced to recant by the Inquisition, heroically still muttering under his breath that the Earth moves. And so Galileo has been awarded his iconic status as the archetypal hero of scientific evidence, the great rational opponent of superstitious Catholic tyranny.

The myth somehow neglects to mention the money that Galileo made from casting horoscopes, or the time when the Church rebuked him for the belief that the movement of the planets determines when people will die.[43] It also draws no attention to the lack of other examples of Catholic controversy about astronomy. Plenty of other Catholic thinkers explored different ideas about the structure of the universe without getting into any trouble. The Galileo myth has greatly distorted the popular understanding of the history of astronomy and of the relationship between faith and science. Many people have enjoyed the myth that Catholicism is inherently irrational and opposed to evidence, but it simply is not true.

In fact, the Roman Catholic Church did more than any other institution to support astronomy from the 13th to the 18th centuries.[44] Today, there is still a Vatican Observatory, which is very active in cutting-edge astronomical research. And all of Galileo's writings present him as a Catholic scholar seeking to learn more about God's creation.

43   See Nicholas Campion and Nick Kollerstrom (2003) *Galileo's Astrology* Culture and Cosmos

44   John Heilbron (1993) *The Sun in the Church: Cathedrals as Solar Observatories* Harvard University Press, p. 3

VIEWS OF THE COSMOS FROM KEPLER TO EINSTEIN

Copernicus and Galileo were, in fact, still wrong about planetary orbits, because they had not understood their correct shape. They remained committed to the traditional view that orbits are formed from circles. The discovery that they were incorrect was made by another astronomer, Johannes Kepler (1571–1630), whose work was deeply inspired by the philosophy of Plato.

Kepler was a German Protestant, who had studied to be a Christian minister and had been given a job as a teacher of mathematics and astronomy. Those two professions seemed far more closely connected then than they do now. Influenced by Plato, Kepler saw mathematics and geometry as a window into the mind of God. He was convinced that the universe had a beautiful, harmonious and mathematical structure. He thought that the cosmos itself should be seen as an image and revelation of God, believing that the study of astronomy involved 'thinking God's thoughts after him.'[45] And he regarded the sun, the source of all light, as a representation of divinity. So it seemed entirely appropriate to him that the heavens and the earth should be in orbit around the sun.

Analysing large quantities of data, he discovered that the planets had elliptical rather than circular orbits. Each ellipse could be precisely described by a mathematical equation, so that a calculation could show where a planet would be at any given time. There were no remaining errors requiring correction by epicycles. This was the third great breakthrough, since Kepler's system could now predict the positions of planets more accurately and more simply than either Ptolemy's or Copernicus's, providing strong evidence that it was correct.

Kepler's theories spread around Europe along with Galileo's, and were widely discussed in its Christian universities. Among those who took careful note of their work was a Cambridge scholar who is usually regarded, along with Einstein, as one of the two greatest scientists of all time. Isaac Newton (1643–1727) was a deeply religious man

---

45   Quoted in J H Brooke (1991) *Science and Religion: Some Historical Perspectives* Cambridge University Press, p. 22

who spent much of his time writing about theology. He described the cosmos in this way:

> This most beautiful system of the sun, planets, and comets, could only proceed from the counsel and dominion of an intelligent and powerful Being. And if the fixed stars are the centres of other like systems, these, being formed by the like wise counsel, must be all subject to the dominion of One; especially since the light of the fixed stars is of the same nature with the light of the sun... This Being governs all things, not as the soul of the world, but as Lord over all.[46]

Newton looked for mathematical patterns in the universe because, like Kepler, he believed that a supreme intelligence structuring the universe would use the unchanging perfection of mathematics. However, he saw this divine action not just in the design of the universe but also in its continued operation. Newton realised that the force which pulls an apple from a tree to the ground is related to the forces which constantly act to keep the planets in their orbits. He discovered that Kepler's elliptical orbits could be accounted for perfectly by a force of gravity which follows a simple equation. Newton also developed laws of motion, and with the same simple kit of mathematical formulae he could describe and predict the elliptical orbits of planets around the sun or the trajectories of cannon balls on the Earth. And his comprehensive account of motion and gravity fully explains why we can hurtle through space on the surface of a spinning planet without feeling any awareness of its movement.

In the natural laws he uncovered, Newton saw the continuous action of God, governing the universe by acting in a uniform, constant, reliable way. Newton wrote: 'There exists an infinite and omnipresent spirit in which matter is moved according to mathematical laws.'[47] For example, without gravity, the Earth would travel onwards through space in a

---

46   From the *General Scholium* in the *Principia Mathematica*. Here quoted from the English translation by A Motte, 1846, p. 504

47   From the Portsmouth Papers, additional manuscripts in the Cambridge University Library, 3965.6, f. 266v. Quoted by R S Westfall (1980) *Never at Rest: A Biography of Isaac Newton* Cambridge University Press

straight line. But the gravitational force from the Sun bends the Earth's path into an elliptical orbit around it. This force reaches invisibly across an average distance of 150 million kilometres of empty space. Newton regarded gravity as the action of God in the present, following a perfect and unchanging mathematical pattern, and working in this same way throughout the vast universe.

Newton's mathematical genius operated within a deeply religious view of the cosmos, in which he believed he was contemplating the beautiful works of God. His work took shape within a specific Christian heritage, which had directed him to look at the book of nature as a revelation of God, and which had passed on the Platonic emphasis on the perfect beauty of mathematics.

There have been huge numbers of people before and after Newton who have pursued the rational study of nature and have been Christians or members of other faiths. But, the routine lack of any exciting conflict has meant that the faith of religious scientists is very rarely noticed. And the Galileo myth has completely overshadowed the facts of history. Very few people know that the first direct evidence for the motion of the Earth around the sun was actually finally discovered the following century by the Revd James Bradley, a Church of England vicar who became the Astronomer Royal. Through painstakingly detailed observations made with a telescope from 1725 to 1728, he detected tiny changes in the apparent positions of stars at different times of year caused by the movement of the Earth through space.

Another of the many devoutly religious scientists was James Clerk Maxwell (1831–1879), to whom we owe our understanding of electricity and magnetism. His equations describe the behaviour of the radio waves that your mobile phone receives, along with the electricity that powers it. He also produced the first ever colour photograph. He was the first director of the Cavendish Laboratory in Cambridge, the university's physics department, and he chose to have the following verse from Psalm 111 engraved on its main door: 'Great are the works of the Lord, studied by all who delight in them.' He was a man with a strong faith, who regarded his scientific research as an investigation into the wonderful deeds of God, part of a life of worship and discovery.

The myth that Christianity is bad news for astronomy is so overwhelmingly strong that it is very unlikely that you have heard of a more recent figure in the history of science, Georges Lemaître (1894–1966). The world has hardly noticed him, because he does not fit the mythology which has dominated our understanding of the history of western thought. But he is the man who in 1927 developed our current scientific view of the origin of the universe, the Big Bang theory. He presented a revolutionary solution to Einstein's equations which indicated that the universe had been expanding from an initial explosion billions of years ago, a theory which has been supported by subsequent observations. And he was also a Catholic priest.

Perhaps, you might still assume, Lemaître was a rebellious priest who did some cosmology in his spare time as a dark secret, wrestling with his conscience, struggling with his faith, listening in terror for the footsteps of the Inquisition and hiding his shameful work from his disapproving superiors. That would fit our usual myth about science and religion. But, no. Lemaître studied physics and mathematics as part of his preparation for the priesthood, and then became a lecturer at the Catholic University of Leuven. And his theory was inspired by a Christian view of creation, the idea that the universe has a beginning.

Lemaître called his theory the 'hypothesis of the primeval atom'. The rather more flippant term 'Big Bang' was jokingly coined by an atheist, Fred Hoyle, who disliked the idea because he did not believe in God. Hoyle preferred his own theory of a 'steady state', a universe which has no beginning and thus does not suggest any kind of first cause or creator. But subsequent observations of background radiation in the universe showed that Lemaître was right.

Lemaître's story has largely passed unnoticed because we have been trained by the Galileo myth to assume that religion, especially Catholicism, is the enemy of science. But Lemaître's work should be a deep embarrassment to those who insist that science and faith are incompatible. They will want to say that he somehow managed to be a good cosmologist *despite* being a Catholic priest. But the truth is that it was Lemaître's faith which pointed him in the right direction, while Hoyle was misled by his atheism. Theology is not just compatible with science, it has made a number of decisive contributions to it.

Atheists tend to ignore or misunderstand the significance of the religious faith of scientific geniuses. Hitchens, for example, asserts that 'religion comes from the period of human prehistory where nobody had the smallest idea what was going on.' He insists that 'all attempts to reconcile faith with science and reason are consigned to failure and ridicule.'[48] And when Dawkins mentions Newton, he concedes only that he 'did indeed claim to be religious', insisting that was true of almost everyone at the time.[49] But any serious biography of Newton will mention the vast amount of time he devoted to the study of the Bible. His faith was deeply important to him. And as I have already described, Newton's scientific understanding of the universe was closely related to his view of God.

Albert Einstein commented that it was a 'cosmic religious feeling' which gave Newton and Kepler the strength 'to spend years of solitary labour in disentangling the principles of celestial mechanics.'[50] This is how the man who was arguably our greatest ever scientific genius understood the pioneers of his field. Einstein linked their 'deep conviction of the rationality of the universe' to a belief in a divine mind which structured the cosmos. He described a religious feeling which 'takes the form of a rapturous amazement at the harmony of natural law, which reveals an intelligence of such superiority that, compared with it, all the systematic thinking and acting of human beings is an utterly insignificant reflection.'[51] He declared that 'the laws of nature manifest the existence of a spirit vastly superior to that of men, and one in the face of which we with our modest powers must feel humble.'[52] As I mentioned in Chapter Two, he found a great sense of beauty in the mathematical equations of physics, as well as rationality. Although he was not a practising member of any religious

48   C Hitchens (2007) *God is not Great* Atlantic Books, p. 64
49   R Dawkins (2006) *The God Delusion* Transworld Publishers , p. 124
50   A Einstein (2007) *The World as I see it* BN Publishing, p. 35
51   A Einstein (2007) *The World as I see it* BN Publishing, p. 35–36
52   Quoted by M Jammer (1999) *Einstein and Religion* Princeton University Press, p. 93

organisation, he said that 'science without religion is lame, religion without science is blind.'[53]

When scientists established their independence as a profession in the 19th century, many of them encouraged a mythology which suggested the importance of keeping science away from outside influences. And yet, as I have described, many of the greatest figures in the history of science got their inspiration from a vision of reality which was broader than the field of modern science. Newton saw the action of gravity across the vastness of space as an expression of the rational and powerful workings of God. Kepler found a great beauty in the mathematical structures of the solar system, which he thought was a window into the divine mind. And Lemaître developed the Big Bang theory because of his belief that the universe had a created beginning.

History shows that many scientists have understood their scientific theories within a wider religious or philosophical framework which has inspired their view of nature. Science itself is compatible with the view that the cosmos is shaped by a divine mind, and has often benefitted from the work of those who think in that way. There is nothing in the nature of reality itself, or in our ideas about the cosmos, which means that science cannot be connected with spirituality. The only division is a human, institutional one. It is simply that different aspects of reality are today studied by different professions, and that each group of experts jealously guards its own territory.

HOW SCIENCE WORKS

Modern science is a human endeavour which assumes that all questions of meaning, purpose and faith should be left outside the door of the laboratory. This clear focus for science has advantages and disadvantages. On the positive side, individual scientists may have a wide range of personal beliefs and motivations, but are able to find a unity with each other by leaving those beliefs aside. A Jewish astronomer can happily study a nebula alongside a colleague who thinks that the

---

53   A Einstein (1941) *Science, Philosophy and Religion, A Symposium*, published by the Conference on Science, Philosophy and Religion in Their Relation to the Democratic Way of Life, Inc., New York

cosmos popped spontaneously out of a meaningless void. Together, they can focus on trying to make sense of patterns in the data from their telescopes. It is a great strength to be able to unite a diverse assembly of people around a common goal, and the great success of science is partly due to the way it works as a global project.

But there is a serious disadvantage in the way that science has been detached from all wider questions about its meaning. It seems to me that this isolationism has allowed science to flourish on its own terms, but has hindered our ability to perceive how science fits in with a view of reality as a whole. This is why science both impresses people and also seems coldly impersonal to many. It is both technologically very powerful, and yet also very hard for many people to connect with.

In particular, the isolation of science is connected with two serious errors in the mechanical view of the cosmos. I have already been arguing against the first idea, which is that reality consists of only those things which scientists can measure. The second idea is that science has a unique ability to produce proven, objective facts, whereas everything else in our heads is a jumble of subjective beliefs and opinions.

Perhaps surprisingly, I would like to suggest that there is nothing at all special about the scientific method. It is not the case that science has a unique claim to rationality which could not be found elsewhere, or that science consists of proven objective facts. I think that such exalted claims greatly confuse our understanding of the human quest for truth. Various grandiose theories about scientific proof and disproof developed from the rhetoric of the Enlightenment and flourished into the 20th century, but they have gradually lost their philosophical credibility. The trouble is that they rarely match up to the messy human reality of what scientists actually do.

So what is it that scientists do? They make observations of some aspects of the natural world, such the orbits of planets, the energy levels of sub-atomic particles, or the genetics of fruit flies. They spot patterns in the data, and notice ways in which those patterns do not fit their existing theories. Perhaps they find that a planet is not where they thought it should be, or that a fly's wings are an unexpected size. Then comes a stage which is surprisingly creative, involving intuition, day-dreams, and leaps of imagination, when they develop new theories which might account for the anomalous data. And finally, they make more observations to see if the new theories work. If the data fits a new theory better than the old one, then the new one takes over. If it does not, then the scientists continue to muddle along with the old theory.

At any given time, in any field, there is always a lot of data which does not fit the best current theory. Often it is hard to tell whether the data is inaccurate or the theory is wrong. In physics and cosmology, for example, there are currently major puzzles about the ways in which the universe has expanded. And the gravitational forces between the galaxies do not seem consistent with the amount of matter they appear to contain. The most popular explanation for these anomalies is that there is a vast amount of 'dark energy' and 'dark matter' lurking somewhere out there in the universe which we have been unable to detect. But we therefore have no direct reason to believe in it. And it is equally possible that there are serious problems with our understanding of gravity. Meanwhile, as I mentioned in the first chapter, the two fundamental theories of physics (quantum mechanics and general relativity) do not fit together.

So there is a high degree of provisionality about all scientific beliefs. We cannot say for certain that our understanding of gravity has been proven to be true, or that it has been disproven. However, our current understanding of it is reliable enough for us to predict the motion of cricket balls or send spacecraft around the solar system. So it does seem to be successfully connecting with reality, just in a rather incomplete sort of way.

In my view, there is nothing special about this scientific approach. It is the kind of process of trial and error which all intelligent people apply to many aspects of life. We find that some of life makes sense to a certain degree and some of it does not. We have theories about the world, and we try to improve them when we come across surprises. And we muddle along with the bits that we cannot get the hang of yet.

For example, imagine that I meet someone for the first time. I immediately form an initial impression, which is based on my observations of matters such his body language, his age, his facial expression, his accent and his clothing. If he is waving an axe and screaming, then I run away. If he smiles, greets me politely and holds out his hand, I shake it. I am already generating a set of ideas about the kind of person he might be based on my understanding of people I have met before or seen in films.

If he is wearing a very smart suit then I assume at first that he rich, and guess that he is possibly an investment banker. However, if he then explains that he is on his way to a job interview in a library, then I drastically revise my theory. As we talk, I will probably find that he gradually makes more sense to me, and that the ideas about him in my head get gradually closer to reality. However, there will still be a great many things about his behaviour that I have not myself observed, and some things that I have observed that puzzle me. If we happen to become friends, then I shall gradually solve some more of those mysteries. Occasionally, however, he will do something that takes me completely by surprise.

This is the active process of trying to make sense of the world around us, which we have all been engaged in since our earliest memories. Some people are more consciously systematic and deliberately rational about it than others. And a lot of people prefer mostly just to go along with what other people tell them to think. But we all have some kind of set of theories about the world in our head, and we all, to some extent are in the process of actively revising them.

To give another example, I have been buying my shoes from the same shop for twelve years. So far I have found them comfortable, long-lasting and smart. But if my next pair falls apart after two weeks, then I will note that my theory about the shoe shop may need to be revised. I will gather new data, by getting a replacement pair of shoes from the shop and seeing what other people are saying about it on the internet. If the new data is also disappointing, then I shall start to develop theories about why the shop started reducing the quality of its products.

The longevity of shoes is something which a scientist could measure, whereas the personality of a human being is rather more complex. The strength of leather, stitching or glue can be tested and turned into a single number. But the character of my new friend is something that far transcends any attempt to reduce it to some measurements. And that, when all is said and done, is the only difference between science and the rest of our ideas about life. Science is based on things that can be reduced down to measurable physical quantities. Some things can, and some things cannot. I might be able to weigh my new friend (although he would be surprised by the request), but I could not fully describe our friendship with any set of numbers. I could measure the size of the *Mona Lisa*, but I could not quantify its beauty. Weight, length, friendship and beauty are all genuine aspects of reality, but only two of them consist of a measurable physical property. The special clarity of science comes simply from the fact that it is easier to agree about things that we can measure, because we can all gather around the scales or have a look at the ruler. And the great error of the mechanical view of the cosmos is the assumption that it is only those measurable things which are the true basis of all reality.

RATIONALITY BEYOND SCIENCE

Science has its limitations because many of the important aspects of reality cannot be reduced to measurements. But I am arguing in this book that these unquantifiable truths are nevertheless real and that we have evolved human faculties which engage with them in reliable ways. Our ability to empathise with each other, to evaluate the character of others, and to form friendships connects us with something immeasurable that is far greater than the sum of its physical properties. The same could be said of our ability to respond to beauty, and our ability to gain a sense of the meaning of life.

I would also like to suggest that it is possible to be very rational in our approach to any of these aspects of reality and to any of our human faculties. Rationality does not only apply to things that we can measure. Just as we can engage in a rational process of trying to understand and predict our observations of planets, we can engage in a rational process of reflecting on our experiences of beauty and goodness, or on our relationships with other people. In each case, we are exploring something real and consistent which we can gradually make sense of.

In the example of beauty, we can develop our appreciation of the finer forms of art, or learn to identify the greatness of literature. And we can gradually develop our understanding of what is meaningful in life by exploring different activities and thinking about our experiences, gaining a deeper understanding of how we can put our talents to good use.

The process of trying to understand a person, or seeking to evaluate a philosophy of life, or learning to appreciate an unfamiliar style of painting can be a complex one. We are unlikely to agree with each other as quickly as if we were making a simple scientific measurement, such as finding the melting point of silver. Nevertheless, we can still go through a similar process of making observations, developing theories, sharing them with each other, and seeing if they fit with our subsequent experiences. We are still seeking to understand the same reality, in all its wonder. And it is still possible to be systematic and rational in our thinking even when reflecting on the aspects of our experience which cannot be reduced to numbers.

What I mean by rationality is therefore not something that is confined to science. It is not necessarily all about gauging the physical properties of nature. It is simply an active process of examining all our experiences of reality, both the measurable and the immeasurable, and gradually enlarging our understanding of them. It is potentially a very sociable activity, because it involves articulating a set of ideas about the reality we share, and anything that we can articulate we can communicate. It is therefore possible together to apply reason to experiences of beauty, of meaning, of spirituality, of religion, of love, of goodness and of friendship.

But to say that there can be a rational exploration of religion and spirituality may surprise or disturb many people. It breaks the assumption that has been widely held since the 19th century parting of the ways between science and faith. It is assumed today that reason belongs with science, while spirituality belongs in its own private realm of intuition, mysticism and whimsical subjectivity, or among dusty old scrolls and unfathomable dogmas.

I have mentioned before that I consider it a loss on both sides when science and spirituality are divorced from each other. In the case of spirituality, there is a kind of flight into esotericism and irrationality which can sadly result. Since that great 19th century separation between science and religion, there has been a strong tendency for religious groups to retreat to ways of thinking which they can defend as their own special areas of expertise. They have safely preserved their traditional teachings, but have often failed to find ways of joining together with other groups in the project of making sense of reality. I think that this rigid compartmentalisation of human knowledge causes a new set of problems, and think that we need to take a critical look at the ways in which both scientists and religious leaders can be so eager to defend their own territories.

In the Renaissance, Christians thought that it was rational to believe in God because it seemed to be the most powerful way of making sense of the whole of reality. By the 19th century, rationality was increasingly associated with the independence of science, and religious people were getting nervous about it. Pope Pius IX published a 'Syllabus of Modern Errors' in 1864, condemning the idea that 'human reason, without any reference whatsoever to God, is the sole arbiter of truth and falsehood.' He also derided the idea that 'the Roman Pontiff can, and ought to, reconcile himself, and come to terms with progress, liberalism and modern civilisation.'[54] In 1870, the Catholic bishops gathered at the First Vatican Council declared for the first time that the Pope himself has the ability to make infallible proclamations of Christian doctrine. Meanwhile, in Protestant circles, the fast-growing Evangelical movement was proclaiming the infallibility of the Bible. Both groups responded to the perceived certainties of science by emphasising that they had their own special sources of unquestionable truth which were not accountable to anyone else's view of rationality. It is no surprise that stories about the battle between science and religion flourished at this time.

I understand the good intentions behind this careful guarding of cherished beliefs. But I worry that these proclamations of infallibility can promote a kind of fortress mentality which lacks vision. It retreats

54   Pius IX, *Syllabus of Modern Errors*, paragraphs 3 and 80.

from an attempt to make sense of reality as a whole, and would seem surprisingly limited to the people of the Renaissance. I am disappointed by a scientific rationality which believes only in things that can be measured; but I am also disappointed by an over-defensive faith which tries to cut itself off from the mainstream of human thought and from scientific progress.

Those who believe in some kind of infallible revelation are claiming to have a source of truth which is at least as impressive as the experimental data of the scientists, but which is largely detached from it. On this basis, scientists and religious teachers usually keep to their own clearly identified territories and use their own completely separate methods. One group measures the physical properties of the natural world, and the other consults a set of authoritative documents about how to live a good life and to find salvation. Stephen Jay Gould has labelled these divided territories as 'non-overlapping magisteria'. Apart from the occasional fundamentalist squabbles over creation and evolution, the two approaches can mostly keep carefully out of each other's way.

But it is not only the religious traditionalists who may keep their distance from other areas of human thought. Even without a belief in an infallible truth, more liberal religious people can also practice a form of isolationism. There is another approach to faith which has become very popular since the 19th century. It follows on from the way in which Schleiermacher aligned theology with the Romantic movement's reaction against the Enlightenment. This is the claim that spirituality is something which goes beyond words, doctrines, definitions and rationality. It is something intuitive, experiential and personal. It is an awestruck, wordless silence in the face of the transcendent wonder of reality, or a deep sense of human frailty and of our absolute dependence on God.

Those who take this approach can therefore also be happy to accept a divide between rationality and spirituality. They may see rationality as something pedantic, small-minded and cold, while regarding spirituality as something deep and personal which can confront the awesome mysteries of the universe and the divine. They are happy to see religious teachings as symbolic and mythological, rather than trying to fit them together systematically. This is an approach which has been common among many of the more liberal Protestants, who regard a compassionate life and an experience of spirituality as more important than any rigid adherence to a set of doctrines.

This approach also strongly characterises the New Age movement. It has grown in the last few decades as a loose alliance of people in the west who are interested in spirituality but who have been alienated by the strict and old-fashioned dogmas of traditional religions. The New Age movement is enthusiastically inclusive, drawing together ideas and practices from all over the world which seem spiritual, including eastern meditation, tarot cards, yoga, feng shui, crystal healing, contacting the dead, astrology, reincarnation, angels and aliens. From my perspective, it seems to be a mixture of the inspiring, the well-intentioned and the highly dubious.

Its underlying assumption is that any attempt to form one rational system out of all these experiences would be intolerant and irrelevant. William Bloom, for example, has a view of rationality which worries me. I admire him when he talks about compassion and wonder, but not when he describes our minds as the first of the great problems that get in the way of our spirituality. He uses the term 'monkey-mind' to ridicule the way in which the human brain keeps chattering away, seeking to create narratives which explain our experiences.[55] Prayer and meditation are important to me, but so also is thoughtful and rational reflection. I think that seeking to understand our experiences is a key part of being human, and that careful discernment is a key part of spiritual growth. An approach which simply affirms everything that sounds spiritual is lacking in intellectual substance. Members of the New Age Movement often like to claim to be being scientific. But I think that Richard Dawkins speaks accurately for most scientists when he dismisses New Age therapies as superstition and a retreat from reason.[56]

One of the great attractions of the New Age Movement is an interest in being holistic, seeking to bring together the best of the ideas about

---

55 William Bloom *The Power of Modern Spirituality* Piatkus, 2011, p. 145–6

56 From the review in the Sunday Telegraph of 4 August 2007 of the Channel 4 programme *The Enemies of Reason*

life which they can find from eastern and western thought, combining an emphasis on the mind, the body, the spirit and the cosmos. It is an admirable goal, and the movement has successfully opened up the exploration of spirituality to many people. However, this haphazard collection of different ideas can only be brought together because of an underlying rejection of rationality. Wildly different ideas about reality are thrown together without any logical search for coherence. In my view, this rejection abandons any attempt to be genuinely holistic. To affirm human spirituality and to dismiss human rationality is to adopt a lop-sided view of ourselves and of the whole of reality. It means using one part of the brain and not another, and it means dismissing one of our most important faculties. I have great sympathy for those who are reacting against the spiritual deadness of the mechanical view of the cosmos, and seeking to avoid a verbal barrage of religious dogma or atheist cynicism, but the rejection of rationality greatly diminishes us. And it provides an easy target for those who wish to dismiss the exploration of spirituality as self-indulgent wishful thinking.

But many who are attracted to the New Age Movement are in fact objecting to the western fragmentation of knowledge which I am seeking to overcome in this book. I admire the fact that they seek to emphasise holistic thought and to explore the relationship between people and the cosmos. They are trying to find a sense of balance and harmony which makes sense of all their experiences and enables them to grow in wisdom and love. However, I do not think that they will find the answers to the problems of western thought by piling an assortment of eastern ideas about spirituality on top of them. That approach seems to me to bring more confusion rather than harmony. Instead, there is important work to be done first in piecing together the fragments of our compartmentalised western view of reality.

A TRULY HOLISTIC VIEW OF LIFE

I have objected to several self-contained and highly territorial views of reality. One is a view of science which says that all that exists can be fully described by a set of scientific measurements, and which regards other inquiries into truth as inherently irrational. Another is a view of religion which claims that there is some infallible source of doctrines which is far exalted above all other sources of truth. And another is a view of spirituality which considers itself to be superior to any attempt to evaluate it rationally. To me, these are all incomplete and disconnected views of reality which make only partial use of our various human faculties. They are associated with the fierce guarding of territories by different factions of experts, and have arisen from the great fragmentation of modern thought.

Instead, I want to suggest that it is much more rewarding and interesting to seek to make sense of the whole range of our experiences. We can apply our rationality to all that we can learn about reality through our senses of sight, hearing, touch, taste and smell, our scientific measurements, our awareness of beauty, our sense of meaning, our intuition, our ability to empathise with others and to form relationships, our awareness of goodness, our sense of wonder, and anything which we might wish to call our spiritual awareness or our sense of the presence of God. We are missing out on a bigger picture of life when we artificially divide the data from all those sources into different areas of expertise. It is time to look for a bigger picture.

I have been delighted to see signs that many atheists would like to move beyond the narrow-minded and strident campaigns of Richard Dawkins and others like him. Alain de Botton's book *Religion for Atheists*[57] offers a much more realistic and insightful view of life than anything that has been written by the New Atheists. Where Hitchens had unconvincingly described *How Religion Poisons Everything*,[58] de Botton recognises that faith has produced many positive results. He describes a much broader view of life than the New Atheists, noting that religions have been very successful in encouraging community, art, architecture, morality and education, and in nurturing a sense of hope, gratitude and perspective. His aim is to show how atheism could emulate and develop the positive aspects of religion.

What I admire about de Botton is that he is open-minded and generous in recognising goodness wherever he finds it, rational in his

---

57   Alain de Botton (2012) *Religion for Atheists* Penguin Books
58   Christopher Hitchens (2007) *God is Not Great: How Religion Poisons Everything* Atlantic Books

attempts to make sense of the world, and skilled in writing in a very accessible way about the things which enable human beings to flourish. There is something responsible and sociable about his approach, in that he is happy to acknowledge where other people have gained genuine wisdom about life. It is a very helpful way of opening up those ideas for discussion. It is also a great improvement on the territorial mud-slinging that has often taken place between atheists and religious people.

The great difference between de Botton and me is, of course, that he regards a belief in God as obviously irrational, whereas I see God as the most rational way of making sense of the whole of reality. I regard the various successes of religion that he mentions, across a wide range of aspects of life, as strong evidence that it is a powerful theory as a whole. But there is much about his approach that I like. Mirroring his methods a little, I wish to emphasise the advantages of science and rationality much more than many religious people have done. And I also think that religions should be far less tribal and defensive about the great treasury of human wisdom and experience which is contained within their traditions. We should be delighted when someone like de Botton wants to explore it, and should encourage his search for the truth.

Underneath all the territorial bluster about infallibility, faiths hold a vast treasury of testimony to the genuine human experience of reality. The reason why religions have developed in every part of the world, and the reason why they show no signs of disappearing, is that they express real and widespread human experiences which feel profound and urgent. Alongside all the institutional structures, illuminated manuscripts and ancient rituals are ordinary human beings, people who are dealing with the challenging and exciting business of living.

Any religion, philosophy or spiritual tradition which has grown by honest and peaceful means has done so because it has impressed and convinced people. It has gained new members because they have looked at the lives of those in its community and have recognised something good, authentic, meaningful, beautiful and life-affirming in its vision. They have been attracted by an approach to life which evidently enables human beings to flourish, to develop their talents, to enlarge their minds, to face up to their failures and their bad habits, to care for each other and to learn to love. And when a religious community has come to cherish particular scriptures, it is because those words ring true to a wide range of people and connect with their experiences. This, it seems to me, is an exploration of reality which can be rational and has much in common with science. The whole breadth of people's experiences of life – their sense of meaning, their struggles to break destructive patterns of behaviour, their ways of encouraging each other, their ways of celebrating achievements, their ways of building community – all of these are true aspects of their experimental quest to make sense of their place in the universe.

One of my favourite writers is the eminent physicist and theologian John Polkinghorne. He regards scientists and theologians as being engaged in a similar kind of task, seeking to make sense of our experiences. He describes himself as a 'bottom-up' thinker, one who starts from tangible evidence. He therefore advocates a philosophy which he terms *critical realism* for both theology and science. *Realism* indicates a belief that there is a genuine and increasing correspondence between our ideas and reality. We are making contact with something real when we say that ice is a form of water and that murder should be illegal. But *critical* realism indicates that our beliefs are incomplete and should always be open to question. We need to cherish the humility, the curiosity, the scholarly rigour and the sense of wonder that are needed to allow us to go on learning. Polkinghorne therefore sees theological accounts of divine revelation not as fixed and unquestionable truths, but as the records of moments of great insight and illumination. He writes:

> Scripture, such as the Bible, is not a kind of divinely dictated textbook laying down the correct answers to the examination questions of life, answers that we had better learn by rote and unfailingly reproduce. Scripture is not an unchallengeable set of propositions demanding unquestioning assent, but it is *evidence*, the record of foundational spiritual experience, the laboratory notebooks of gifted observers of God's ways with men and women.[59]

59   John Polkinghorne (2000) *Faith, Science and Understanding* SPCK

I believe that we all need to step outside our familiar areas of expertise and talk to each other about the full breadth of reality. Polkinghorne's approach presents theology as a developing tradition of enquiry into human spiritual experience which can connect fruitfully with our developing scientific theories about the cosmos. My suggestion is that the rationality and usefulness of theology is demonstrated by its ability to form connections with all areas of knowledge and experience. And so I wish next to demonstrate how theology can help to place the scientific study of nature in a meaningful context, while also supporting a strong commitment to liberty and rationality.

SCIENCE IN A THEOLOGICAL PERSPECTIVE

A social understanding of the cosmos indicates that the physical properties of nature are not themselves the most significant aspect of reality. But they are the purposeful framework within which human consciousness can develop, and within which we can grow as people who know love, goodness, courage, integrity, faithfulness, wonder and truth. The mathematical patterns of nature are like the paint and canvas which make possible a great work of art.

I believe that nature is full of regular patterns not because it is a giant, independent mechanism, but because of the continuing faithfulness of God. Nature's order is a sign of purpose and trustworthiness, the workings of a patient and loving intelligence. Similarly, I believe that the beautiful mathematical structures of nature should be understood in terms of a living relationship, not as a dead piece of engineering. It has been God's intention to provide for us a consistent and intelligible environment, within which we can evolve, flourish and develop as rational creatures. The universe is an expression of God's faithfulness and providence, enabling us to live.

Consistency and regularity are necessary and important features of the processes by which the intelligent God facilitates the development of intelligent life. We can only breathe and digest food because a whole set of complex chemical reactions inside our bodies follows unchanging patterns. Carbohydrates, stomachs and enzymes behave the same way today as yesterday. We can only learn to walk because forces and movements work the same way all the time: the signals to our leg muscles which we learned yesterday will have the same effect today. We can only develop our minds because the cosmos is set up to follow consistent patterns and is open to our investigation. It rewards enquiry and is not chaotic or capricious.

An ordered universe allows the evolution of intelligence and the development of stable relationships. It also enables an awareness of good and evil. A predictable arrangement of cause and effect enables us to take responsibility for our actions, supporting our growth as moral individuals. Just as a loving parent will treat a child in ways which are consistent, reliable and faithful, so God enables the universe to provide us with a home in which it is possible for us to flourish, to learn and to love. The order and mathematical structure of the physical processes of the cosmos are an expression of the faithfulness and love of God.

Like Newton, I see the continued operation of the laws of physics as part of the continuing action of God in the present, not as the actions of an impersonal clockwork mechanism. The universe is God's way of opening up a hospitable space in which intelligent beings have room to evolve and develop.

Each of us therefore has a genuine independent identity of our own. As seen in the processes of evolution and in the probabilities described in quantum physics, God has placed a degree of openness in the order and structure of reality. That openness gives us the freedom to make real choices. We are not like tiny cogs being controlled by the inevitable workings of a giant mechanism or actors forced to stick rigidly to a script. The universe seems to be configured to give rise to living beings and to involve their responses in its functioning. Reality is a social environment, shaped for relationships. For all these reasons, it seems to me that the discoveries of science connect happily with a theological view of reality. Rationality, like beauty, is an aspect of reality which fits well into the belief that there is a divine intelligence underlying all that exists.

I can draw another analogy by comparing the cosmos to a piece of music. If I carried out a scientific analysis of a symphony, I would find that it was full of mathematical patterns. Musical harmonies arise when notes are played whose frequencies are related. If one note has a frequency which is double that of another, for example, we hear an octave. A ratio of 3 to 2 produces a perfect fifth (like C and G). And a ratio of 5 to 4 gives a major third (like C and E). All those notes together make a major chord, a very pleasing and harmonious set of sounds. Rhythm also is mathematical: four semi-quavers make a crotchet, for example. And tunes often fall into phrases of equal lengths, such as repeated sets of eight bars. Many books could be written about the mathematical patterns of just one symphony. And, having discovered them, I could adjust them. I could change the sound of the music, and gain power over it.

But I would not have understood the music if I thought that the mathematical patterns were the only point. I would not have understood the music, however intricately I knew its structures, if I thought that the structures were all that it was about. I would not have understood the music until I experienced it as music, and until I felt the emotions that the composer wanted me to feel. In and through the intricate mathematical structures of the music can come a form of communication which may engage and delight my soul. The symphony can speak from one heart to another. It is a message, a part of a relationship between people. And you cannot reduce the truth of the symphony, or its meaning and purpose, to its many mathematical patterns, even though they make it possible. They find their true context within the realms of consciousness, beauty and relationship that are enabled by the mathematics. And similarly, the mathematical patterns of the cosmos find their true meaning within the creative love of God, within his communication with us, and within his invitation to a relationship.

Therefore, I have suggested in this chapter that science has mostly flourished very well within a religious view of reality, and that theology has the potential to illuminate the context of science. Taken in artificial isolation, science can give the mistaken assumption that it is the mathematical properties of nature which are the only real and important aspects of existence. But the true shape of reality is known when all of our experiences are taken seriously. The true shape of reality is known when science, rationality, beauty, goodness, human consciousness and love are all understood together in the context of the creative love of God. I believe that a belief in God has a unique ability to bring together all these different aspects of reality and show how they relate to each other. I think that this potential is very significant.

Within science, it is thought to be a great breakthrough when diverse phenomena are understood within the same theoretical framework. One of the most impressive features of Newton's work on gravity and motion is that the same equations can describe both the fall of an apple and the orbit of an asteroid. But I think that a theological understanding of the universe has the potential to illuminate an even broader and richer view of reality. As I am describing in this book, it can bring together science, rationality, beauty, goodness, consciousness, love, meaning and purpose within one open framework. That open framework shows the context for the continued scientific exploration of the mathematical patterns of nature, showing how these patterns relate to the other aspects of reality.

The many scientists who are religious will happily testify that the enterprise of science can fit peacefully and fruitfully within a spiritual understanding of life. Those who believe in God should greatly value the truths uncovered by those who seek to explore the mathematical patterns within God's creation. The book of nature is a revelation of God, and we are discovering more and more about the astonishing beauty of that revelation. Those of us who have watched the orbits of the moons of Jupiter or photographed the swirling gases of the Orion nebula or looked into the microscopic structures of living cells have even more reason to marvel and to worship than those who have not. The accomplishments of God are even greater than our ancestors thought, and we should delight in this knowledge.

And so I believe that science and faith share a common history, belong together and can continue to benefit each other. Religion should be open to rational scrutiny and ready to learn from the discoveries of science. And science, I would like to suggest, may be able to learn from religious faith.

THEOLOGY AS A RESOURCE FOR SCIENCE

The suggestion that theology has something to offer science may surprise or alarm many people, but religion has already done much to point scientists in the right directions. I have described how Kepler and Newton found mathematical patterns in the cosmos because their faith inspired them to look for them. And I have described how Georges Lemaître developed the Big Bang theory because his faith told him that the universe had a beginning. In these cases, we remember them because they made discoveries and found evidence, but it was their faith which gave them their perspective on reality and which inspired them to follow these lines of enquiry.

I have a hunch that there are other ways in which faith could still point scientists in useful directions. My main message to scientists would be that reductionism has its limits. If you keep explaining big, complex phenomena in terms of lower levels of simpler, smaller phenomena, then you are doing something interesting and useful, but you may be missing something greater. I would recommend that research also looks in the other direction, and considers more than our ability to make measurements and formulate equations. I think that human consciousness is the most significant feature of the cosmos that we have yet discovered, and that the universe and all its particles and forces exist to make it possible. The most fundamental and important features of nature are not its mathematical patterns, but rather the phenomena of life and relationship which they enable. I would therefore like to propose two particular avenues of enquiry, one which approaches an answer to the greatest puzzle in modern science, and one which explores a direction of my own interest.

As I mentioned in the first chapter, modern physics is built around two big theories which totally refuse to fit together. Quantum mechanics describes the surprising behaviour of the smallest known components of matter and energy. Meanwhile, general relativity describes the workings of gravity, space and time on an astronomical scale. Both theories are now about a century old, and physicists have been trying for a very long time to amalgamate them into one Theory of Everything. But they have failed. Thinkers as great as Albert Einstein and Stephen Hawking have considered the problem, staring long and hard at the two sets of equations, and trying to find ways of fitting one into the other. But the holy grail of modern physics has always eluded them. Great mathematical ingenuity has been employed, including detailed speculations about many hidden dimensions and tiny vibrating strings. But the two mathematical systems remain stubbornly incompatible. The history of theoretical physics contained a rollercoaster ride of transformative breakthroughs throughout the late 19th and early 20th centuries, but has ground to a halt at this problem for a very long time.

My guess is that mathematical physicists will never find the unity that they seek, because it does not exist in the realm of mathematics. They are looking in the wrong place. My guess is that the real interface between these two separate branches of physics is not equations but consciousness. What these two theories have in common is that they both, in their very different ways, have a weirdness which suggests a central role for the observer. In the quantum realm, as I described in chapter 1, things seem only to take a definite form when people examine them. Meanwhile, up on the vast scale of relativity, the all-important concept is the observer's frame of reference: whether I am lying on a beach on my spinning planet, or sailing past in a boat, or hurtling away in a rocket. When we push space and time to extremes, we find that they are not fixed and absolute frameworks, but that they twist and stretch depending on the movements of those who observe them. The same object can be different sizes in different people's frames of reference. And events that are simultaneous for me can happen at different times for someone else. In relativity, as in quantum mechanics, the universe does not behave as a fixed and impersonal clockwork machine. The perspective and experience of the observer is central.

But physics has been studied by those who love mathematics, and who may feel a little less at home in a more personal realm. For a very long time, they have worked on the assumption that reality is fundamentally mathematical, and that life is an odd side-effect that can be safely ignored. 'Shut up and calculate' is a favourite slogan of those who dislike being asked about the human significance of quantum mechanics. But I would suggest that it is consciousness which is the fundamental reality: the mind of God underlying the cosmos, and the experiences of the living creatures which evolve within it and observe it. The quantum realm and the relativistic realm are different aspects of the scaffolding which enables the possibility of *us*. In a theatre, the pigments in the scenery and the beams in the great archway over the stage only make sense together in terms of the drama that happens within and which they enable. No other grand unified theory of paint and girders will ever work.

I therefore suspect that no amount of mathematical ingenuity will in itself overcome the century-old impasse of modern physics. It is time to bring in the poets, the novelists, the philosophers and the theologians: any who will take the central role of consciousness seriously.

The universe is shaped and sustained by the mind of God, and is configured to be a place within which life and consciousness and community will develop. Consciousness, beauty, goodness and love transcend the physical properties of nature which support them, and cannot be reduced to equations. But my second suggestion is that there is much about the human experience of consciousness, beauty, goodness and love which could be studied. I would wish simply to point to these aspects of reality, and to say to scientists, 'Look, this matters—see what you can find out.'

I will mention just one thing that intrigues me, which will draw together the themes of this chapter and the previous one. There is a good reason why men and women have evolved in such a way that men find women beautiful: it brings an attraction which helps the human race to reproduce. And there is a good reason why plants and insects have evolved in such a way that bees are attracted to flowers: bees get free food and flowers transmit pollen. And there is a good reason why peacocks and peahens have evolved in such a way that a peacock's colourful tail feathers attract the interest of a peahen: again, it is part of the way their species reproduces.

But why do I find flowers and peacocks beautiful, as well as women, even though we have evolved these various interactions separately? Obviously, there are physical aspects of my attraction to women which are missing in my response to the other two cases. But the appearance and the scent of flowers is not just some kind of private language between plants and bees, like the coded electrical pulses exchanged by my mobile phone and the nearest transmitter. It is something which human beings can appreciate too. I think the answer is that people, flowers and peacocks are all tapping into the universe's potential for beauty, just as an artist might. And I respond with joy to the beauty of flowers, peacocks and so many other delights in the world of nature. I would suggest also, therefore, that bees and peahens have something of an appreciation of beauty, even if perhaps they have very narrow tastes. But I find myself wondering whether peahens enjoy the appearance of flowers, and bees appreciate peacocks, and whether they all enjoy a good sunset. Even if beauty itself is beyond scientific definition, perhaps some future brain-scanning device can tell me more about the ways in which living creatures respond to it.

It seems to me that the universe is a social environment, configured with the potential for relationships. It is set up to cause the evolution of conscious life. And it makes possible this phenomenon of attraction, which draws living creatures together. For many of us, the beauty of the whole of nature is a reflection of the glory of God, inspiring within us a response of wonder, thankfulness and adoration, an invitation to a relationship of love.

But I still need to discuss the most famous current dispute relating to science and religion: the argument about creation and evolution. Are we really made in the image of God, or is our tiny presence in this vast universe only a brief and meaningless accident? The next chapter will suggest a way of answering that fascinating question.

SUGGESTIONS FOR FURTHER READING

A very helpful introduction to the philosophy of science is *What is this thing called science?* by Alan Chalmers (Open University Press, 2013).

A good introduction to the study of the relationship between science and faith is *Science and Religion: A Very Short Introduction* by Thomas Dixon (Oxford University Press, 2008).

A detailed textbook covering many aspects of that field is *God, Humanity and the Cosmos* edited by Christopher Southgate (T & T Clark, 2011).

I have been greatly helped and inspired by the writings of John Polkinghorne, a man who has been both a professor of mathematical physics in Cambridge University and a Church of England priest. I think I have found many of his ideas so convincing that I have forgotten that they were his, and there are probably more places than I realise in this book where he deserves to be warmly thanked. I would recommend any of his books, but a good summary of his work can be found in *Science and Religion in Quest of Truth* (SPCK, 2011).

For a highly enjoyable debunking of 25 myths about science and religion, see *Galileo Goes to Jail*, edited by Ronald L. Numbers (Harvard University Press, 2009).

Further debunking, in impressive detail, can be found in *God's Philosophers: How the Medieval World Laid the Foundations of Modern Science* by James Hannam (Icon, 2009).

Allan Chapman's *Stargazers: Copernicus, Galileo, the Telescope and the Church* (Lion Hudson, 2014) contains a wealth of fascinating detail, getting behind the myths to describe Galileo in his true context.

And for the truth about Columbus, see *Inventing the Flat Earth: Columbus and Modern Historians* by Jeffrey Burton Russell (Praeger, 1991).

Chapter Four
The Evolution of Consciousness

THE VITRUVIAN MAN

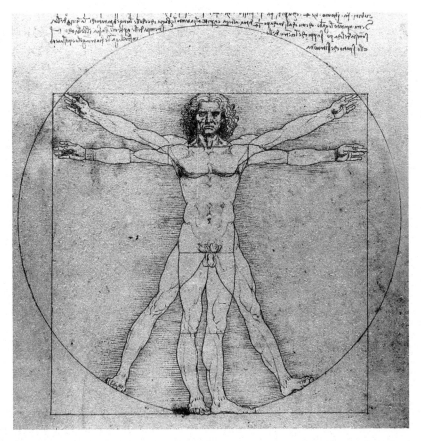

Leonardo da Vinci's most famous drawing is his pen and ink sketch of the Vitruvian Man. It illustrates the belief that human beings embody a set of universal principles, so that there are connections between the proportions of our bodies and the principles of geometry.

Vitruvius himself was a Roman architect in the first century BC. He believed that the natural figure of the human body was connected to the universal geometrical forms of the square and the circle, and was also related to the art of constructing beautiful buildings. He wrote about connections between the proportions of hands, heads, arms and shoulders and the proportions of an ideal temple. This ancient philosophical view found an appreciative home in the world of Renaissance man, combining biology, mathematics, engineering and aesthetics.

The Vitruvian Man has become the best-known symbol of the belief, held by Leonardo and many others in the Renaissance, that a human being is a microcosm: each of us is a lesser world which mirrors the wider structures of the cosmos. This relationship includes the way that the universal principles of mathematics and geometry are reflected in 'nature's design' of the human body, as Vitruvius describes it.[60] The idea of the microcosm held by the Christian thinkers of the Renaissance also includes the belief that a human being is both physical and spiritual. We each have a physical body which works in the same way as the physical world around us, and we have a rational soul which reflects something of the intelligence, love and consciousness of God. Our physical nature functions in the same ways as the bodies of animals, but our spiritual nature is an image of the divine.

This is a very positive view of our place in the cosmos, regarding us as people whose entire nature reflects the whole of reality. It connects with the claim that I am making in this book that all of our faculties are responses to genuine aspects of that reality. Those faculties include our five physical senses, along with our abilities to think rationally, to love, to empathise, and to perceive goodness and beauty. It is a view which lends itself to a unified, harmonious understanding of all human knowledge and experience.

However, many people today would regard this view as a quaint historical curiosity. They would see it as a misunderstanding which has been disproved by science. And they would think of it as self-indulgent, naïve or hopelessly arrogant. The people of the Renaissance were confident that they had been created by God and placed at the

---

60   Vitruvius *De Architectura*, translated by M H Morgan, Book III, chapter 1

centre of a purposeful cosmos. But, since then, we have discovered that our sun is only one among many billions of stars in our galaxy, which is itself only one of many billions of galaxies. Since the work of Charles Darwin (1809–1882), we have also discovered that we are the products of a long process of evolution caused by random mutations, so that our place on this one tiny planet is the result of a long series of accidents. Is there any future for Vitruvian Man?

THE INTERPRETATION OF GENESIS

The debate for Christians is famously associated with the beginning of the Bible, the first chapter of Genesis. The well-known opening passage describes God creating the heavens and the earth in six days, including the stars, the plants and the animals. It culminates in the creation of men and women, who together are made 'in the image of God'. This is the origin of Christianity's very confident sense that people have a privileged position within the universe. However, the familiar six-day story notoriously does not fit well with the account given by scientists. Although both narratives begin with a burst of light and end up with human beings, creation in Genesis 1 all happens within a week, rather than over billions of years. It is also out of sequence with the evidence, as seen in the way that the trees appear before the sun is created. Furthermore, the purposeful divine actions it describes seem very different from the random processes discovered by scientists. Evolution involves atoms rattling around randomly for billions of years, happening by chance to form themselves into groups which can reproduce themselves. They eventually form organisms which, over vast numbers of generations, become better adapted to the task of surviving in their various environments. Evolution sounds very different from six days of divine construction. When God is understood within the mechanical view of the cosmos, this contradiction is highlighted, because he is pictured as the one who designed and assembled everything at the beginning of time.

This is probably the strongest reason why many sceptics would consider a Christian theory of everything to be an impossible project. The Bible and the science of evolution seem to them to be contradictory and irreconcilable, suggesting that Christian faith can only continue among people who are stubbornly committed to the ignoring of evidence. Meanwhile, Richard Dawkins has described the discovery of evolution as the breakthrough that makes it possible to be an intellectually fulfilled atheist,[61] (a possibility that would have seemed remote during the Renaissance). Nevertheless, like the majority of the world's Christians, I do regard creation and evolution as compatible ideas, and will explain why. In this chapter, I will describe how science can actually shed new light on Genesis's declaration that we are made in the image of God.

It is worth first of all taking a closer look at what the Bible itself actually says. It is important to note that Genesis contains not one but two accounts of creation, which themselves give contradictory details of the order of creation. It would appear that the two texts come from different original sources which have very different styles. The divine name in chapter one is *Elohim*, simply meaning God, but in the account beginning at Genesis 2.4, he has the distinctive Jewish name *Yahweh*, meaning 'I am'.

The first account describes the famous sequence of six days of creation that I have already mentioned. Within this, the heavens and the earth are created on the first day, the plants on the third day, birds and fish on the fifth day, and animals and people (both men and women together) on the sixth day. But in the second account in chapter two, a single man, Adam, is created first of all, on the day of the creation of the earth and the heavens. His creation is followed by that of the plants, and then the animals. Finally, after the lonely Adam has finished naming every single living creature and assessing them all as potential helpers (which must have taken a good few weeks), Eve is created as his wife. The order and timescales are completely different in the two accounts, which suggests to me that the order and timescales were never meant to be the real point.

If we attempt to interpret both chapters literally, they do not fit together at all. And yet, they provide a set of powerful, moving and meaningful images to illustrate the purpose of the universe. They

---

61   R Dawkins (2006) *The Blind Watchmaker* Penguin, p. 6

convey a clear sense that creation is ordered, meaningful and good, and that human beings and our relationships have a special place in the purposes of God. And they describe how the universe depends on God for its existence. But whoever combined them made no attempt to harmonise their details, and so does not seem to have thought that the detailed mechanisms and timescales of creation were the real point of the texts. It seems clear to me that the real meaning and purpose of the combined document is not to be a textbook about the mechanisms of how things began.

Those who are determined to see chapter one as a literal scientific account have to go through all kinds of ingenious manoeuvres of rein-terpretation to make the second chapter fit in, or quietly ignore the differences. It is much more logical to notice that the combined text simply does not work that way. And I am not just saying that because I know about evolution and am looking for excuses to explain away Genesis. Theologians in the early church were happy to interpret these biblical passages as symbol and allegory. They asked how there could be days and daylight three days before the creation of the sun in chapter one. They wondered if a day might represent a much longer period of time. And, reading chapter three, they said that God would not literally walk around in the Garden of Eden having to search for Adam and Eve. Most Jews and Christians have been content to regard these two stories as having a poetic, symbolic meaning, since many centuries before Darwin. Those who insist a literal six-day creation tend to be some (mainly American) Evangelical Christians from the 20th century onwards, who feel that this is the only way they can demonstrate a place for God within the mechanical view of the cosmos.

The Genesis accounts show the divine purpose behind creation. They are written within the limited scientific understanding of the ancient world, making sense to an audience who knew very little about cosmology. They are not meant, in a few short pages, to be the last word about the complex workings of the universe and to rival all the subsequent discoveries of scientists. On the contrary, they show a sense that the cosmos has a goodness and an order which comes from God, and which should therefore be worth investigating. The fact that this investigation has uncovered huge amounts of evidence for evolution seems to me to be something which adds to the picture given by the creation accounts in Genesis, rather than replacing it.

Among many Christians today, it is therefore perfectly normal to regard evolution as the mechanism used by God in creation. Such a view combines a theological belief in the purpose of the cosmos with a scientific account of the details of its functions. Science has greatly enlarged our understanding of the cosmos, but it has in no way ruled out a belief that the universe has a purpose behind it. In fact, as I shall next describe, there are various aspects of modern science which provide a powerful validation for the view that human beings are a microcosm of reality. Far from disproving God, science can actually breathe new life into the Renaissance understanding of the cosmos.

THE HISTORY AND THE
FINE-TUNING OF THE UNIVERSE

Until the 19th century, Christians assumed that the universe had been created in the way that we see it now. Stars, planets, oceans, animals, birds, plants and people all had been given their places within one harmonious structure at the very beginning. This picture was reinforced by the development of the view of the mechanical cosmos. It appeared that the divine clockmaker had assembled all of the cogs and wheels in their final positions at the dawn of time. But the discoveries of science have added an extra dimension to this picture, the dimension of time and change. Science affirms that the universe has a beginning, but shows that what we see now is the result of a long and complex series of processes of development.

When the universe began, about 14 billion years ago, the first matter to appear was composed of hydrogen, the simplest of all elements. A universe made up of hydrogen does not look like a very promising start. But the clouds of gas were drawn together by the forces of gravity to form giant stars, and within them the processes of nuclear fusion began. Hydrogen atoms were joined together to form heavier atoms, releasing colossal energies and sending starlight out across the blackness of space. In this first generation of stars, the elements which now comprise our world and our bodies were forged: carbon, oxygen, nitrogen, silicon, iron and many others. And, after billions of years, when those stars ran low on hydrogen fuel and died, they flung those elements out across the universe in enormous explosions. When those ingredients collected together, later generations of stars and solar systems were formed, including our own sun with its rocky planets and moons.

When the Earth was formed about 4.5 billion years ago, it was composed of a far more varied collection of materials than those early clouds of hydrogen gas. There were lava flows and then rocks, and then running water and an atmosphere of oxygen and nitrogen. But, for a long time, it was a barren place, with no one to see its lifeless grandeur. But its carbon, nitrogen, oxygen and hydrogen held a hidden potential which began to be seen after perhaps nearly a billion years. Life developed, first in the form of simple microscopic organisms which could reproduce. And then, in increasing complexity, in the form of larger creatures which could swim, walk, run, climb and fly. At first, these creatures responded only to blind instinct, but then intelligence developed, and consciousness. There were people who stood upright, and painted pictures and looked at the stars and told stories to their children.

This 14 billion year history was unknown to the people of the Renaissance, but in my view it adds to the grandeur of their vision of the cosmos rather than detracting from it. A universe whose natural processes lead it to turn hydrogen gas into philosophers and strawberries is even more wondrous than one in which every species is manufactured in one go by its creator. These astonishing processes of development show, if anything, a greater sense of purpose than a universe which is static. And, the more we understand about those processes, the more remarkable our existence appears.

There are many details about the laws of physics, the structures of atoms and the conditions of the Big Bang which seem to be precisely balanced to cause the cosmos to be a life-giving environment, a setting within which living creatures can evolve. When cosmologists have simulated the results of tweaking any of the universe's parameters, working out how it would have developed under very slightly different conditions, the results have been startling. They only have to change the strength of gravity by a tiny amount, or give the merest nudge to the balance of forces within atoms, or make an infinitesimal alteration to the way in which the universe first expanded, and then life becomes impossible. The tiniest adjustment can mean that the universe collapses back in on itself long before any planets have appeared, or that it flies apart too fast for galaxies to form. Or it could have the result that the carbon atoms which are the basis of life are not stable, or that there is no water. In fact, many physical different parameters have to be fine-tuned to within one per cent of their current setting for the universe to be an environment within which life can evolve. And the probability of them all being just right is absurdly small. The physicist Fred Hoyle found that his atheist beliefs were deeply shaken by his discoveries about energy levels in carbon nuclei. It looked like a 'put-up job', he said, as if a super-intellect had been 'monkeying' with the laws of physics.[62]

Before the discovery of evolution, people used to marvel at the intricacies of different living creatures, and it seemed obvious to them that the elephant's trunk, the eagle's wings and the salmon's gills had all been specially and individually designed by a creator. But Darwin showed how all those adaptations to different environments could arise through processes of random mutation and natural selection. And, to some people, this has seemed to show that the whole universe is a gigantic and meaningless accident. However, subsequent discoveries have revealed more and more about the wonders of the processes of cosmological development and biological evolution which have given rise to the appearance of life.

Our existence as conscious, living beings depends on a whole series of natural processes being precisely balanced in exactly the right way. It is an extraordinary situation, in which the wonders of the universe very clearly demonstrate that there must be a lot more going on in reality than just this one physical cosmos. The universe is such a startling place that it seems very clearly to point beyond itself for an explanation. And there are two leading possibilities.

---

62   F Hoyle, 'The universe: past and present reflections' in *Annual Review of Astronomy and Astrophysics*, vol 20 (1982), p. 16

One cosmological explanation, whose supporters include Stephen Hawking and other atheists, is the multiverse theory. This accepts that the universe is an extraordinary place which happens to look deeply purposeful. But, notes the theory, it is hardly surprising that our universe is one which is exactly right for us to survive in, because we would not otherwise be here to be surprised. The theory then suggests that there must be an infinite number of universes, each with a slightly different set of physical parameters. And, in all the universes where life cannot evolve, there is no one there to notice. So, says the theory, our universe may happen to look purposeful and meaningful, but this is just an accident. We exist within an infinite assemblage of universes which are, as a whole, lacking in any kind of higher purpose.

There is, it should be noted, no evidence for the existence of these other universes. And to imagine the existence of an infinite number of parallel universes is a rather extreme step to take. It seems more plausible to many people to look at the only universe we know about, and to pay full attention to its wonders. For the second possible explanation is that our astonishing universe is the way it is for some good reason. There is some kind of meaning, purpose and intelligence behind this extraordinary reality. We belong here, in this social cosmos. Our existence as rational, conscious beings mirrors the existence of a divine mind which shapes the whole of reality. God remains a credible and powerful theory today.

HUMAN BEINGS AND THE SHAPE OF REALITY

The Renaissance belief in the human person as a microcosm describes a strong correspondence between human nature and the nature of this purposeful cosmos. That account of correspondence has an interesting similarity to our modern understanding of evolution, which describes how living beings develop to become adapted to their environment. As species develop, they evolve forms and abilities which enable them to maximise their ability to survive. There is then a strong correspondence between their nature and the nature of their surroundings.

It is interesting to explore the ways in which human have been shaped by the reality we inhabit. We have evolved within the cosmos, and all our various faculties have developed in response to the environment around us. There are fascinating connections between the nature of reality and the functions of all our human faculties, including our physical senses, our rationality, our conscience, our ability to empathise with others, and our appreciation of beauty. One example is our vision, which has evolved in response to the properties of light and the ways it interacts with matter.

The evolution of the eye is something which some people have been very sceptical about. They have asked how such a sophisticated organ could arise by chance. The eye is a very complex optical device, and it requires some impressive brain hardwire to process its signals. But some degree of sensitivity to light can be found even in bacteria, and plants can grow to face the light. The evolution of the eye has been able to proceed in tiny steps, because any increase in an organism's ability to respond to light is useful and helps it to survive by gaining a better understanding of its environment.

Perhaps the most fascinating thing about the eye is that it seems to have evolved independently in very different kinds of living creatures. Worms, octopuses and humans have all acquired similar kinds of eyes through separate evolutionary processes. And their eyes have a lot in common with the cameras that we have invented: a lens projects an image onto a sensor. This seems to be the simplest way of receiving and processing light in order to view the detailed layout of our surroundings. So here is the really remarkable thing: given the structure of reality, given the laws of physics, given the way that light behaves and interacts with matter, given this potential inherent within the cosmos, the eye is the solution which arises repeatedly to make use of that potential. It has happened independently a number of times on Earth, because separate evolutionary processes have converged on the same solution. If there is life on other planets, we can reasonably expect aliens to have eyes. It is likely, also, that they will have two eyes so that they can judge depth and thereby perceive the three dimensions of space. So the existence and structure of eyes is determined by the structure and functioning of the universe. Evolution involves a large number of random mutations and a very long time, but the end result is shaped by the nature of reality itself. The eye, amazingly, follows directly from the very parameters of physics which were built into the Big Bang.

This view of evolution is more time-consuming than the picture of a creator who designs eyes and then calls them into existence in a day. But I think it is an awe-inspiring discovery to find that this universe, which is precisely structured to enable the evolution of life, is also structured in a way which leads to the evolution of eyes. The same could be said about all of our other senses and faculties: they have developed in response to our environment. Our physical bodies are, in a sense, a reflection of the shape of reality, as suggested by Leonardo's *Vitruvian Man*. Simon Conway Morris, Professor of Evolutionary Palaeobiology in Cambridge University, has therefore written about evolutionary convergence and 'inevitable humans'.[63]

The development of consciousness can be understood in a similar way to the development of vision. The potential for human consciousness has been there, woven into the nature of matter right from the very beginning, just like the potential for sight. Consciousness greatly enhances human abilities. There is a clear evolutionary advantage to developing it, in the same way that it is useful to have sight. Conscious beings are better at understanding themselves and their surroundings, and so are better at surviving. Conscious beings are better adapted to their environments, and reality is structured in a way which causes conscious life to evolve. The evolutionary process draws out the advantages of this potential for consciousness, which is part of the fabric of reality. Our souls, we might say, are a reflection of the shape of reality. And that thought brings us back very closely to the Renaissance idea of the microcosm. Our physical and spiritual faculties are an image of the cosmos and of the divine mind that shapes the universe.

The evolutionary process as whole, therefore, is not random. Nor, I would suggest, is it purposeless. Over time, creatures evolve which reflect the shape of reality, and I can illustrate that process with a couple of analogies. Suppose, for example, I have a box with lots of marbles in it, which I shake around and tilt. The marbles will roll and fall in lots

63   S Conway Morris (2003) *Life's Solution: Inevitable Humans in a Lonely Universe*
Cambridge University Press

of complex ways and end up in a random order. But they will tend to settle into a regular pattern made of triangles and hexagons, which is the most efficient way of filling the space. Atoms do something similar when they fit together to form crystals. The process of being thrown around was random, and could have happened in countless different ways, but the final pattern is determined by the shape of the box and the shape of the marbles, along with the geometrical properties of space. A similar thing happens if I make my bed by holding on to one end of the duvet and throwing it all in the air. It makes a rather chaotic shape while it is all billowing up and down. But it settles tidily onto the flat surface of the bed, taking the ordered form which is given to it by the shape of the environment. In a similar way, evolution involves a huge amount of activity which may look random and disordered in its details. But, as organisms become more and more adapted to their environments, life takes on a form which responds more and more closely to the nature of reality.

This shaping of life could be seen as a very surprising accident, or as an impenetrable mystery, but it can also shed new light on the idea in Genesis that God made men and women in his own image. Jews and Christians understand this to be a spiritual resemblance, meaning that we share something of God's abilities to think, to make choices, to love, and to form relationships. As I have been describing, we human beings have evolved to reflect the nature of reality, and reality itself is shaped and sustained by God. There is a direct correspondence between us human beings and the structure and purpose of the cosmos, and the cosmos itself is an expression of the divine mind. As philosopher Thomas Nagel has written, 'mind is not just an afterthought or an accident or an add-on, but a basic aspect of nature.'[64] So here is a new and perhaps more wonderful way in which we can regard ourselves as being formed in the image of God: our consciousness has evolved to reflect the divine consciousness which shapes the whole cosmos. We have evolved to be people with the intellectual and spiritual capacity to respond to God.

---

64   Thomas Nagel (2012) *Mind and Cosmos: Why the Materialist Neo-Darwinian Conception of Nature Is Almost Certainly False* Oxford University Press, p. 16

THE WONDER OF HUMAN CONSCIOUSNESS

I have been making a strong claim about a deep connection between human nature and the nature of the cosmos which will surprise many people today. Are we really all that special? Human beings have existed for only a tiny fraction of the 14 billion-year history of the universe. We live on a planet orbiting a star which is one of hundreds of billions of stars in a galaxy which is one of hundreds of billions of galaxies. The fraction of the universe's space and history taken up by human beings is absurdly, vanishingly tiny. The vast majority of space and the vast majority of time seem to have nothing to do with us human beings. The cosmos's story is more about bacteria, dinosaurs, barren craters and, above all, colossal empty voids.

The scale of the universe and its age should fill us with awe. However, despite all our space probes, despite all the observations we have made of the universe with optical telescopes, radio telescopes, x-ray telescopes and other ingenious devices, despite all the ways we have looked out into this vast cosmos, and despite all our investigations into the history of the Earth, one extraordinary fact remains. We have not found anything anywhere in the universe which is more remarkable, sophisticated, complex and extraordinary than a human being. The rings of Saturn, the Orion Nebula and the Niagara Falls are nowhere near as wondrous as one single human child. And what seems to me most wonderful of all is the phenomenon of consciousness which we human beings experience. As I described in chapter 2, our role as conscious observers seems to play an important part in the way that the universe becomes what it is. It is well worth taking some more time to consider how special that consciousness is, for it is the most remarkable phenomenon which the universe displays.

Research by physicists at the University of Leicester has suggested that Star Trek's transporter beam may never be possible because of the vast amount of data needed to fully map a human brain.[65] Even with the kind of colossal bandwidth which would put our fastest Wi-Fi connection to shame, it would still take more time than the age of the

---

65   D. Roberts, J. Nelms, D. Starkey, S. Thomas: 'Travelling by Teleportation' in *Journal of Physics Special Topics*, University of Leicester, November 2012

universe to transmit a full analysis of the mind of one person. Crew members from the Starship Enterprise would need to find a much faster way to escape from any impending crises.

I have met many people and have got to know some of them well, but I have never come across two people with identical personalities. Even identical twins have remarkably different characters. Each of us is the result of a long story, a highly complex product of experiences, choices and relationships. People can spend years exploring the complex inner workings of their own minds, emotions, fears, hopes and abilities. There are many ways of measuring aspects of human personality, but there is no meaningful way of reducing human consciousness to a simple set of numbers. To know a person well requires a long friendship, and much time spent listening to their life story and their feelings about the future. Even then, we can still surprise ourselves and those who know us best. Our consciousness is an extraordinarily complex phenomenon which sets us apart from the great variety of other living creatures in the world around us. And the civilisation we have formed together is, as Brian Cox has written, 'the most complex emergent phenomena in the known universe.'[66]

The simplest forms of life are bacteria. They do not exhibit what we would call intelligence, but they can respond to their environment in various ways. For example, they might swim towards light, or towards a higher concentration of a particular nutrient. It would be quite easy to build a robot which could do the same kind of thing. A car with automatic windscreen wipers which turn on when it rains displays that level of sophistication. Looking at something bigger, the chickens in my garden have small brains and show some signs of intelligence. From when they first hatch, they know how to run around and can jump accurately as soon as their wing feathers grow. They recognise food and they peck it. They make noises to warn each other about potentially hostile creatures in the garden. When it gets dark, they move into the coop and onto their perch. They have a limited ability to learn, and know that when they hear me opening the door it is worth running over to see if I have brought them any food. But, in other ways, they are remarkably

66   Brian Cox (2014) *Human Universe* William Collins, p. 271

unable to analyse their own decisions. When they have laid a number of eggs, they follow an instinct which tells them to sit on the eggs and incubate them for three weeks. But a broody hen will still stubbornly sit in her warm nest box even if we have already removed and eaten all the eggs she wants to hatch. She does not understand why she feels she has to sit there, and is unable to make the judgement that there is no longer any point. It is only if we move her to a cold wire-bottomed cage that she will give up and carry on with normal life. It is obvious that chickens are following a number of instincts, and are learning to associate some sounds and sights with food. But they have very little ability to solve problems and to think about the limitations of their instincts. I do not know if anyone has ever tried, but I think it would be possible to construct a convincing robotic chicken.

But what about us? We certainly have a strong set of instincts which cover our basic survival needs. We have powerful urges which lead us to find food, water, shelter, warmth and safety, to form social groups and to mate and reproduce. But we also have the ability to make intelligent judgements, to override our immediate instincts and to solve problems. Other living creatures are confined to the environments within which they evolved. But humans, with the aid of clothes, fires, tinned food, transport networks and other inventions can live among penguins, among camels, or in the vacuum of space. We have evolved abilities which enable us to explore the cosmos far more than any of the other creatures of this world.

But the distinctiveness of human nature involves more than just intelligence. I am more than just a logical mechanism which solves problems and responds creatively to its environment. I am more than just a computational device which can optimise its behaviour to meet a set of programmed goals. *I am aware that I am me.* I am conscious. I know that I *am*, that I exist. I have an understanding of myself. I know what it feels like to be me. I ask all kinds of awkward questions about my existence and about reality. I am a lot more than just an arrangement of atoms which has developed highly sophisticated survival and self-replication strategies. I listen to symphonies and climb mountains and look at the stars and wonder what it all means.

In the earlier stages of the evolution of life, it seems to me that living creatures were tapping into the same kinds of properties of matter that we make use of when we build machines. But human beings have accessed a much deeper and more wonderful property of the universe than physical forces or chemical reactions. We have become conscious. And it is this consciousness that I am referring to when I say that we have not found anything more wonderful than a human being. The most amazing thing within the cosmos is our presence looking out at it, marvelling at its beauty, and pondering its meaning

The people of the Renaissance understood human nature in a dualist way, which they had inherited from the Greek philosophers: they regarded human beings as having a physical body and a spiritual soul. Our bodies are similar to the bodies of animals, and they exhibit the same kinds of physical properties as machines. Yet we also have a rational, spiritual side to us, an ability to make intelligent choices, and to perceive beauty and goodness and wonder. In Plato's philosophy, it is the soul which connects us to all that is eternal, beautiful, good and true, while the body exhibits the tendency of all material things to break down and decay.

This dualistic understanding was easily absorbed by Christian theology, even though the Jewish view of human nature found in the Bible sees human beings as a more integrated union of body and spirit. Many Christians today still hold to a belief in a detachable soul which is implanted by God at conception. The Catholic Church, for example, although it now accepts the evolutionary account of the development of human bodies, still insists that we have a divinely-installed eternal soul which distinguishes us from the animals.

However, science has produced many fascinating insights into the ways in which human consciousness is actually something that arises from our material bodies, rather than being a contrasting addition to them. Much about the human brain is still a mystery to us, but we know far more about it than the people of the Renaissance did. We have discovered many ways in which drugs can greatly affect our perceptions, moods and behaviour though their effects on the biochemical systems of our brains. Physical injuries to the brain can also have drastic effects on our personalities, changing our abilities to process language or vision or to stabilise our emotions. Our state of mind also has an observable impact on our physical health: people more likely to recover from an illness if they are in a calm and optimistic mood and believe that they are being given an effective treatment. All the evidence seems to suggest that we function as an interconnected unity of body and mind. My consciousness, my sense of who I am, very much arises from my body, from my brain, and from all my physical senses.

Knowing all this, we are in a good position to outdo the people of the Renaissance. Where they saw dualism, we can find a greater sense of unity. Our understanding of consciousness can be connected even more deeply to our understanding of the whole of reality.

It seems to me that consciousness is something which we as a species have acquired through evolution, and which each new human being acquires gradually as he or she grows. The first creatures which ever flew were making use of a property of matter which had not previously been utilised. And the first occurrence of human consciousness was similarly making use of a potential hidden within matter which had not previously been accessed.

But although I do not believe in a separately created soul, I do want to emphasise that the consciousness which arises from each physical body also far transcends it. My consciousness, along with my sense of identity and my personality, is far greater than the sum of my physical parts. It is not something which can be described and predicted according to any mathematical pattern. It cannot be reduced to any equation or brain scan. Yes, there are ways in which you could control and manipulate my experience with drugs, surgery, lights or sounds. Yes, there are various phenomena related to consciousness which can be studied and influenced by scientists. But there is something about me which is private, which is who I am inside, which is who I decide to be. The experience of being me is something which could be conveyed far more authentically in poetry or drama or autobiography than it could be in any graph or equation. Consciousness is one of the most significant and complex aspects of reality.

There is a huge amount which has been learned and a huge amount which remains to be learned by those who study the connections between the properties of the brain and our experience of consciousness. But, as I described in the first chapter, scientific reductionism has its limits. We will not grasp the full significance and meaning of human consciousness if our only approach is to try to break it down into components and mechanisms. Consciousness arises from the physical properties of the human brain and body, but it is far greater than the sum of the parts which make it possible.

There is much about who we are, as individual people and as people in communities, which transcends anything which could ever be explained mathematically. You cannot deduce the fact that I like choral singing, astronomy and eating raspberries from the properties of a hydrogen atom. Culture, literature, love and civilisation exist because of atoms and forces, but I am not waiting with any realistic expectation for all these forms of knowledge to be reduced to equations and derived from the laws of physics. The soul arises from the body and all its atoms and molecules, but it then far surpasses them, as do the communities and relationships we form.

MORE ABOUT THE CREATIONIST CONTROVERSY

I have been writing enthusiastically about how modern science can shed new light on the idea that human beings have a meaningful place within a purposeful cosmos. I want to talk very positively about a view of reality which can encompass both science and spirituality, and which takes all our experiences seriously. But, of course, there is a notorious and bitter argument raging in some quarters about creation and evolution, and that needs some further attention.

I find this argument very disappointing, and regard it as one of the saddest divisions in the fragmented landscape of human thought. It seems obvious and straightforward to me to think that our discoveries about the evolution of human consciousness have great spiritual significance. And I do not see any inherent contradiction between a theological view of reality and an enthusiastic interest in the findings of modern science. The two seem to me to belong very happily together.

My sense of wonder encompasses both a love of spirituality and a delight in the scientific exploration of nature.

Nevertheless, it is well-known that not all religious people would agree with me. One of the most notorious clashes of worldviews today involves a bitter set of arguments about creation and evolution. A noisy minority of Christians, and various members of other faiths, are convinced that evolution is an inherently atheist ideology which must be resisted fiercely. Their attitude encourages some admirers of science to think that religion is a dangerously irrational ideology which must be resisted fiercely. Each side thereby manages to confirm the other's worst fears. On one side, there are religious fundamentalists who think that evolution is a cunning deceit which is intended to undermine all that is good and true. On the other side, there are some passionate supporters of science who think that all religion is a barbarous rejection of rationality. The more noise they make, the more they alarm each other and the less they listen.

The one thing they agree on is that creation and evolution are incompatible. But that perceived incompatibility has nothing to do with the ideas themselves. The ideas, as I have been describing, can fit together in fascinating ways. The problem is simply that creation and evolution have become tribal slogans, rallying-cries for two opposing communities of people who misunderstand and mistrust each other. This is a distinctively American phenomenon, part of the polarisation of a country which is now very deeply divided along political and religious lines. It is a row which began to flare up in the 1920s because of disagreements about the place of religion in publicly-funded American schools.

By then, evolution had long since been peacefully and thoughtfully accepted by religious people in Europe and elsewhere. After Darwin published his book *On the Origin of Species* in 1859, there was much lively discussion among all kinds of people, but his conclusions were soon widely believed in Britain. Theologians noted with interest that the discovery of evolution revealed more about the mechanisms by which God created all the different forms of life. One of those who warmly welcomed Darwin's discoveries was Frederick Temple (1821–1902), who later became Archbishop of Canterbury. He and many others found it fascinating to think of God creating a universe within which life could evolve in so many diverse forms through just one process. They recognised a life-giving cosmos as a greater divine wonder than a world in which God needed to act in different ways to make each individual species. Darwin's ideas became widely accepted in the Church of England in his lifetime, and he was given the very rare honour of a state funeral in Westminster Abbey.

Sadly, the American creationist rejection of evolution seems now to be becoming more well-known around the world. Accounts of Christians in England rejecting evolution were rarely heard 20 years ago, but seem more common now. And the atheist protest against creationism is also becoming more famous. This angry division greatly saddens me, because good people on both sides are missing out on a greater vision of the whole of reality. There is still a wide middle ground of people who are sympathetic to both science and religion, but we do not make the headlines in the way that the campaigners on each side of us do.

The fundamental problem is that we have all got into the habit of trying to separate our investigation of the physical mechanisms of the cosmos from our exploration of its meaning and purpose. There is only one reality, and both of those enquiries are important aspects of the ways we use our various faculties to relate to it. But those different processes of enquiry are now occupied and policed by different professions, each of which gets very protective of its territory.

It seems to me that religious people who reject the evidence for evolution are closing their eyes to a wealth of fascinating discoveries about the universe. Since they believe that it is God's creation, they ought to enjoy finding out more about what he has done. To refuse to use our senses and our minds to explore the world shows a strange lack of faith in the one who gave us those abilities and who made the world. The evidence for evolution is extremely strong, found within ancient fossils, within the patterns of DNA, and in the distribution of different species in different places around the world. For me and for a great many other theologians, evolution seems to fill in some of the details of our picture of the works of God, rather than to overturn the picture. On the other hand, it seems to me that those who love science but reject any sense that the universe has a higher purpose behind it are also missing out. It takes an odd kind of tunnel vision to explore the wondrous story of the cosmos without developing any ideas about its meaning.

For me, the discoveries of science and the insights of faith seem to belong very happily together. They can each help us to enlarge our awareness of the wonders of the cosmos, and I have often enjoyed pondering the potential interactions between traditional spiritual wisdom and modern discoveries. I used to work in a church which was built in 1170, a beautiful Romanesque building whose elegant design and fabulously-carved stonework tell a story of centuries of human life, community, art, faith and spirituality. But we now understand an even older story which is hidden within the fabric of the stone walls. Little fragments of shells can be seen here and there, trapped within the solid rock. They tell us about an ancient sandy sea bed millions of years ago in the Jurassic era, when dinosaurs walked the earth, and when the English countryside was submerged in warm water somewhere near the tropics. This planet is ancient, and we are part of its long story. But there is yet another story, older still, hidden within the fabric of those shells. They were made from atoms which were forged in the hearts of stars billions of years ago, and then flung across the universe in colossal explosions. And we are here because they came to form a planet which was just right for living creatures. I used to think about those three long stories when I sat in the still, prayerful atmosphere of that church. The history of the development of the cosmos and of life on earth is a wondrous thing. I see it as a marvellous unfolding of a divine purpose which stretches across the vastness of space and time. Its immensity is awe-inspiring. It captivates my mind, and draws my heart to worship.

The discoveries of science seem to me to connect in fascinating ways with a spiritual belief in the purpose of the cosmos. Those who try to set evolution and faith against each other are engaged in a battle which I find entirely unnecessary. But it is beyond the scope of this chapter to try to unpick all the great religious and political divisions of America.

Instead, I am going to proceed more positively by seeking to return to the Renaissance vision of the unity of all truth, drawing together all that I have been saying about a Christian way of making sense of the evolution of consciousness.

GOD AND EVOLUTION

In the Renaissance, people believed that they were living at the heart of an ordered, purposeful cosmos. Within that divine order, they believed that they had been given free will and the opportunity to grow in love and virtue. They believed that they had a physical nature, like animals, and also a spiritual nature. They believed that they had the potential, therefore, to become brutish if they thoughtlessly followed only their bodily instincts, or to develop the life of the soul through appreciating reason, beauty, goodness and virtue. They saw the human condition as having both a deeply flawed predisposition towards sinfulness, and also a glorious potential for spiritual transformation. In my view, the scientific discoveries of the last five centuries do not undermine that vision of life; they actually add depth and colour to it.

Firstly, the discoveries of evolution and of the history of the cosmos open up an extra dimension in our understanding of the order and purpose of the cosmos, as I have described. The dramatic story of the development of an ancient universe provides even more insight to stimulate our sense of wonder. And this understanding of a purposeful, developing cosmos provides a very meaningful background to our understanding of our own growth as individual conscious beings, and the development of our society.

Secondly, there is an interesting combination of direction and openness in the evolutionary picture of the cosmos. In my analogy of the box of marbles, the patterns formed by the marbles when I shake the box are inevitable consequences of geometry and physics; but the movements of any individual marble are impossible to predict. In the same way, the universe proceeds purposefully towards the evolution of consciousness; but many of the details of what happens within it appear to us to be determined far more by various small local circumstances, random events and human choices. The universe provides us with both an experience of divine purpose and a genuine sense of freedom. I will talk more about the place of openness, risk, evil, conflict and suffering within the cosmos in the remaining chapters.

Thirdly, our understanding of evolution sheds more light on the human experience of being pulled in different directions by different instincts, ideas and aspirations, both physical and spiritual. We now understand that we are evolved animals, who exist because our biological nature is well-suited to survival. We have urgent instincts, therefore, to find food and water, to protect ourselves, and to reproduce. We are social creatures, with much to gain from being part of a group, but also with a strong desire to gain status within the group. Much of our instinctive thinking therefore centres on a preoccupation with food, sex, possessions, territory and competition.

Many of the details and foibles of our default human nature make sense in this evolutionary way. Food is essential to our survival and is one of life's great pleasures, especially in meals shared with those we love. But we have a natural tendency to eat too much, and especially to eat too many sweet and salty foods, because the human race evolved under conditions when food could be scarce, and sugar and salt were rare and important. We have also hunted species to extinction, having evolved under conditions where the resources of nature seemed limitless.

Sex is another of life's great joys, and is necessary for the existence of the next generation. It is especially meaningful in the context of a loving relationship where there is real trust, intimacy and commitment. Love, partnership and parenthood are important parts of most people's lives. But we can end up giving a large proportion of our attention to our sex drives in ways which are either pointless or actually harmful, seeking multiple affairs and encounters with prostitutes, or amassing huge collections of pornography, or treating others in ways which are thoughtless or predatory. The urgency of the human sex drive means that some forms of behaviour may instinctively feel important and necessary which actually do little to enrich our lives and may even be damaging.

Many of the skills used by people playing team sports such as football also seem to relate to our evolutionary origins. They are similar to the skills used by our ancestors when hunting animals or fighting other tribes. We still feel instinctively drawn to this kind of behaviour, which is generally a healthy form of exercise and shared fun. But instincts for hunting and for defending territory are not always ideally suited to the smooth functioning of modern life. Some of the gangs of bored teenagers who hang around on street corners together, occasionally carrying out random acts of vandalism or getting into fights, might adjust far more naturally to life in the kind of environment we first evolved in. If they were in a tribe which trained them to take a valued place as warriors, hunting for food and defending the camp, they might feel much more fulfilled. Instead, our society tends to be wary of them and to make them feel like outcasts, while they drift around in confusion with a troubling sense that something is wrong and that no one understands them.

Our normal instincts, therefore, have equipped us well to survive, but may have serious limitations and may be ill-adapted to aspects of our present circumstances. However, we also have the intelligence to reflect on our situation and the potential to grow beyond it. We have an awareness of goodness, honour, faithfulness and virtue, alongside our tendency towards selfishness and defensiveness. Human maturity involves the ability to understand and control ourselves, and to act with wisdom and insight rather than blind instinct. And human consciousness gives us the ability to perceive a set of spiritual ideals, to ponder the beauty of the cosmos, and to become aware of the ways in which our lives can contribute meaningfully to the good of the world.

Nevertheless, we often struggle to live up to our ideals. We may have a view of the kind of people we would like to become, but we get lost in our anxieties and bad habits. We have a sense that things feel broken within us and within our society, and that we are not yet the individuals and the communities that we know we ought to be. As St Paul wrote in Romans 7, 'I can will what is right, but I cannot do it.' Christian spirituality has always been very familiar with this awareness of a gulf between the people we are and the people we are meant to be. It is the difference between our default sinful nature and the virtues which God calls people to develop gradually through the transforming power of the Holy Spirit.

The most famous biblical account of the human struggle with our own troublesome desires is found in the third chapter of the book of Genesis. Adam and Eve eat the fruit which God has told them not to eat, with the consequence that they are expelled from the Garden of Eden. Beginning with the fourth-century writings of St Augustine, western Christianity described this gulf by interpreting the myth of Adam and Eve in Genesis chapter 3 as a catastrophic fall into sin from an original state of perfection, unleashing chaos and death into the whole world. That approach conveys vividly the sense that something feels broken and messed up within us. But the theme of a perfect paradise at the dawn of human history is actually something that the Bible itself hardly ever refers back to, and which we have no external evidence for. Eden seems to be legendary rather than geographically and historically real.

There is an earlier Christian way of reading Genesis, developed by the second-century theologian St Irenaeus, which has been influential in eastern Christianity and has become more well-known again in the west in recent decades. It does not think in terms of an initial state of perfection followed by a sudden descent into depravity, but of a slow process of growth. It reads the story of Adam and Eve as an account of human beings beginning in a state of naive childlike immaturity, becoming aware of good and evil, and beginning to learn to live with the consequences of their choices. Irenaeus' approach fits better with a scientific account of the universe as a long process of development, within which life and consciousness gradually evolve. But either view symbolises the deep human awareness that there is a great gap between the way we are and the way we ideally should be.

The wisdom of many faiths and philosophies, with their explorations of the inner life and their calls for self-examination and holiness, centres on the need for us to learn to direct our bodily instincts appropriately, with love, moderation, self-control, delight and thoughtfulness. Such wisdom contrasts with the way that today's very individualist and commercialised society encourages us to follow our desires and to maximise our ability to control resources. It is important to recognise that our primitive survival instincts can be very short-sighted and foolish, and that we need to gain a greater vision for our spiritual development and for the needs of the world around us. Greed and impatience are deeply destructive to our souls and to our environment.

The Christian message calls people to respond to God's love with thanksgiving, trust and a change of heart, in ways which lift us out of our selfishness and give us a greater vision. It tells us of a future in which we can lose our sinfulness and learn to live in harmony with the divine consciousness that shapes this social cosmos. This understanding seems to me to connect very fruitfully with a belief that we are evolved animals who have acquired the spiritual awareness to sense a higher calling and a greater destiny.

But what can we say about the one who calls us, and about the significance that our lives can acquire when we follow that higher calling? The next chapter will address the central theological question of God.

SUGGESTIONS FOR FURTHER READING

For an example of the Renaissance view of human nature as a micro-cosm, see the Fourth Exposition in the *Heptaplus* by Pico della Mirandola ((1463–1494). This can be found in the volume entitled *On the Dignity of Man* (Hackett, 1998), which also contains notes relevant to this theme on page xv.

The Goldilocks Enigma: Why is the Universe Just Right for Life? By Paul Davies (Allen Lane, 2006) gives a useful account of the fine-tuning of the universe and sets out a range of possible explanations. Rodney Holder's *Big Bang, Big God: A Universe Designed for Life* (Lion, 2013), brings cosmology and theology together very persuasively.

Simon Conway Morris's work on evolutionary convergence can be found in his weighty volume *Life's Solution: Inevitable Humans in a Lonely Universe* (Cambridge University Press, 2003), or summarised in one chapter as *Evolution and the Inevitability of Intelligent life* published in *The Cambridge Companion to Science and Religion* (edited by Peter Harrison, Cambridge University Press, 2010).

Much has been published about the arguments over creation and evolution. Richard Dawkins, writing from an atheist perspective, is famous for his accounts of evolution in works such as *The Selfish Gene* (Oxford University Press, 2006), *The Blind Watchmaker* (Penguin, 2006) and *The God Delusion* (Transworld, 2006). Alister McGrath, a theologian with a background in science, argues that Darwinism is compatible with religion in *Dawkins' God: Genes, Memes and the Meaning of Life* (Blackwell, 2005). Thomas Dixon's *Science and Religion: A Very Short Introduction* (Oxford University Press, 2008) contains a good overview of the debate and its history. More details from a wide range of perspectives can be found in the documents contained in Mary Kathleen Cunningham's *God and Evolution: A Reader* (Routledge, 2007).

For more about the comparison between Irenaeus and Augustine, see *Evil and the God of Love* by John Hick (Macmillan, 1985).

Chapter Five

Personality and the Meaning of Life

THE PERSONAL GOD

This social view of the cosmos attributes great significance to human consciousness and character, and to the relationships that we build. It also suggests that our consciousness reflects something of a far greater consciousness that underlies the whole of reality, a divine mind to which we can relate in a personal way. To do so is to follow one of the deepest instincts which human beings have evolved in response to reality.

Worship and prayer are found in some form throughout the many traditional cultures of the world and throughout human history. A sense of spirituality can be seen in the pyramids of ancient Egypt, in the cathedrals of modern Brazil, and among the pilgrims who visit the sacred river Ganges, to give just three examples. Many have therefore suggested that we have some kind of 'God-shaped hole' within our being, a spiritual hunger for relationship which senses that we are incomplete without a connection to a divine power. I believe that these instincts point to something which is as real and significant as the targets of our instincts to find food and shelter. As St Augustine prayed: 'You have made us for yourself, and our hearts are restless till they find their rest in you.'[67]

But many sceptics regard this instinctive longing for God as a childish and superstitious way of thinking which modern people ought to grow out of. They single out this aspect of our natural response to

67 Saint Augustine *Confessions* I.i

reality and label it as delusional, misleading or self-indulgent. This rejection seems to me to be a very curious judgement. I find it strange that some people suggest that we should ignore our spiritual intuitions, while continuing to take very seriously all our other faculties. Such people usually think that we should still pay great attention to our rationality, our five physical senses and our sexual desires, believing that they tell us important things about our identity and the reality surrounding us. I would not dispute that at all. But I would also insist that our spiritual instincts have evolved like all our other faculties in response to the shape of reality – they are tuning into something real about ourselves and our universe. As I argued in the previous chapter, there are good reasons for continuing to believe that a human being is a microcosm of reality, and reflects the image of God. It is very significant that human beings across many cultures and ages find it natural and meaningful to address the divine in a personal way.

But God is the ultimate reality, greater than the universe, the source of all being, and one who is far greater than any set of ideas which we can fit in our heads. When we talk to God, or about God, we inevitably do so with a mental picture of him that is much smaller and much more simplistic than the reality of God. All language about divinity faces this risk, including the language of personal relationships. When we address God in a personal way, we may make the sustainer of the cosmos sound like our invisible friend, or Father Christmas, or a distant bureaucrat. It is also tempting to see God as a large version of our own culture, treating him as a national mascot, and thinking that he identifies especially with our own great nation, whatever that might be. Although the hierarchical view of the cosmos gives a sense of the greatness of God by positioning him as the most highly-exalted person of all, it runs the risk of giving the impression that he is a remote, detached, grumpy old man.

There are therefore many who recoil from the limitations of these images. Perhaps they still want to describe themselves as spiritual, but they say that they do not believe in a *personal* God. They tend to say this in a way which distances themselves from traditional religion and its very human squabbles, but which still affirms a sense of wonder and goodness. They have a feeling that life is meaningful and that there is something bigger than us going on in this fascinating universe. But they may see this greater power as something mysterious and indescribable which goes beyond the views of divinity found in any faith. They may perhaps talk about some kind of spiritual force of goodness, or destiny, or a life force. They may worry that organised religion is just a very human way of propping up empires or supporting the careers of the ambitious.

Einstein, for example, did not practice the Jewish faith he was brought up with, even though he believed in God. He thought that a belief in a personal God was closer to the truth than atheism, and that traditional religious faith was the most accessible approach for ordinary people, but he did not think it was the best possible answer. His view was that the most perceptive spiritual geniuses were distinguished by a 'religious feeling, which knows no dogma and no God conceived in man's image'.[68] For him, the idea of God as personal was limited by being anthropomorphic: it regarded God as a large projection of ourselves.

I think that there is some value and wisdom in Einstein's caution, for the reasons I have already stated. But I am still going to suggest that personal, narrative language can be the best way of talking about our experiences of the divine. Inevitably, when trying to make great big statements about the realm of the infinite, we have to make comparisons with things that are simpler and more familiar. And the clearest example of making 'progress' away from a personal deity is the transition from the hierarchical to the mechanical view of the cosmos. Yet, projecting our own industrial successes out onto the universe is just as anthropomorphic, if not more so. It is also more simplistic to think of the whole of reality as a giant piece of engineering, since any clockwork mechanism is far less sophisticated than a living personality.

As I described in the previous chapter, the most advanced and complex features of the universe known to us are consciousness and the loving relationships formed by conscious beings. Personality and love are actually the most sophisticated and highly evolved aspects of

---

68   A Einstein (2007) *The World As I See It* B N Publishing, p. 34

reality that we have discovered, not its most naive and primitive. The language of character and love is therefore the most advanced thing we have available to us when we are trying to describe God.

But talking about a consciousness which sustains the whole cosmos is about as far away from our confident scientific reductionism as we can possibly get, which is another reason why some people are very doubtful about it. It is much easier to reach an agreement about those aspects of reality which we can measure and quantify. By contrast, the stories which human beings tell about one or more deities are very diverse, describing many different perspectives. And the failure of human spirituality to converge on one tidy answer leads many people to conclude that the whole task must be completely futile.

However, I have been arguing throughout this book against the assumption that reality consists only of those things which we can quantify and agree about. Human consciousness is more complex than any set of agreed measurements, yet it does exist. I would suggest that the same is true of God. People and God are all, it seems to me, vividly and excitingly real, and yet have a wondrous complexity which makes them impossible to reduce to a few agreed statements.

Leaving God aside for a moment, suppose for example that I wanted to find out about *you*. One way of doing that with unchallengeable precision would be to call in several different teams of scientists to carry out a series of tests on you. They could weigh you, measure you, determine your blood type, scan your brain and x-ray your teeth, and they could come up with a precise set of data about you which could be cross-checked by all the different teams. And their findings then would be an interesting collection of verified knowledge which could be presented as the scientific facts about you. Those facts would have the great advantage of being entirely uncontroversial and universally convincing. However, they would be extremely limited.

Now suppose that, instead of sending in the scientists, I invited you to have lunch with me and we had a good long chat. I could then gain a very different kind of knowledge of you. I could ask you about your life, your hopes and dreams, your likes and dislikes, your occupation, your hobbies and interests, your friends and your family. I could try to tune in to your sense of humour, to develop a rapport with you, and maybe even start to become your friend. I would then acquire a knowledge of you which would be of a very different character from the data gathered by the scientists. It would be less precise and more qualitative. But, unless they found evidence of a medical condition requiring urgent treatment, I would regard my lunch with you as something which produced a far more significant kind of knowledge.

However, other people would know you in very different ways from the view I would gain of you. That is how relationships work. People are all different and they form different relationships with each other. Knowing someone in a personal way is complex. Someone else might have things in common with you which I do not, or might dislike aspects of your character which I appreciate. You would relate in different ways to parents, friends, children, colleagues or a partner. You might have some bitter enemies as well as some good friends. And if we all got together to have a discussion about you, we would almost certainly find that we had formed some rather different impressions of you. We would have some very different stories to tell. We might even sometimes wonder if we were all talking about the same person. But we would not be impressed if a team of scientists arrived and suggested that we should all stop arguing about your personality and stick to the uncontroversial facts about your cholesterol level or the sizes of your toes.

Knowledge of the infinite consciousness who sustains the universe is a similar kind of knowledge. It cannot be reduced to a few tidy measurements, but it is genuine and powerful. A high proportion of the human race have seemed to display some kind of an emotional connection with a divine figure. And their knowledge of God is closer in nature to the understanding which we find in friendships with each other. It contains mysteries, surprises, paradoxes, and truths which are impossible to capture perfectly in words or numbers. We relate most authentically to the mystery behind the cosmos through our ability to love, to trust, to argue, to question and to tell stories. Most of the books of the Bible and the sacred texts of many religions consist of narratives which show people just doing that. It is the life of faith and prayer.

It should not be a surprise or a problem when we do not immedi-ately arrive at one, single, standardised view of God if we regard the divine as personal. A personal approach regards God as much more complex and multi-faceted than any agreed set of scientific data. It means that the sacred is best described through stories, rather than definitions. No set of statements about divinity could ever be the full and final truth. There will always be things about God which surprise us, and ways in which other people will rightly see him (or her, or them) differently. There may be people who describe God very differently from me, but who are still encountering the same reality.

But this line of argument is likely to make admirers of science and rationality very nervous, as well as unsettling many people who are very clear about the infallibility of their religious beliefs. They will worry that I am advocating an approach within which anything goes, within which anyone can dream up any weird and wonderful legend, and within which there is no procedure for putting theories to the test. We could choose to believe in one supreme being, or a whole Greek mountaintop of quarrelling gods and goddesses, or the infamous Flying Spaghetti Monster (a satirical deity invented by atheists). There appears to be nothing in what I am saying here to restrain any excess of deluded invention. And, as has often been noted, the choice of one religion rather than another usually results from our upbringing and the people we happen to live among.

But, again, I think this is no more of a problem than the familiar fact that we have different opinions about each other. Many people believe many different things about any President of the United States, for example, and many of those beliefs owe a lot more to their own backgrounds and prejudices than to any accurate observations of an occupant of the Oval Office. Some may think that he is the greatest hero of the free world, and others that he is an evil tyrant, and their own views may often have more to do with the values of the people they live among than they do with the man himself. But the President himself is still real, and there are still meaningful and rational ways in which we can and should talk about him. Some people have a more accurate view of him than others, and there are ways in which those views can be scrutinised, even if we never fully manage to agree.

Similarly, people can to different degrees be right or wrong about God, and it is perfectly possible to have rational and helpful discussions about those beliefs. We can compare our ideas about God and judge them against our experiences, drawing on the records of other people's experiences, our rationality, and our awareness of meaning and goodness.

The overwhelming majority of those who believe in God would say, for example, that terrorists who claim a religious affiliation have completely misunderstood the love of God and the sacredness of life. We are rightly shocked by the histories of holy wars and inquisitions. And a wide range of religious people have converged on an agreement about the importance of compassion, forgiveness, fairness, reconciliation between enemies, the growth of virtue and the protection of life. When others use faith as an excuse for hatred, nationalism or racism, they are wrong about God and the rest of us can say so. And people are increasingly pointing out that discrimination on the grounds of gender or sexual orientation is also contrary to the vision of a loving God who longs to see people flourish and to grow in close relationships. Aggressive people are much more likely to get into the newspapers, but there are many more peaceful thinkers who know that it is possible to believe in God in a way that facilitates important discussions rather than shutting them down.

THE STORY OF JESUS CHRIST

So what is God actually like? I cannot attempt to discuss all the religions of the world, even though I believe that truth is widely found in different degrees among them. My theme in this book is the Christian understanding of the personal nature of God, the theory about life which has convinced the largest number of people in the world.

Back in the Renaissance, Christianity might have seemed like a European faith, even though it had begun in the Middle East. But it has today spread all around the globe, and is enthusiastically embraced by people from all continents. It is actually now even more widespread in the southern hemisphere than the northern, and continues to grow in the world as a whole. A diverse range of people in many cultures and many centuries have perceived there to be something compelling and convincing about Christianity. For a great many human beings, it accurately expresses and nurtures spiritual experiences which are deeply important to them. It rings true with regard to their most profound longings and religious feelings. For them, the Christian account of God is at the heart of an understanding of life which they find convincing, enlightening and life-enhancing. People trust in this understanding of God because they perceive that it *works*. It makes sense of life, it helps them through dilemmas and challenges, and it inspires them to live more authentically. It seems to connect very powerfully with reality.

And the heart of Christianity is indeed a person. The centre of this faith is not a book, or a ritual, or an institution, but it is the person of Jesus Christ—the most famous man in the history of the world. His story is told from four perspectives in the four Gospels of the New Testament. Together they give a vivid portrayal of his character in multiple dimensions, offering multiple levels of meaning.

Part of that presentation of his character is the demonstration of what human life looks like when it is lived entirely in harmony with God. Jesus revealed the true potential of humanity in a human life of abundant goodness, courage and love. And, by showing what life looks like when it is lovingly, fully devoted to God, he thereby showed us what God himself is like. By living whole-heartedly according to the guiding light of divine goodness, Jesus gave the world a unique window into the nature and character of God.

Jesus was someone whose remarkable life attracted the attention of great crowds. But, where others sought status, comfort and power, he was content to live in simplicity and vulnerability.[69] He was born in conditions of squalor and hardship, among animals.[70] As an adult, he remained single, without wealth, without a settled home, without worldly security. He was a friend to those who were social outcasts:

69   Luke 9.58
70   Luke 2.1–12

lepers, prostitutes and traitors.[71] He was a humble man who completely ignored the usual human tendency to chase after status and power.[72] He did not defer to hierarchies, or attempt to climb them, or seek to establish new ones. Instead, he got on with making himself useful, showing great compassion to those who were in need. He was content to be a friend to the friendless, to sit alongside the poor and the unlovely, and to embrace those despised by respectable society.

From his childhood, he eagerly sought after wisdom.[73] He could silence learned opponents in keenly-argued debates, or use everyday imagery to explain himself to the uneducated. His days involved long and hectic periods of interaction with crowds who were seeking his help, and precious times of spiritual refreshment when he went to pray in solitude in deserted places.[74] He was familiar with the horrors and the sufferings of the world, as well as with its goodness and its beauty.

Living in the Middle East, at the meeting point of three continents, he inhabited a war-torn country which had long been attacked by mighty empires from all directions. Its people resented their Roman rulers and many longed for a great military leader to start the fight for independence. But, even though Jesus had the charismatic presence to draw and persuade the crowds,[75] he chose instead to live and teach a life of non-violence. His message was that we should love our enemies and pray for those who persecute us.[76] He lived and taught the practice of extravagant generosity and forgiveness.

Jesus did not seek political or military power, but neither was he a submissive, passive or cowardly person. His approach to life undermined and disturbed the comfortable social hierarchies of the wealthy, the well-connected and the religious. As a guest at an expensive dinner, he might observe loudly that those who ceremonially washed their hands still had hearts of greed and wickedness.[77] Or he might scandalise

71   Mark 2.16, Luke 7.36–50
72   Mark 10.42–45
73   Luke 2.41–52
74   Mark 1.35–39
75   John 6.1–15
76   Matthew 5.38–48
77   Luke 11.37–41

the respectable guests by declaring God's forgiveness to a gatecrasher notorious for her life of sin.[78] He advised rich people that they could be closer to God if they gave their money to the poor.[79] And he called religious leaders hypocrites for enjoying their grand titles and fine robes while failing to show the love of God in their lives.[80] He broke his own people's strict religious rules when there was a good reason to, choosing to act always in ways of compassion and integrity which far surpassed any predictable set of laws and customs.[81] And he showed a form of goodness which could never fit easily into the comfortable compromises by which human society usually operates. In doing so, he earned the hatred of those with status and privilege. The aristocrats and religious leaders in the hierarchy began to plot to kill him.[82]

But neither was he a stern kill-joy. His enemies called him a glutton and a drunkard.[83] He loved meals with friends, and served over 100 gallons of very good wine at a wedding.[84] He displayed overflowing generosity and love. His advice to those throwing parties was that they should invite the poor, the disabled, the blind and the lame, rather than those they wanted to impress.[85] He taught and lived by two great commandments: to love God with all our heart, soul, mind and strength; and to love our neighbour as much as we love ourselves.[86] And he taught his followers to relate to God in a personal way, as they would relate to a loving father.[87]

The Gospels are full of accounts of extraordinary encounters between Jesus and troubled people. He once unexpectedly came to stay with a corrupt tax-collector called Zacchaeus, a man who had worked for the occupying powers of Rome and who had been extorting money from his neighbours. As a result of Jesus' unlikely friendship,

---

78   Luke 7.36–50
79   Luke 19.21
80   Mark 12.38–40
81   Mark 2.23–28
82   John 11.45–57
83   Matthew 11.19
84   John 2.1–11
85   Luke 14.12–14
86   Matthew 22.34–40
87   Matthew 6.5–13

Zacchaeus gave half his possessions to the poor and returned to all his victims four times the amount he had stolen.[88] On another occasion, Jesus rescued a woman who was about to be stoned to death for adultery. He calmly suggested that whoever was without sin should cast the first stone. [89] He startled people in his choice of associates, calling ordinary, uneducated fishermen to be his disciples, and training them to take his message to the world.[90]

THE SIGNIFICANCE OF THE LIFE OF JESUS CHRIST

What does this famous set of narratives mean? At its most straightforward level, the story of Jesus Christ is the story of a human being who lived a life utterly devoted to God. In doing so, he gave a powerful demonstration of the character of God, offering a way for us to see what God is like.

But that insight leads to a deeper level of meaning, which was explored in detail by theologians over the following centuries. The Gospels suggest that Jesus Christ was not just a random holy person who succeeded in living a very godly life. He was not just an ordinary human being reaching out to God. In addition, his life can be understood as God's way of reaching out to us.

Jesus can also be understood as God himself stepping into our world in human form in order to make himself known and to build a relationship with us. For Christians, therefore, Jesus Christ is the fullest answer to the question of the character of God. He is the image of the invisible God, as St Paul wrote.[91] To see Jesus is to see God, as Jesus himself said.[92] The personal nature of God is revealed by Christ, who brings the wondrous mystery of God close to us in the form of a human being.

This leads to something of a paradox. Jesus appears both to be a human being who relates to God in the ways that we do, and he also appears to be God making himself known in human form. Christians have always wanted to tell the story in both ways, since it seems to be

88   Luke 19.1–10
89   John 8.1–11
90   Mark 1.16–20
91   Colossians 1.15
92   John 14.9

overflowing with meaning at both levels. Jesus can therefore be understood as fully human, and he can also be understood as fully divine.

When Jesus is understood as divine, another dimension of the nature of God is revealed. The Gospel accounts of Jesus praying give us a surprising glimpse of God relating to himself. This encounter suggests a sense of duality and relationship even within God. Not only that, but the New Testament also describes the Holy Spirit, the divine presence who comes to dwell within us. In time, the Church therefore explored the understanding of God as a Trinity of three persons: the Father, the Son (Jesus Christ) and the Holy Spirit. This suggests, as I mentioned in Chapter One, that God from all eternity exists as a community, as a three-fold network of loving relationships.

Stated as a system of ideas, the Trinity is mysterious, paradoxical, and the inspiration for much fascinating theology as well as much scratching of heads. There is something irreducibly complex and surprising about God, and rightly so. But the Trinity can be grasped intuitively simply as a sign that God is inherently relational. God exists in a way which includes love and relationships within his own nature.

That divine love began to spread when it overflowed in the creation of other living beings. From then onwards, God has sought to enter into relationship with us, drawing us into the eternal love of the divine Trinity. That invitation to community centres on the actions of Jesus Christ, who was born in human form and lived as one of us. He revealed the personal nature of God in a way that we can relate to, and he led the way in bringing humanity into relationship with God.

I recognise that these are rather big claims to make about one human being who lived so long ago. He was just one man who walked the Earth two thousand years ago, and he did not even write a book. Nevertheless, he has had a greater impact on the world than any other person. When I first looked seriously at the accounts of his life and teachings in the Gospels, I soon found myself captivated. I was intrigued, fascinated, baffled and disturbed by the way in which this man seemed so unusual and yet seemed also to have grasped the deepest truths about my own life and experiences. Vast numbers of other people in many times, places and cultures have found him equally significant.

There is no other person in the history of the world who has caught the attention of the human race so effectively. There is no other figure who has been referred to in art, literature, music, philosophy, politics, culture and education in so many ways, in so many countries, and over so many centuries. There is no other person who has so many buildings dedicated to him or named after his most inspiring followers. There is no other person whom so many human beings have known about. No one else comes close. He is worshipped by Christians, who are now thought to be more than two billion in number. And the world's Muslims, thought to be over a billion, recognise him as a great prophet and Messiah. Many others have been profoundly inspired by his life and teachings. Mahatma Gandhi, a Hindu, sought to follow his example when he offered non-violent response to tyranny. And, despite his thoughts about the limitations of a personal view of God, Einstein said that he was enthralled by the luminous figure of Jesus.[93]

Jesus Christ appeared within human history at the crossroads of continents, in a small country where travellers and invaders from Europe, Africa and Asia meet. He lived at a time which might be called the crossroads of history, within the Roman Empire, the most powerful civilisation the world had ever seen. His people, Israel, had endured centuries of being bullied and enslaved by successive empires from different directions. But they had gained a remarkable resilience based around a faith in God who, they believed, would one day send a Messiah to them. Christians and Muslims understand Jesus as the fulfilment of that hope. The Bible sets the Gospels within the context of a long narrative which describes God's faithfulness to the people of Israel, and his goal to bless all the peoples of the world through them.[94]

The full significance of Jesus for Christians is shown in the opening of John's Gospel, which describes how the *Logos*, the rationality underlying the cosmos, took human flesh and dwelt among us. Earth's life and civilisation had developed to a point where it could now provide a vehicle for God himself to step into his creation, making himself known in a new and deeper way. A human being, whose evolution had been

---

93 Quoted in Max Jammer (1999) *Einstein and Religion* Princeton University Press, p. 22

94 Genesis 22.17–18

shaped by the reality created by God, could now provide a physical form for the transcendent consciousness underlying the whole cosmos. Jesus was God made visible, and, as I shall describe in the next chapter, he was God's way of confronting the problem of the evil of the world.

JESUS CHRIST AND THE NATURE OF LOVE

Jesus spent much of his time teaching, and his central theme was the joyful proclamation of a deeper relationship between people and their creator, known as the Kingdom of God. He began his mission with this announcement: 'The time is fulfilled, and the Kingdom of God has come near. Repent, and believe in the good news.'[95] This reference to a Kingdom fitted with the long-standing Jewish hope that God would one day send them a powerful new leader, a Messiah descended from the great King David. And this regal theme sounds at first like a powerful mandate for a hierarchical view of the cosmos, a strict environment arranged around male power structures. But Jesus' teachings greatly subvert all traditional understandings of monarchy.

Monarchs in the ancient world were dictators who exercised absolute power, and ordinary people had no choice about whether or not to accept it. Kings were powerful military leaders who took charge using brutal force, and a kingdom was something that was imposed on a whole society all at once. However, Jesus refused to wield military power, and described the Kingdom of God in very different terms. He described the Kingdom not as a regime imposed from the outside, but as an experience of great significance which was there for individuals to discover when they chose, something which depended on the response of each person.

He said that the Kingdom 'is like treasure hidden in a field, which someone found and hid; then in his joy he goes and sells all that he has and buys that field.' He also said that the Kingdom 'is like a merchant in search of fine pearls; on finding one pearl of great value, he went and sold all that he had and bought it.'[96] The Kingdom is there for all to find,

95   Mark 1.15
96   Matthew 13:44–46

but it is up to each individual to notice it and to choose it. Those who recognise it realise that it is of more value than anything else.

Jesus tended to teach using vivid stories and examples, and his most famous account of the relationship between people and God is his parable of the prodigal son.[97] In the story, the younger son rudely demands his share of his future inheritance early, and then disappears and squanders all the money in a faraway country. When he has nothing left, he decides to return home, acknowledging that he is no longer worthy to be called his father's son, but preparing to ask him for a job as a farm labourer. But the father sees him while he is still far off, runs to greet him, hugs him and welcomes him back into the family with a great party. That is how Jesus described God's love for every erring human being.

The father in the story treats the son's choices with great respect. He does not impose his authority on him, but allows his son to choose his own path and to make his own mistakes. Instead of keeping his son financially dependent on him, forcing him to stay at home in deep resentment, he allows him to have the resources to find his own way in the world. Even though the father knows that the son will do some things that are foolish, wasteful and deeply disappointing, the father takes his son's freedom very seriously. The son eventually finds that his chosen hedonistic lifestyle leads to disaster, and comes to recognise that what he really needs is the nurture and security he could find at home. He fears that he has ruined the relationship with his father, but when he makes the choice to go home he discovers that he is very deeply loved.

Jesus' parable offers various deep insights into the nature of loving relationships. Even though the father knows that the best life for his son will be at home, he has to let him discover that for himself. He has to allow him to make his own choices, including making his own mistakes, and to go on a long journey. The son's freedom is of great importance. Forcing the son to stay at home would not bring the close relationship that the father longs for. A genuine loving relationship can only develop when all power is set aside and the parental relationship can be rejected or accepted. It is only by handing over his financial

97 Luke 15.11–32

advantage to his son, and then by waiting and longing and hoping for his return, that the father can enable the genuine mutuality and closeness that he knows will be the best outcome.

Love requires freedom, vulnerability and the risk of rejection. It is not the result of the exercise of power. The most ingenious creator imaginable cannot force the existence of love, because the deepest relationships are those which are not brought about by compulsion or trickery, but where one chooses to grow close to another. That is why other parables of Jesus' draw on the uncertainties of nature: a farmer sows seeds, some of which grow and some do not, just as some people respond to God's invitation and some do not.[98] God cannot compel the development of love, but he can provide a space within which it will in some cases grow. He invites and he welcomes, but he does not force. And when some accept and come home, when some realise where the true treasure is to be found, there is great rejoicing in heaven.[99]

This central Christian emphasis on freedom and love is found in the New Testament and has been explored again more deeply by recent theology. Jesus himself can be seen as God's way of making himself vulnerable and drawing close to us, in order to make relationships between him and us possible. St Paul writes that Jesus 'though he was in the form of God, did not regard equality with God as something to be exploited, but emptied himself, taking the form of a slave, being born in human likeness.'[100] The Greek word for emptying, *kenosis*, provides the name for a theme which has been notably explored by various Protestant theologians. Jesus chose to set aside all his divine advantages in order to live as one of us, taking the role of a servant.

Jürgen Moltmann sees even creation itself as something which is not primarily an act of power, but a form of kenosis.[101] When God enables the existence of other beings who can make their own decisions, he does so by freely deciding to limit his own authority. He makes a space for people and for their choices, allowing them to find their own way, and

---

98   Mark 4.1–20
99   Luke 15.7
100 Philippains 2.6–7
101 Jürgen Moltmann (1985) *God in Creation: An Ecological Doctrine of Creation* SCM, p. 86–93, and John Polkinghorne, ed (2001) *The Work of Love: Creation as Kenosis* SPCK

giving them the ability to reject him. Moltmann refers to St Paul's affirmation that we live and move and have our being in God, saying that God restricts himself when he chooses to make his presence the dwelling place for creation. God makes room for us within himself, giving us space to be ourselves, and yet remaining close enough for us to seek and find.[102]

This understanding of loving relationships was obscured both by the hierarchical view of the cosmos and by the mechanical view of the cosmos. An enthusiasm for hierarchies can enable our thirst for power to assist in the development of a stable society, but it can fail to notice the more fragile and subtle dynamics of love. Climbing up the career ladder or gaining entrance to the most exclusive parties means nothing compared with building a friendship on an equal basis. And the father in Jesus' parable is not the kind of authority figure who rants about his honour or demands elaborate apologies from his underlings. The hierarchical view of the cosmos places too much emphasis on the kind of power which God himself seems content to lay aside for the sake of the development of love. But the mechanical view of the cosmos is even worse in that it fails to highlight the importance of relationships of any kind.

A social understanding of the cosmos can provide a much more convincing, healthy and life-affirming picture. God is a Trinity of love, a divine community which seeks to create and to welcome others in. God is one who gives space and freedom to others to be themselves. And he is also one who makes himself vulnerable in order to draw close to us. He is Jesus Christ, the one who laid aside his divine glory in order to make friends with the poor and the broken. That is why I feel able to claim that good theology provides the best possible basis for a belief in human dignity and liberty.

FAITH AND FREEDOM

For me, an authentic faith in Jesus Christ seems to establish the importance of liberty. But European society has become very nervous about sharing big ideas about life, worrying that they are a threat to freedom.

---

102 Acts 17.26–28 and Moltmann (1996) *The Coming of God: Christian Eschatology* SCM, p. 299

It is not just the old hierarchical view of the cosmos which has frightened us, but we have also had bad experiences of the non-religious ideologies of communism, fascism and nationalism. We look back with embarrassment on the era when Europeans confidently expanded their empires around the globe, and with horror on the two world wars which brought that era to a disastrous end. Since then, post-modern philosophy has warned us that any attempt to declare a grand narrative about the meaning of life is a bid for power by the group making the declaration. We worry that conversations about big ideas may lead to violent military campaigns led by people who think that they have a duty to impose their superior grasp of ultimate truth on everyone else. It seems safer to be an isolated individual in a world with no shared sense of meaning than to get caught up in an angry ideological battle. A book like this, offering a grand narrative about the meaning of life and the nature of reality, may seem rather alarming to many.

However, in the picture of reality that I am describing, the optimum situation would be one where individuals have a high degree of freedom over their ways of life, while living in an environment where important ideas about life can be peacefully shared and enthusiastically discussed. Western society at its best has often been able to move a long way towards that ideal. Progress came initially not through the rejection of all religion but through the development of Protestantism. In fact, Protestantism has a very honourable track record in its association with the development of western ideals about democracy, liberty and human rights, inspired by the teachings of Jesus Christ.

After rejecting the authority of the Pope in the sixteenth century, Protestants began to explore new ways of running churches. Some, like the Church of England, remained for a long time closely tied to monarchies and aristocracies. But other more radical movements began, undermining the old hierarchical systems. Congregationalists said that the Christian Church was not primarily about a big power structure, but that it was each local community of disciples that really mattered. Christianity was about ordinary people choosing to follow Jesus and then joining together with others nearby who had made the same decision. Baptists and others began to emphasise that the decision to become a disciple had nothing to do with the king, but was the concern of each individual. Protestants emphasised that all Christians should read the Bible for themselves, and many took more seriously the idea that ordinary people could be guided by the Holy Spirit within them, seeing more significance in the spiritual experiences of lay people. Many Protestants therefore began to understand the Church through its local roots, rather than seeing God's grace flowing down through a powerful male hierarchy. Within this new approach, the gifts of women as leaders and preachers began slowly to be noticed and affirmed, including among Quakers in the 17th century and among Methodists in the 18th century. Women began to play prominent roles in Evangelical revivals and new missionary movements which grew rapidly from the 18th century onwards. And there has been huge popular support for Evangelical and Pentecostal Christianity in many local contexts around the world. These movements take very seriously the choice of the individual to follow Jesus. They emphasise the value of a lively and supportive local Christian fellowship, expecting that ordinary people will experience the work of the Holy Spirit through the life of the local church.

The western shift from monarchies to democracies is deeply interwoven with the transition, led by Protestants, from a hierarchical view of the Church towards one which greatly values the individual. Theological ideals about liberty have inspired political ones, as famously seen in the American Declaration of Independence of 1776:

> We hold these truths to be self-evident, that all men are created equal, that they are endowed by their Creator with certain unalienable Rights, that among these are Life, Liberty and the pursuit of Happiness.

The full significance of those ideals are still being explored. But the exploration was taken a stage further in America in the campaigns led by Baptist minister Martin Luther King Jr (1929–1968). He led the African-American Civil Rights Movement which successfully ended racial segregation through a form of non-violent protest inspired by the example of Jesus Christ.

I am suggesting that authentic Christianity is something that promotes a belief in human dignity and liberty, rather than being something that is inherently a source of oppression. Protestant countries have led the way in developing democracy in the modern world, and the Roman Catholic Church, since the Second Vatican Council (1962–5), has been catching up with these developments. It has translated its services from Latin into locally-understood languages, and placed far more emphasis on the importance of the whole people of God, rather than simply its hierarchy. It has also finally recognised that salvation can be found among those who do not accept its leadership. Over a similar period, the traditional Catholic love of hierarchical societies has been supplemented by the development of Liberation Theology in Latin America, an approach to faith which seeks to challenge unjust social structures and to prioritise the needs of the poor, a cause which is close to the heart of Pope Francis.

THE SPIRITUALITY OF A RELATIONSHIP

Christian spirituality is therefore the spirituality of an open, honest, freely-chosen relationship, a conversation of love. God's side of the conversation is found above all in the revelation of himself in Jesus Christ. But his voice is heard also through our encounters with the goodness, beauty and wonder of creation, our awareness that we have our being in him. He is heard in the promptings of the Holy Spirit in our hearts, in a great variety of spiritual experiences that encourage us from evil and towards goodness and love. And he is heard in community, especially when people seek God together and try to help each other to become the people God calls them to be.

The Christian experience of hearing the voice of God is celebrated most clearly in the library of texts found in the Bible. They centre on the story of Jesus Christ, showing both the background to his coming and the impact he had on those who first encountered him. These texts are very personal accounts of a personal figure. They cover many genres, but the dominant mode of writing is narrative, the vivid portrayal of God through his actions and through people's experiences of him.

They are a notoriously messy set of narratives, famous for their disturbing passages and their ponderous genealogies as well as for their verses of sublime and visionary beauty. Many of them show clear evidence that they were written by people trying to survive great crises and violent conflicts. Theologians have therefore often seemed to want to convert the Bible into something rather more settled, logical and respectable. In the early centuries, logic and respectability meant Greek philosophy, and a great effort went into to grappling with technical questions about the being of God that were important in ancient Greek thought. In the Middle Ages, logic and respectability meant a carefully-choreographed deference to hierarchy. In recent times, logic and respectability has meant the mechanical view of the cosmos, and a great effort has gone into reprocessing the biblical narrative into precise statements that can sound as confident as scientific laws. In various ways, people have carefully tidied up the narrative of the Bible into creeds and doctrinal statements, or talked proudly about infallibility, or made it sound as if Christianity was mainly about accepting some particular theory about who Jesus is and what his death accomplished, or about participating in some precise set of rituals.

Yet there remains something stubbornly messy about the narrative of the Bible, which bears witness to the complex world of genuine and honest relationships. Karl Barth has led the way in reminding Protestants that God's Word is something dynamic and active, rather than something that we can master and reprocess as a set of tidy ideas. God is revealed in and through a complex set of actions and interactions, rather than fitting neatly into a philosophy. The Bible itself offers a vibrant, disturbing, chaotic and yet hopeful world, a drama within which the kindest pilgrim and the cruellest tyrant can find a place and can experience redemption. There are disciples who fall asleep while their master prepares for his arrest; a prophet who sulks because God wants to forgive the foreigners he hates; an apostle who perseveres through beatings, imprisonments and shipwrecks to write the world's most famous description of love; jealous siblings who sell their brother into slavery and then receive his help many years later; a philosopher who grumbles that life seems meaningless; bereaved people who mourn; and a central character who prays for those who are hammering nails through his wrists.[103]

The Bible opens up a world of dramatic and honest relationships. It invites us into a human story of encountering God in a messy world, and invites us to develop our side of the conversation, expressing our deepest thoughts and feelings to God. It invites us to be open about our failures, our painful memories and our confusions, as well as our nobler thoughts and our higher ideals. It is full of vivid examples of the life of prayer: Job complains, David dances for joy, Abraham negotiates, Sarah laughs, Moses asks God to send someone else, Jacob wrestles with God, Thomas demands evidence, Peter makes promises that he cannot keep, and Mary obediently accepts her unique role in history.[104]

The Psalms offer templates for prayer which convey the heights and depths of human experience, offered honestly and passionately to God: impatience, desolation, intimacy, depression, triumph, fear, guilt, dedication, hope, trust and joy. They are a powerful invitation to be real with God. They show a path of faith which many millions of Jews and Christians have found profoundly meaningful. It involves the courage to be honest about the horrors and the joys of our own broken and wondrous souls, drawing the full reality of our human nature into a relationship with God.

And those individual relationships with God are brought together in the prayers and songs of Christian congregations. Worship, at its most authentic, has the potential to gather up all the forms of knowledge and experience which I am writing about in this book. It is an experience of awe, with a sense of delight and amazement at the glory of God. It is an encounter with beauty, engaging all our senses, through wonderful music, the drama and colour of processions and ceremonies, banners, stained glass and soaring architecture. The love of God is made tangible through the sounds of poetic words and joyful singing, the taste of bread and wine, the smell of incense and candles, the cleansing touch of water and the handshakes of friends, and all the sights of these

---

103 Mark 14.32–42, Jonah 3.10–4.5, 2 Corinthians 11.25–33 and 1 Corinthians 13, Genesis 37–50, Ecclesiastes, John 11.38–26, Luke 23.34

104 Job, 2 Samuel 6.12–15, Genesis 18.16–33, Genesis 18.12, Exodus 4.13, Mark 14.26–31 and 66–72, Luke 1.26–38

interconnected experiences. Prayers and hymns wrestle with a sense of the meaning of life, and good preaching may contain both rational enquiry and a challenge to love. The whole experience draws together a community which is ready to be hospitable and inspired to do good in the world.

Talking to God, aloud or in the silence of our own thoughts, alone or with others, follows a human religious instinct which is genuine and significant. Our ability to pray engages with the reality of ourselves and the reality of God, in a way which is as genuine as the use of our other human abilities and instincts. It enables us to respond to God with honesty, and to play our part in the development of a relationship of love. For love is what matters most. A love which can well up in our hearts for the transcendent glory which sustains the universe. A love which can overflow in care for our neighbour, in concern for the world, and in humble service for the good of others. In a social cosmos, that love is the key to the meaning of life.

THE MEANING OF LIFE

Today, however, many people find it amusing even to ask about the meaning of life. When we think of the cosmos as a vast machine, any discussion of its meaning seems futile. Douglas Adams famously wrote the story of a supercomputer which performed millions of years of calculations and concluded that the answer to the ultimate question of life, the universe and everything was 42. He then suggested that another more powerful computer would be needed to work out what the question meant.

When the hierarchical view of the cosmos was universally shared, it gave everyone a way of understanding and talking about the meaning of their lives. Everyone had a place in the hierarchy, a role given to them by God, and an obvious set of tasks to perform. Whether they were called to plough fields or to reign over a nation, each person had something to do which gave them a way of contributing to the good of all. And they understood that their faithful service was their way of growing in virtue as they were prepared for the life of heaven. However, when our shared view of the cosmos is a depersonalised and mechanical one, the various cogs and wheels add up to no particular meaning, and 42 seems as good an answer as any.

Nevertheless, we do understand very well what it means to ask about the meaning of life, because we do know what meaning means and what it feels like. We do sometimes have a profound sense of the meaningfulness of particular experiences. Many of our most cherished stories describe events which are experienced as very meaningful, or which have the pain and emptiness of being devoid of any sense of purpose. Our ability to detect meaning is another of the human faculties that has evolved to respond to reality.

This Theology of Everything indicates that life has a deep and evident meaning, because the cosmos has a divine creative purpose behind it. The cosmos is God's way of enabling the development of consciousness and love, and we find life meaningful the more that we join in with that divine purpose. We find life meaningful the more that we grow in love, wisdom and character, the more that we learn to help others to flourish, and the more that we work together to build a compassionate and civilised society. We find life meaningful the more that we grow closer to each other and to God. And all that we learn as individuals and in communities prepares us to live together in a greater world which is still to come.

There are, therefore, many things in life which people find meaningful, because they are actions which join in with that divine creative purpose. Caring for others is meaningful, especially the long and demanding process of bringing up children. There is something very rewarding about nurturing and protecting others, and there is a deep sense of satisfaction to be found in seeing them grow and flourish as a result. There are many other ways in which people may seek to enrich the lives of those around them, building up a sense of community and aiming to make the world a better place. Someone who campaigns for social justice, or seeks to improve standards of healthcare, or who protects the vulnerable from crime, or who takes meals to the housebound elderly, is likely to find a great sense of meaning in those actions. Teachers and nurses often find their work very meaningful, even when their pay and working conditions are not as good as those of their friends in other professions. It feels rewarding and significant to seek to make a positive difference in the lives of others, helping individuals and communities to thrive. Even tending gardens and looking after seedlings can carry a deep sense of purpose connected with the flourishing of nature.

A strong sense of meaning may also be found in developing our own knowledge and abilities and setting ourselves new challenges. Life can feel very rewarding for those who seek after truth for its own sake, perhaps as scientists or archaeologists, or who develop their appreciation of beauty, or who learn to speak a new language, or who stretch the limits of their abilities to contribute to the success of a team.

Meaning therefore seems to be found in activities which enable us to grow as individuals, or which involve caring for others, or which build up relationships in families and communities, or which have a pioneering sense of seeking to make the world a better place. All these activities carry a sense of purpose which can leave people feeling hopeful, positive and connected to an important cause which is greater than themselves. Activities which are constructive of personalities and communities are joining in with the divine purpose of this social cosmos, and we have the ability to feel aware of that sense of meaning.

A rewarding sense of purpose contrasts with the feeling of emptiness which results from actions which do not develop our abilities, challenge our minds or make any difference to the world around us. An approach to life which simply consists of maintaining our existence is a predictably disappointing experience. Alternatively, we may be captivated for a time by strong and primitive desires which seem exciting, but which turn out to be surprisingly unsatisfying. Those who dream of revenge will gain no lasting sense of fulfilment when they have made their enemies suffer. Those who seem to thrive on competition against others will often find that their victories have a hollow sense of anti-climax, leaving them searching restlessly for the next opportunity to prove themselves. Similarly, many of the products which look so thrilling in adverts do surprisingly little to make life any more rewarding. Owning a more expensive car than the people next door does not really do anyone any good. And someone who restlessly seeks after casual sexual encounters will find life far less meaningful than someone who learns to care faithfully for a spouse and family over several decades.

We are vividly aware of meaning and emptiness, just as we are vividly aware of beauty and ugliness. In both cases, we have a significant human faculty which has evolved to connect with a genuine aspect of reality. Someone who does a dull, repetitive job, filing reports which no one will ever read, in an office where there is no hope of change, will feel a numbing sense of emptiness, however much he earns. So will a prisoner who watches TV all day while sitting out a long sentence. On the other hand, I find writing this book very meaningful, and the same is true of my teaching and pastoral work. A scientist searching for a cure for cancer and an architect designing energy-saving buildings are similarly likely to find a deep sense of meaning in their work. A stockbroker who makes millions by betting on the rising and falling of the stock market may feel energised by the daily risks, dilemmas and potential profits of that work. But a far greater sense of lasting satisfaction will be experienced by someone who invests directly in small businesses and enjoys guiding young entrepreneurs in bringing useful inventions to market.

Many people make great changes to their lives as they search for a deeper sense of what is meaningful in life. They gain the wisdom to recognise the activities which bring them a deep sense of fulfilment and purpose, and to distinguish them from the ones which merely hold their attention for a while. I have come across many who have accepted big pay cuts in order to go into teaching or into Christian ministry later in life, finding such work far more meaningful than their previous jobs. There is an active process of exploring meaning which many people feel inspired to engage in, sometimes from a young age or sometimes after a deep crisis at a later stage in life.

Our ability to perceive meaning is an attribute of our consciousness, like our ability to perceive beauty. It is a faculty which we have evolved to acquire, since it increases our ability to understand reality and to flourish together within it. Our awareness of meaning helps us to move beyond the basic tasks of acquiring food, protecting territory, competing for status and reproducing ourselves. It detects the divine calling which encourages us to make a greater contribution to the world, to give something back to society, to build, to create, to nurture, to inspire, to heal, to invent, to donate, to investigate and to explore. Like our awareness of beauty, it is a faculty which promotes the development of civilisation.

A Theology of Everything shows how this human instinct to seek to live meaningfully connects with the purposeful nature of the whole universe. The nature of reality promotes the evolution of conscious life, and our consciousness is drawn towards the actions which lead both to our own personal development and to the development of civilisation. The microcosm of our own search for meaning connects with the macrocosm of a universe which develops in a very purposeful way. There is a drive for growth and development which is seen in individual lives, in societies and in the cosmos as a whole.

MEANING AND VIRTUE

Some may be surprised that I have been talking here about meaning, instead of other terms often associated with Christianity, such as goodness, righteousness, justice and holiness. I have not given the expected sermon about absolute standards of morality. Instead, I have chosen to talk about meaning because I think that it relates well to the creative character of God, and connects with the very purposeful, developing, dynamic, constructive way in which God is described in the Bible. It is true that the Old Testament does present the Lord as a giver of laws, including most famously the Ten Commandments, but the relationship between God and people goes beyond a demand for the keeping of a timeless set of rules. The Old Testament greatly prizes wisdom, the ability to sense the right thing to do. It even personifies wisdom, saying that she calls out to people, and that she leads people in paths of pleasantness and peace. Wisdom offers to inspire kings to rule well, and she enables people to live constructive lives that lead to security and prosperity.[105]

The New Testament presents Jesus as someone who sees the limitations of legalism and seeks to put people in touch with the true meaning of the laws. Sometimes he breaks laws where there is a good reason to do so, such as when healing on the Sabbath, a day when people were commanded to rest from their labours.[106] At other times, he urges people to go beyond the law and to think about their hearts. As well as not committing murder, people should also avoid being persistently angry, and should urgently look for ways of finding reconciliation.[107] In both these cases, he is seeking the flourishing of human beings and relationships in ways which are constructive and which go beyond a blind obedience to the rules.

St Paul's letters repeatedly emphasise that Christianity is about the generosity of God and the life of the Spirit, rather than about legalism. 'The letter kills, but the Spirit gives life,' he says.[108] His understanding of life in the Spirit involves each person being given a different vocation by God, rather than everyone simply following the same set of orders in the same manner. All are called to serve God in distinctive ways, using their own particular talents. Paul explains this with the analogy of a human body, in which we are all different parts and all have different functions.[109] A healthy body could not consist entirely of eyes, he points out. But each person in the Church has a distinctive and meaningful role to play. The New Testament emphasises the priesthood of all believers,[110] without the rigid distinction between priests and lay-people that developed in later centuries. Paul's argument is that there is a diversity of essential roles, and that all people have something vital to contribute. He explains that there is an overall constructive purpose, the building

105 See Proverbs 3 and 8
106 Mark 3.1–6
107 Matthew 5.21–26
108 2 Corinthians 3.6
109 1 Corinthians 12.12–31
110 1 Peter 2.9, Revelation 1.6

up of the whole body, as all people use their various gifts for the common good.[111]

The Holy Spirit is seeking to draw us towards ways of life which are meaningful and constructive, which cause people and relationships to flourish. Goodness is therefore not just about keeping the rules, but it is about catching a vision for the true potential of each moment, sensing the spiritual inspiration which can bring extraordinary new achievements out of even the darkest situation. It is very important that we have a conscience which reminds us of our obligations to others and which helps us to realise when we have acted harmfully, but a truly flourishing life goes beyond simply staying safely within the law. It is about joining in with the constructive purposes behind the universe.

Unfortunately, while the mechanical view of the cosmos has been dominant, our western understanding of goodness has turned into something much more static, without that emphasis on the development and flourishing of people and communities. It has centred around two legalistic, mechanistic and impersonal approaches. Ethicists have looked for ways of talking about ethics that sounded like the kinds of things that scientists were doing and fitted with the approach of seeking to understand a great machine.

The first approach is associated with Immanuel Kant (1724–1804). He tried to understand goodness entirely in terms of absolute ethical principles, which he thought were as unchanging and universal as the laws of physics. He believed in moral laws which could be discerned by human reason, just as the laws of nature could be uncovered by scientists. He thought that we should tell the truth in every situation, for example, and even argued that we would have a duty to be honest to a murderer who asked us for directions to his chosen victim.

The other modern approach to ethics seeks to judge our actions by pleasure they produce, copying the scientific habit of making careful measurements of observable quantities. It is known as utilitarianism, and is especially associated with Jeremy Bentham (1748–1832) and John Stuart Mill (1806–73). Utilitarianism says that we should always act in the way which will bring the greatest amount of happiness to the

111 Ephesians 4.12

greatest number of people. Giving false directions to a murderer is easier for utilitarians to justify, because the murderer's annoyance will be more than outweighed by the preservation of the happiness of the intended victim and those who care about him (although this calculation would be chillingly different if the victim were widely disliked). But a utilitarian approach is difficult to use when we struggle to predict how an action will affect everyone's happiness. And utilitarianism finds it harder to safeguard the rights of minorities, especially if a great multitude can be protected or amused by suffering inflicted on a few.

Both of these mechanistic approaches have their limitations in modern ethical discussions, and their mechanisms sometimes clash with each other. Most episodes of *Star Trek*, for example, involve the crew agonising loudly about the conflict between their deeply-held principles and their awareness of the possible consequences of their actions. Should they break the Prime Directive again this week in order to avert another impending disaster? Or should they stand by their principles whatever the cost to them and to others? The trouble is that life cannot be reduced to any set of rules, nor can we ever fully understand how much happiness will result from our choices.

But recent decades have seen a fruitful rediscovery of another approach: the ancient tradition of virtue ethics. This focusses on people and their qualities, rather than on laws or quotas of pleasure. It examines the abilities that people develop as we learn to live good lives and to flourish. Virtues are skills which we develop, rather like moral muscles: they give us the strength to do the right thing in the complex situations that arise in life. Renaissance philosophy and art was much concerned with the depiction of virtues, and these can include qualities such as trustworthiness, courage, integrity, patience, wisdom, self-discipline, perseverance, loyalty, fairness, compassion and generosity. The more that we develop those virtues, the more we will be equipped to live good and meaningful lives. The best people to deal with murderers seeking directions are those who have already developed the virtues of courage, compassion and quick-witted inventiveness. Virtue ethics fits well with the account I am giving of reality as being the purposeful setting for the development of human beings. And virtues are seen most clearly not in definitions but in the stories of the people who exemplify them.

I find it very interesting that the most of the Bible is narrative, rather than laws and commandments. Most of us engage far more deeply with a sense of the morality and meaningfulness of life through stories rather than through statements of principles, which is why there are still plenty of enjoyable bits in *Star Trek*. We enjoy finding out about other people's struggles, temptations and scandals, whether that be in talking about our neighbours or reading about the achievements and follies of celebrities. And most of us, through TV soaps, radio dramas, novels or films, immerse ourselves somehow for a time most days in stories. We are captivated by accounts of moral dilemmas, of tragedies and triumphs, of danger, cowardice and bravery, of adultery, betrayal, love and faithfulness, and of villains who cheat and steal and heroes who act with honour and truthfulness. This aspect of reality is deeply important to us. We consume vast quantities of fiction, most of which shows people grappling with moral choices and searching for a sense of meaning. It illustrates the development of virtue and personality within a social cosmos shaped by a personal God.

MEANING AND MEASUREMENTS

Sadly, the mechanical view of the cosmos has trained us to regard our love of stories as rather frivolous. Instead, we often assume wrongly that the really important things in the world are the quantities that we can measure. Our main shared ways of assessing the well-being of our society are now economic statistics, such as gross national product, inflation or share indexes. In the absence of any other joint vision of life, the prominence we give to these financial graphs makes it seem as if we have all agreed that the point of life is the acquisition of wealth. In fact, wealth is only a limited measurement of the degree to which people are flourishing and living meaningful lives. It is certainly true that unemployment is very bad news, since those who cannot find work have lost the most obvious avenue for making a meaningful contribution to society. But the very wealthy can also find that there is a surprising lack of fulfilment in a life of ease and luxury. And those in the middle can waste far too much time feeling envious of their richer neighbours. Meanwhile, some people with comparatively little may be finding a greater sense of purpose simply in growing food for their families.

Finances can be very useful, but they are not in themselves the key to the meaning of life. Jesus warned that we cannot serve both God and wealth,[112] and St Paul diagnosed the love of money as the root of all kinds of evil and much suffering,[113] advising the wealthy to be rich in good works, generous, and ready to share.[114] A meaningful and rewarding life comes from learning to use our resources wisely, compassionately and responsibly for the good of all. Economic statistics tell us less than we might expect about the happiness and well-being of people. Unfortunately, a preoccupation with money itself and with the challenges of the global economy can distract us from having the conversations which really matter.

Our own individual sense of meaning may be at its strongest in the work that we do, since that may be the main positive contribution we make to society. However, much of the world of work is now cursed by a tendency to regard human beings as components in a machine. One of the most chilling aspects of the mechanical view of the cosmos is that we now talk about 'human resources', as if people were expendable materials in some vast impersonal engine. Earth's most intelligent species should not be described with language which makes us sound like barrels of oil.

A healthy workplace is one where every person knows that they have an important and appreciated role to play, and that they are doing something worthwhile which contributes towards the well-being of society. A true understanding of meaning requires a clear sense of what it means for human beings to grow and to flourish together. However, people tend to opt for the simpler approach of looking for some numbers. In some cases that is relatively easy, as when a worker can be seen as a way of turning a quantity of materials into a quantity of a finished product. If someone's job is to turn fabric into shirts, then

112 Matthew 6.24

113 1 Timothy 6.10

114 1 Timothy 6.18

we can pay her according to the number of shirts that she makes. But that ignores the ways in which she might have interesting ideas about new styles, or might step away from the sewing machine for a while to help someone else, or might have a warm sense of humour that helps the whole department to run happily. Treating the worker as one of the resources required for one sewing machine is a dehumanised and empty approach. Yet, even people who do not work in factories suffer from this industrialised view of life.

In my own working life, I am most familiar with the world of education, which is constantly plagued by foolish and self-defeating attempts to reduce people to numbers. One of our strongest and most meaningful instincts is the desire to pass on our knowledge of all that is best in life to our children, and it is a very rewarding experience to help young people to grow and to flourish. But, when we try to work together to improve our schools, we often try to reduce this wonderful and complex reality to a small set of measurements, thereby causing great problems.

Politicians like to look as if they are helping in this task, and so every new government in Britain attempts to shake up the education system with another new wave of dramatic reforms, restructurings, league tables and targets. Many people have found it impossible to resist the temptation to believe that this project can be reduced to a tidy set of measurements. It has therefore become more and more popular to find ways of redefining education as something that can interface smoothly with our familiar systems of market economics. For example, most of the recent discussion about higher education in Britain has centred on the fact that a university degree enables graduates to earn higher salaries. Studying involves an investment of time and course fees, which can be expected to deliver a profit in later years. The value of a degree certificate can therefore be quantified and treated as a commodity like any other, something that turns a person into a more valuable resource.

This financial approach provides an attractively straightforward way of understanding education. It says that schools exist to enable people to earn money. The best education is therefore one which most efficiently enables people to acquire the qualifications needed for the most highly paid jobs. This approach presents the value of education to society as an economic one, since education equips people to become wealthier. It fits with a belief in prosperity, while completely avoiding all of the bigger questions about life.

Like most exercises in reductionism, the financial approach to education can be very successful, but in a limited and dehumanising kind of way. When it works well, it brings the market forces of supply and demand to bear on our system for producing educated people. If the market produces a demand for particular skills, then the salaries of those people educated in that field will rise, and therefore the motivation for people to invest time and money in gaining those skills will rise. When it works well, education can function efficiently as part of our great shared project of seeking to increase wealth. Ideally, it produces the kinds of labour which are currently in demand in the global marketplace.

There is some good in this approach, but it rests on a limited vision of life and on a shallow understanding of what it actually means to grow to maturity as a human being. If these economic factors are all that we manage to address together, then we are in trouble. There is far more to life than learning to earn as much money as possible. There is far more to growing up and fulfilling our potential than learning to serve the market by becoming a cog in a giant economic machine. People are more than commodities, and human society should be more than an efficient way of making sure that our gross national product keeps on rising. An appreciation of literature, ethics, music, art, justice, community, history, philosophy, virtue and poetry is important in a civilised society, even if that appreciation is not as lucrative as the ability to get a job in banking or plumbing. But there is a great crisis in the humanities in our universities today, as they struggle to justify their existence to policy-makers who only know how to talk about economic benefits. Engineering degrees are valued as a way of training people to make money through industry, but we are losing the ability to say that an appreciation of the history of art is a good thing in itself. We losing the ability to say that philosophy can help us become more civilised people, and we are losing the ability to say that our lives are enriched if we understand the languages and cultures of others. Meanwhile, all students are under pressure to think that education is simply about exam results.

Fortunately, there are still many wonderful teachers who can convey a sense that their subjects are meaningful and valuable in themselves, not just useful as a means to a certificate and an economic end. They show a genuine interest in the welfare of their students, and enjoy seeing their pupils come alive with the excitement of learning new ideas and new skills. They offer an attractive example of what it means to be someone with an enquiring mind, someone who takes delight in exploring the truth. They are role models, people who offer a vision of a way of life, a glimpse of the advantages of virtue, and an example to which others can aspire. They show how the knowledge and the skills they teach fit into a meaningful and rewarding approach to life. They transmit the example of being a flourishing person, rather than simply the skills to get good marks.

Good education transmits a complex human reality from one generation to the next. It is a vision of how to live well, rather than just a collection of facts. It is far more than simply being a means to an economic end, and it is far more than anything which could ever be captured by a set of numerical measurements. But our mechanised world finds it difficult to talk about any broad vision of human life beyond the pursuit of wealth, with the result that attempts to improve education sadly tend to rely on the blunt instruments of reductionism. I have seen, with much sadness, what this crude oversimplification does to schools, teachers and pupils.

When I was a primary school teacher, I was responsible each summer for administering a series of tests which the government had demanded for all seven-year-old children. The goal was to seek to raise educational standards, setting targets for improvement in every school and every local education authority. Our success as a school was judged according to the proportion of our pupils who scored highly enough in tests in reading, writing and mathematics. So far, that all sounds very laudable. But as soon as we take a complex human reality and reduce it to one number in a spreadsheet, the dehumanising nightmare begins.

I still feel horrified when I remember the shameful advice which we received from a senior local education advisor about our targets.

It turns out that, if you try to reduce the well-being of a whole class to one single measurement, then most of the children do not matter anymore. For example, if 80% of our children were reaching the desired level in mathematics and our target was 83%, then the difference we needed involved only one child in a class of thirty. There was no point, we were told, in giving any attention to those children at the middle and the top of the class, as they would comfortably be able to pass whatever we did. Nor was there any point in giving any extra help to those children at the very bottom of the class, since they had no hope of passing whatever we did. But the three or four children who were close to the boundary suddenly became immensely important. If we could push one more of them over the pass mark, then our target would be met and everyone would be delighted with our educational triumph. It would not matter to the authorities if we were neglecting most of the children as a result. Nor would it matter if we were spending most of our time training children to answer a particular kind of exam question. As long as the statistics got better, the bureaucrats and the politicians could announce that their project was a great success.

Those of us who love teaching enjoy a sense that we are passing on to the next generation an inheritance of learning, an approach to life, and a love of civilisation which will enable them to flourish. But attempts to reduce education entirely to numerical targets are short-sighted and self-defeating. If you ask good teachers how and why they became good teachers, they will never say that they were energised by the targets which some bureaucrats set for them. Instead, they will talk about the teachers who inspired them, and about the ways that they have enjoyed seeing others learn. The way to elevate the success of education is by celebrating the examples of excellent teachers, with all their human complexities and intriguing eccentricities, rather than by seeking to reduce an entire profession to a mechanism for improving statistics. The way to improve education is to celebrate the deep sense of meaning which is found in helping human beings to flourish and to fulfil their potential, rather than turning education into a means to an economic end.

Doctors, nurses, social workers, police officers and many other public-sector workers suffer under similarly bureaucratic regimes of reductionist target-setting. These over-simplistic targets are well-intentioned and sound good to politicians and voters, but they actually devalue the qualities of wise, compassionate professionalism which are really needed. People thrive and work hard in their jobs when they find a deep sense of meaning in their work, when they feel valued, and when they can go home at the end of the day knowing that they have made a positive difference in the world. If they are told that all that matters is a statistic on a spreadsheet, they are more likely to become disillusioned, demoralised and cynical. If a complex and responsible profession is turned into the game of maximising one number, then people are likely to find ways of maximising the number that defeat the initial purpose behind the target. They will keep ambulances waiting outside hospitals as a way of minimising the waiting times inside, and then go home feeling miserable and empty.

Similar problems exist in the commercial sector, where companies face fast-changing economic challenges. There is a very strong pressure to understand work entirely in terms of balance sheets and market forces. But there is a kind of spiritual malaise in any organisation which understands its existence entirely in terms of the drive to make money. We have lost any sense of the meaning of life when an employer regards the workers just as a means of generating a profit, and the workers regard the employer just as a means of producing a salary, and the whole company regards the customers just as a source of cash. A much healthier company will have a clear sense that it offering something worthwhile to the world, so that its workers can take a real pride in what they do. Employees can find a great sense of meaning in their work if they are valued as people who make a difference to a situation that they care about. That is an analysis that could never simply be reduced to numbers.

MEANING AND THE SAINTS

The theme that ties this whole chapter together is its focus on persons and their development. The source of all reality is God, who is personal and who seeks to enable the evolution of consciousness and the growth of loving community. Despite our tendency to understand people as statistics and resources, I wish to assert again that it is individual people, their personalities, their virtues and their relationships which are the real point of this social cosmos.

Human beings are amazing, and our lives can be full of meaning. I find it an extraordinary thing that I can keep on meeting new people year after year, and they are all different. Even Cambridge students, who have similar ages with similar kinds of intelligence, outlook and motivation, are all different. They have different interests, foibles and personalities. There is an extraordinary diversity in God's creation, which provides opportunities for people to develop and to grow in character and love. The meaning of life is shown, not in theories or laws or statistics, but in the total reality of the lives, personalities, virtues and relationships of those who have explored their calling to grow and to love.

In Christianity, the supreme example of a meaningful life lived to the full is that of Jesus Christ himself. All Christians are called to become like him in his love for God and for people, but that does not mean turning into identical clones. Instead, we flourish in ways that develop the good potential of our varied interests, talents, quirks and eccentricities, and which draw on the opportunities and challenges provided by our own unique stories and circumstances. As well as celebrating the central example of Jesus himself, Christians therefore also cherish the stories of many of his followers, finding encouragement from the ways that their unique experiences reflect the love of God. Some of their stories are found in the New Testament, while many other famous saints come from later centuries. Leonardo, of course, painted a number of them. I will mention just a few of my favourite examples from those whom the Church of England now celebrates on special days in its calendar.

One is William Wilberforce (1759–1833), who led the campaign in Britain for the abolition of slavery. He became a Member of Parliament at the age of 21, enjoying the lively social life of a wealthy and popular young gentleman. A few years later, he became an enthusiastic Evangelical Christian, which was an approach to religion treated with suspicion by the upper levels of English society. He considered leaving politics, but received the wise advice that there was useful work he could do for God in Parliament. In 1787, he realised that his great task was to be the campaign against slavery, which was at the time bringing great wealth to Britain and its colonies, and causing great suffering for Africans. It was a very long campaign, which faced much opposition and many delaying tactics. The British trade in slaves was abolished in 1807, but the campaign to free those who had already been enslaved took even longer. Parliament finally ordered the abolition of all slavery in British territories in 1838, 3 days before Wilberforce's death. It is hard to imagine a stronger example of a meaningful life, a life which took seriously Jesus' teaching about love for our neighbours.

A second example is Florence Nightingale (1820–1910), who pioneered the professional training of nurses. Women at that time had very few options open to them, and faced the overwhelming expectation that they would become wives and mothers. But Florence had a series of powerful spiritual experiences which led her to think that God was calling her in a different direction, and refused proposals of marriage. She was inspired by the thought of devoting her life to the service of others and, against the wishes of her family, became a nurse. In 1854, she was horrified to hear of the appalling conditions experienced by wounded soldiers in the Crimean War, and trained up a team of volunteer nurses to go and help. By implementing improvements in sanitation and in care for the injured, she was able to greatly reduce the death rate. On returning home, she established the first professional training of nurses in England at St Thomas's Hospital in London, raising the status of nursing to that of a serious medical profession.

An example from much earlier in history is Saint Cyril (826–869), after whom the Cyrillic alphabet is named. Cyril was a skilled linguist and a teacher of philosophy in Constantinople, and was sent to Moravia with his brother Methodius to teach the Christian faith. Previously, the Slavonic language had never been written down, but they invented a way to do so in order to translate the Bible and the liturgies of the Orthodox Church. The Cyrillic alphabet is today used by around 250 million people, and the two brothers are regarded as the fathers of Slavonic literature. They are two examples of a great multitude of Christian scholars whose faith has inspired their contributions to education and learning.

Finally, among the remarkable women of the Middle Ages there is Hildegard of Bingen (1098–1179). Hildegard became a nun at the age of 15, which might sound like the beginning of a life of uneventful seclusion. But Hildegard became an abbess, and her role in the Church enabled her many talents to be widely appreciated. She wrote hymns, chants and songs, and people still sing her hauntingly beautiful music today. She received a series of visions, and was encouraged by her archbishop to write them down. She saw herself as a prophetic figure, and was not afraid to rebuke the powerful, corresponding widely with many other people. Among her many writings are works of visionary theology and texts on medicine and biology. This book's central theme of the divine unity of all truth would seem completely obvious to her.

Each of these saints is commemorated on a particular day of the year, so that their stories and examples can be celebrated. Their dramatic and varied lives are an inspiration to others, showing what human beings can become when we live with purpose, faithfulness, hope and love. It is important to celebrate the examples of those who have contributed to the good of the world through their generosity, wisdom, courage and creativity. And it is important to rejoice in the examples of those who have struggled with hardship, temptation and human frailty, who have grown in virtue, and who have learned to reflect the love that sustains the cosmos. For it is in valuing such lives together that we can get a clearer sense of how to help each other to explore the purpose of our own lives. These colourful, three-dimensional examples mean more than any set of rules, statistics or measurements could convey about human life. The wisdom to perceive the meaning of our lives is a wonderful gift, and it is one that we should celebrate.

I have offered four examples of very eminent people who followed a sense of divine calling, and lived their lives to the full, with a sense of wonder and compassion. Only a few people are called to be as famous as they became, but any local church has its own treasured stories of people whose faith has led them to great saintliness. There are the wise and kindly elders of the congregation who have cared quietly for the lonely and have shown the ways of Christ to many; the troublesome prophets who have grumbled loudly when the community was in danger of losing its way; and the wounded people, broken by the evils of the world, who have gradually found healing.

In this chapter, I have presented the cosmos as a constructive setting, a social and life-giving environment where love and goodness can flourish. And yet, we know that this does not always happen. The next chapter will explore our experiences of evil, and the times when life seems lacking in any beauty or meaning.

SUGGESTIONS FOR FURTHER READING

My favourite book of spiritual guidance for those exploring the meaning of life for themselves is *God of Surprises* by Gerard W. Hughes (Darton, Longman and Todd, 2008).

A theological exploration of meaning, connected with a scientific view of the universe, can be found in *Surprised by Meaning: Science, Faith, and How We Make Sense of Things* by Alister McGrath (2011, Westminster John Knox Press).

The idea of creation as kenosis is explored very movingly in W. H. Vanstone's little book entitled *Love's Endeavour, Love's Expense: The Response of Being to the Love of God* (Darton, Longman and Todd, 2007). It is discussed in more depth by Jürgen Moltmann in *God in Creation: An Ecological Doctrine of Creation* (SCM Press, 1985), especially p. 86–93. It also forms the basis for a discussion among scientists and theologians reported in *The Work of Love: Creation as Kenosis* edited by John Polkinghorne (SPCK, 2001).

For details of the varied lives of holy people from many countries who are commemorated in the Church of England's calendar, see *Saints on Earth: A Biographical Companion to Common Worship* by John H Darch and Stuart K Burns (Church House Publishing, 2004).

An Introduction to Religious and Spiritual Experience by Marianne Rankin (Continuum, 2008) presents a diverse and fascinating account of the spiritual experiences of people from a wide variety of cultures and beliefs. The book draws upon the work of the Alister Hardy Religious Experience Research Centre.

Tom Wright's *Simply Christian* (SPCK, 2006) sets Jesus Christ in his historical context and gives a helpful introduction to the main themes of Christianity. He also explores some of the connections between faith and ideas about beauty, justice, relationships and the issues facing the world today.

In his book *Virtue Reborn* (SPCK, 2010), Wright looks closely at the ways that human beings can grow in character and can take part in God's work of renewing the world.

Tokens of Trust: an Introduction to Christian Belief by Rowan Williams (Canterbury Press, 2007) presents a Christian understanding of what it means to live in the light of the love of God, exploring the meaning of the creeds of the early Church.

An excellent textbook for those who would like to study Christian theology in more depth is Alister McGrath's *Christian Theology: An Introduction* (Wiley-Blackwell, 2011), which offers a detailed overview of the history and content of Christian thought.

Chapter Six
Evil and the Drama of Love

INTRODUCTION

This has mostly been an optimistic book so far, reflecting on positive phenomena such as the beauty of nature and the meaningfulness of life. But you may have found my account of our experiences rather selective. What about the times when life is ugly and painful and meaningless? It is important to confront that question, and to admit that the wonders I have been describing involve an appallingly high price.

God has enabled the cosmos to function as a life-giving space where consciousness can develop, and where individuals have the opportunity to grow in character and to learn to develop loving relationships, if they choose to. The universe therefore provides us with freedom, and it functions in a consistent way which allows us to experience the consequences of our actions. It is an arrangement which often works very well, and it is easy to find examples of human beings flourishing and learning to treat each other with kindness. However, we are also very aware of the many times when it does not work. There is much human behaviour which is selfish, cruel and destructive. And the same intelligible and constructive patterns of nature which lead to beautiful mountains sometimes also lead to devastating earthquakes. There is evil tangled up in the goodness of the world, as Jesus said, like weeds growing among the wheat.[115]

Our experience of life can therefore be agonisingly painful and deeply distressing. Another of our widespread human responses to the cosmos is that of disappointment, anger and outrage. We may feel very strongly that things are not as they should be, and may feel moved

115 Matthew 13.24–30

to complain bitterly to the universe or to God. It may feel as if no reply is ever heard. But the centre of the Christian faith is the narrative of how God became one of us, and confronted the evil of the world in a life that led him through the horrors of betrayal, torture and crucifixion.

FREEDOM AND THE SPACE FOR EVIL

Human consciousness is a wondrous and complex phenomenon. Ordinary matter follows the predictable patterns familiar to science, but we have the capacity to make dramatic decisions. We may choose to act in ways which others would not have foreseen, and we have significant abilities to affect the world around us. We can build or destroy, and bring life or death to others. I am writing this book in a small attempt to interest and inspire others, but I could instead have chosen to spend my time spreading malicious gossip and writing hate mail, or just dozing in front of the television. Human beings can be the universe at its most wonderful, but we can also be the universe at its most dysfunctional. We can write symphonies or we can commit genocide.

The cosmos provides an environment which invites us to mature as intelligent, moral people, allowing each of us to develop our own unique personality. We are surrounded by opportunities which can enable us to grow. The rational structures of nature can enable us to develop as intelligent beings, if we choose to study them. And they provide a stable setting within which we can understand the consequences of our actions and learn to make moral choices. Meanwhile, the beauty of the universe can inspire within us a response of wonder and gratitude, if we take the time to contemplate it. Our awareness of the meaningfulness of life can encourage us to take delight in actions which stretch our abilities and help others to flourish. And our freedom opens up a space in which we may develop genuinely loving relationships.

But this freedom, the intelligibility of nature, and all these opportunities come at a terrible price, for the same space allows the possibility of evil. The liberty of human beings includes the potential to commit acts of great foolishness or of great cruelty. And we are not wrapped up in cotton wool by the cosmos, or rescued from the consequences of our actions and other people's actions. Instead, we have the opportunity together to face up to our responsibilities and to learn to make better choices.

We might wish that we had guardian angels who intervened to rescue us from our faults, and who stepped in to prevent all risks and all harsh words and all laziness. But, if so, we would start to feel like teenagers with ever-present, nagging, over-protective parents, depriving us of the space to work out our own sense of who we are.

We might wish that God would prevent all car accidents. But, if so, we could cruise down the motorway with our eyes shut, and our feet pressed down hard on our accelerator pedals, knowing that divine forces would steer our cars away from crashing into each other. There would be no need for us to exercise any kind of judgement or maturity.

We might wish that the universe would adjust itself to prevent all unfair acts of aggression. If so, we could even fire nuclear missiles carelessly in all directions without having to worry if we were doing the right thing. We could be confident that a target would only be destroyed if it deserved to be, and that the laws of physics would temporarily tweak themselves to divert any warheads heading towards innocent victims. We would not need to feel any sense of responsibility for our actions.

However, to be real people, to make real choices and to develop real virtues, we actually have to grow up and face up to the presence of good and evil for ourselves. Our decisions need to have a genuine effect on the world around us, and we need to take responsibility for them. If we were somehow protected from all the bad consequences of human foolishness and selfishness, then we would remain forever as spoilt infants. And if the behaviour of nature was constantly modified for our comfort and safety, then the universe would be an irrational, chaotic and incomprehensible place. We would never be able to reach any kind of maturity.

We need the universe to behave consistently if we are to develop intelligence and learn to understand it. We need to know that our actions have real consequences if we are to develop a sense of morality and responsibility, which means that human folly and cruelty have to be real options. If we are to have genuine freedom to be ourselves and to grow up, then there has to be a space for bad choices.

But suffering is not just caused by people. The reliable, consistent patterns of nature provide an environment within which we may flourish, but they can themselves have a harshness which may cause us great pain. They do not keep reshaping themselves around our immediate needs and can therefore be highly destructive. The same forces which raised the land above the oceans and shaped the mountains, moving the great tectonic plates over the surface of the globe, also cause earthquakes, tsunamis and volcanoes. The very same potential for mutation in DNA which has enabled life to evolve is also the openness that permits cancer.

These natural processes can sometimes be disastrous for us. But there is an underlying rationality to them which we are able to investigate. And so we have the potential to face the challenge of understanding these hardships and learning to overcome them. It is through dilemmas, challenges and adversities that we develop character and virtue. As a result, the cosmos at times feels like a very uncaring and inhospitable place, but it is, nevertheless, an environment within which human personalities do grow and take shape. It is an environment which enables moral development, within which people can and do learn to love. It is, terrifyingly and wonderfully, a place where people can and do learn to live good and meaningful lives. But this growth comes at a very high price, and we may often wish there could be an easier way.

A DISAPPOINTING LACK OF SHORT CUTS

God's action in the world is primarily one of inviting us towards ways of love and goodness. The Spirit speaks through the beauty of nature, through our encounters with life's potential for meaning, through our experiences of love, through the examples of others, and through words of guidance found in the scriptures and the insights of the wise. God inspires people to become caring parents, talented surgeons, brave police officers and inspiring teachers, and he works through their gifts, but he does not generally seem to use overwhelming force as a way of sorting things out. The Old Testament stories of God imposing his ways through colossal power seem largely to illustrate that such an approach does not bring any short cuts. God rescued his people from slavery in Egypt by parting the waters of the Red Sea, but then had to keep them wandering in the desert for 40 years while they gradually learned to trust him and follow his ways. No exercise of divine power can force the development of genuine love, or speed up the process by which people grow up and learn to live with responsibility, generosity and compassion.

The same is true of human political processes. Many people have assumed that the universal application of some great political ideology, imperial rule or state religion would be able to sort out the problem completely and permanently. It is a common attitude for people to think that the world would be lovely if only everyone shared their particular beliefs. Fascists, communists, religious zealots and military dictators have all tried to impose their own brand of order on the world at various times, but the results have tended to be disappointing or tyrannical. Colossal popular revolutions in France, Russia and China, backed up by plenty of thoughtful philosophy about equality, led to the dictatorships of Napoleon, Lenin and Chairman Mao.

The attempt to sort out the world by imposing one great system fails at one of the greatest challenges faced by the human race: enabling people to flourish as individuals while simultaneously contributing to a close and loving community. This problem is experienced at all levels of human society. It is found within families, neighbourhoods, cities, countries and across the world as a whole. And there is no system of government, no constitution, no political ideology and no religion which has ever been able to provide a full and lasting solution to the problem. As Winston Churchill observed, 'democracy is the worst form of government except all those other forms that have been tried from time to time.'[116]

A strong sense of shared identity and unity of purpose can be enforced by a dictatorship, but at the cost of the freedom of individuals to be inventive, to think for themselves, to notice the opportunities provided by local circumstances, and to pursue their own well-being.

116 Speech, *Hansard*, 11 November 1947

And a nation may be united against a shared enemy, at the expense of conflict on an international scale and a loss of individual liberty. We enjoy great freedoms today in the west, but those advantages come at the price of living in a society which is often unequal, fragmented and marred by selfishness and superficiality.

Many religious people have assumed, wrongly, that the imposition of their faith on the whole of society would solve its problems. However, the history of holy wars, inquisitions and persecutions shows that any joyful sense of unity comes at a very high price. By contrast, some people think that the eradication of religion and the universal establishment of atheism would make the world a far better place. Sam Harris, for example, calls for 'the end of faith', and asserts that 'the very ideal of religious tolerance... is one of the principal forces driving us towards the abyss'.[117] However, the atheist track record is, if anything, even more dismal than the religious one. The communist regimes which have enforced atheism have failed miserably to generate flourishing societies and to show respect for human rights. The same regimes have claimed to set out to eliminate poverty and inequality, but their main achievement has usually been to transfer power to a new elite of unaccountable leaders.

No one has ever found a perfect system which allows individuals the freedom to thrive and which also guarantees the growth of a close, fair, caring society. Yet, life presents every individual and every community with opportunities to build better relationships, if they choose to accept them. Every generation needs to face again the challenge of learning to live together in a supportive and caring way, which is always a task of great importance and meaning, and which is always possible. Remarkably, people do still learn goodness and kindness within the most challengingly unkind situations. After 27 years in a South African prison, Nelson Mandela emerged without hatred or a desire for revenge, but with the message of peace and reconciliation which brought an end to the racist regime of apartheid. And the early Church grew rapidly, despite the cruel persecutions inflicted by the Romans. Life can be extremely tough,

---

117 S Harris (2006) *The End of Faith: Religion, Terror, and the Future of Reason* The Free Press, p. 15

but goodness and hope can still arise within the most unpromising of environments. The cosmos provides a space for each generation and each individual, if they choose, to grow in virtue and in love. It is an essential process of growth and transformation. But it can be a harsh experience, and there are no short cuts.

GOD AND THE ANGER OF THE HUMAN RACE

The evil of the world strains and tests our relationships with each other and with God. There is another natural human faculty which is rather less calm and dignified than our abilities to appreciate beauty, rationality and meaning. It is a deep sense of outrage and anger at the way things are. It leads to a spirituality of complaint and protest, and to a response to God which is full of impatience and even rage. Many religious people are shocked by this response, or ashamed of it, but they are unnecessarily cautious when they think they should cover it up. There is a rich tradition of protest and complaint in the Bible, and our annoyance with God is another important human faculty which has developed in response to reality. It is part of a genuine and honest relationship.

The experience of being a righteous man immersed in pointless suffering is explored in painful detail in the Book of Job. Job's complaints to God shock his devout friends, who attempt to comfort him with religious platitudes, claiming that his suffering must be his own fault. They try to silence him, and to reassure themselves that the world is a fair place. But Job curses the day he was born, and protests bitterly to God. Elsewhere in the Old Testament, Psalm 88 cries out to God from the depths of despair, loneliness, hopelessness and depression: 'You have caused my companions to shun me; you have made me a thing of horror to them... O Lord, why do you cast me off?' The author of Ecclesiastes looks around at the injustice of the world, the emptiness of the pleasures sought by people, and the miserable fate of human mortality, saying repeatedly that all is futile and meaningless. 'Vanity of vanities, all is vanity,' he complains. He observes the same old problems continuing, saying that there is 'nothing new under the sun.' And the prophet Habbakuk pours out his exasperation, saying:

'O Lord, how long shall I cry for help, and you will not listen? Or cry to you "Violence!" and you will not save?' This tradition of protest and complaint reaches its extraordinary climax in the desolate cry of Jesus Christ, dying in agony on the cross, quoting the beginning of Psalm 22: 'My God, my God, why have you forsaken me?'

There is no escaping from the fact that life can be crushingly difficult, and that the freedom we enjoy comes at a terrible price. I think that religious people do no favours to God or to each other when we try to get everyone to be constantly polite and respectful to him. God's decision to create us is in some ways an act of outrageous recklessness. It is rather like leaving some children alone with a loaded machine gun after telling them to be good. Human life is often a bloody and horrible experience, and God is ultimately responsible for all of it. We can be grateful for all of our experiences of beauty, freedom, love and the meaningfulness of life. But it is perfectly valid to shout out in rage sometimes, and to face the terrifying question of whether the possibility of consciousness and love is really worth the cost.

Real faith encompasses this honest tradition of protest, as the Bible itself shows. And this anger is also part of the experience of many people who are deeply suspicious of religion. I was fascinated to see the response of the atheist Stephen Fry to the question of what he might say if he died and met God. This is what he would want to say to a creator:

> Bone cancer in children? What's that about? How dare you?
> How dare you create a world in which there is such misery
> that is not our fault? It's not right. It's utterly, utterly evil. Why
> should I respect a capricious, mean-minded, stupid God, who
> creates a world which is so full of injustice and pain…
> The God who created this universe, if it was created by a God,
> is quite clearly a maniac. Utter maniac. Totally selfish. We
> have to spend our life on our knees thanking him? What kind
> of God would do that? Yes the world is very splendid, but it
> also has in it insects whose whole life-cycle is to burrow into
> the eyes of children and make them blind. They eat outwards
> from the eyes. Why? Why did you do that to us? You could
> have easily have made a creation in which that didn't exist.

It is simply not acceptable. So, atheism is not just about not believing that there's a God, but, on the assumption that there is one, what kind of God is he? It is perfectly apparent that he's monstrous, utterly monstrous, and deserves no respect whatsoever. The moment you banish him, your life becomes simpler, purer, cleaner, and more worth living in my opinion.[118]

Many religious people offered predictable rebuttals, some of which reminded me of Job's comforters. But Fry's response seems to me to be honest, authentic and meaningful. I imagine that it is, among other things, a response to his own experiences of depression and of the cruel way in which religions have often treated people who are gay. I find it fascinating that he would not just say to God, 'Oh, hello, I had no idea you really existed!', as he might if he met the Tooth Fairy or Father Christmas. His atheism is a very emotional response, expressing his own deep disappointment, exasperation and indignation at the evil and suffering he has encountered, even within a universe which is characterised by so much splendour. He is angry about the way that creation is and, despite regarding himself as an atheist, he instinctively knows how to express that anger in a personal way to a personal figure. To me, although I know that it is impertinent to say so, these heart-felt words seem like words of faith. They sound like the words of a relationship which is strained and angry, a relationship which Fry finds exhausting when he thinks about it, but they are within the human tradition of relating to God reported by the Bible rather than outside it.

Similarly, it is worth pointing out that Fry's angry rant is possible because he has been able to learn what fairness, meaning and goodness look like. They are not some strange alien forces which he has never come across. He recognises them, and knows how to seek them, and misses them very painfully when they are absent. He is someone who is able to choose for or against them, and his atheism is part of his own personal journey of seeking to make principled, moral choices. Nevertheless, his wrestling with good and evil seems to me to show that the universe is serving the creative purpose which I have been

118 From the RTE television programme *The Meaning of Life*, broadcast on 1 February 2015.

describing. In another interview, Fry explains what he has learned since he was 18, saying:

> I suppose the thing I most would like to have known or be reassured about is that in the world, what counts more than talent, what counts more than energy or concentration or commitment or anything else, is kindness. And the more in the world you encounter kindness… the better the world always is. And all the big words—virtue, justice, truth—are dwarfed by the greatness of kindness.[119]

Fry's experiences support my claim that the universe is a creative environment which enables the development of consciousness and love: a place where kindness can be valued and can grow. The cost is terribly high, and we may validly rage against it and ask if it is worth it and complain that there should have been a better way, but the evidence is overwhelming that the cosmos does provide a space where kindness is recognised and can flourish. There are many weeds in the garden, but the flowers are growing there among them. And our anger about the problems of the world may turn out to be another of the means by which God energises us to work with him in seeking goodness.

THE NATURE OF EVIL

The world is a space where kindness be learned and love can flourish, but often it does not. Evil, therefore, is stuff that could be good, but which has gone off in its own meaningless direction. It is a result of the freedom and openness of the cosmos, and is what happens when parts of creation fail to join up with others through connections of love. God's work is one of reconciliation, as the New Testament describes,[120] a bringing together of these fragments. Without that reconciliation, evil can function like a tumour formed of cancerous cells, growing in its own pointless way and showing no regard for the well-being of the whole body. Like a cancer, evil can seem to flourish in a terrifying way, dominating its environment. But it is ultimately futile, bringing only

---

119 From an interview for splashlife.com in June 2010
120 See Ephesians 1.10, Colossians 1.20 and 2 Corinthians 5.18–20

destruction to itself and to its surroundings. Those cells would have a far better existence if they could rediscover their true role within the whole body.

A tendency towards evil is found in ourselves, in our relationships, in our communities, our nations, and in our world as a whole. It leads to the traditional Christian understanding of the world as being fallen, and of human beings existing in a state of original sin, turning away from God by default. Evil is goodness that has gone wrong, but it is still redeemable. Evil can become good when relationships are healed, when kindness is embraced, when the prodigal son chooses to come home, and when more and more of God's creation is brought the web of loving relationships nurtured by the Holy Trinity.

It is important to consider evil on an individual level first, seeing it as something which arises from within us, from our own immaturity. Some people respond very actively to their awareness of what is good and meaningful in life. They develop courage, virtue and wisdom, becoming more and more aware of what is right and more and more skilled in doing it. Others remain lazy, fearful, resentful or resistant to change, or become actively selfish and cruel. But most of us are a complex and tangled mixture of allegiances to good and evil. We are imperfect, immature people who may or may not choose to grow towards maturity by faithfully following the good. It is up to us how we respond, day by day. And so human history contains an extraordinary mixture of heroic kindness, dull selfishness and terrible cruelty.

As I described in Chapter Four, we have evolved with a set of instincts which equip us to survive and reproduce, seeking food, drink, sex, territory, status, and the ability to defend ourselves. In the same manner as animals, human beings naturally focus on our own survival needs and those of our family or tribe. But we also have a conscious ability to sense something of a higher calling, to reflect on our choices, and to embrace a greater vision of the good of all. Evil results when we simply follow our own survival instincts without any wisdom, compassion or self-control. It leads to a life of selfishness and conflict which is lacking in meaning.

It is also the case that both good and evil are present outside us: within other individuals, and within families, social groups, communities, sub-cultures, religions, ideologies, institutions and countries, and within the world as a whole. Evil could be present within the discourse of a group of men who habitually talk about women in a way which degrades and objectifies them. It could be present within business practices which protect the privileged and exploit the poor. It could be present within religious institutions which use a distorted view of God to justify sectarian violence and persecution. It could be present within oppressive regimes which have no respect for human rights.

Evil, therefore, is present around and beyond us, as well as within us. But it is important to avoid the self-righteousness assumption that we are especially good, or to see others as irredeemably evil. Reality is very rarely that black and white. And branding others as evil, ironically, predisposes us to commit acts of great wickedness ourselves. When religious people have foolishly set up inquisitions, witch-hunts and other zealous projects to purify the church or society, the result has tended to be hypocrisy, cruelty, savagery and disaster. Crusades and holy wars have created far more evil than they have destroyed, as have witch-hunts and political purges.

Good and evil are present both around and within us: in the world and in the heights and depths of our minds and memories. We feel tugged in different directions by these various influences, and it is a common human experience to feel caught up in a great interior conflict. There are negative influences on our thoughts which drag us down, which move us to despair, bitterness, vengefulness, apathy or hatred. And there are positive influences, which develop our sense of the meaningfulness and wonder of life, which nurture our consciences and inspire us to do good.

The negative influences may tell us that life can never have any meaning. Or that people do not like us. Or that our situation is hopeless and that nothing will ever change. Or that we have no value and no real talent. Or that we must fight for our own interests and establish power over others, because otherwise no one else will ever help us. Or that the most important thing in life is to impress the right people and fit in with the right crowd and to pretend to like the things which other people pretend they like.

There is also our awareness of the reconciling work of God, our sense of the good potential of all that exists. It tells us that there is no dark situation out of which new hope cannot arise. It tells us that we can make a difference in the world, and urges us to develop and use our own unique talents for the greater good of others. It calls us to live with bravery and passion, delighting in all that is good, and struggling resolutely against all that is evil. It tells us that the universe has a beauty and a purpose, that our lives have meaning, that we are loved and that we belong.

In this scientific age, we may smile at the traditional symbolism of angels and demons whispering opposing advice in people's ears. But an interior conflict between constructive and destructive impulses remains part of the ordinary daily experience of human beings. Like most modern theologians, I am going to avoid exploring a literal interpretation of traditional Christian imagery about Satan and his minions. Their few mentions in the Bible seem more symbolic than systematic to me, like the personification of lady Wisdom in the Book of Proverbs. But, I do think that evil exists in the world at multiple levels, from the individual to the global. And I find it fascinating that many of our most popular stories are those which show good and evil in a supernatural way on a colossal scale. The best-selling book series in history is J. K. Rowling's *Harry Potter* stories, and immense popularity has also been gained by Tolkien's *Lord of the Rings* trilogy and by C. S. Lewis's seven *Chronicles of Narnia*. All three authors use a dramatic understanding of good and evil which was inspired by their Christian faith. They show characters who appear to be small, weak and powerless learning to resist mighty forces of evil with courage and love. However much we try to see our world as a mechanical place consisting of nothing but atoms and molecules, we still tend to remain fascinated by stories of dark powers and of the heroes who oppose them with bravery, integrity, kindness and self-sacrifice. In fact, people who spend their days programming computers and working in laboratories can be especially keen to spend their evenings immersed in games and stories about sorcerers, dragons and wizards.

JESUS CHRIST AND THE VICTORY OF LOVE

Christianity has its own central narrative of the conflict between good and evil, presenting Jesus Christ as God's response to the evil of the world. In an exercise of power, God could simply have obliterated all evil from outside. Instead, he made the surprising choice to make himself vulnerable and to step right into the middle of the problem. In Jesus Christ, we see God working from within the mess of our world to bring reconciliation.

Jesus' teaching frequently addresses this central issue of damaged relationships. He often talked about forgiveness and about ways of responding positively to other people's cruelty and aggression. Faced with conflict, our natural instincts are usually either to fight back or to give in, but neither response leads to a healthy relationship. Power struggles involve injury, hatred, misunderstanding, entrenched stubbornness, irrational polarisation of views, petty tribalism, and a failure to respect the humanity of the opponent. They then lead to oppressive hierarchies established by the victors, until the day comes when the defeated rise up again. But power struggles do not in themselves lead to love, trust, kindness, empathy and cooperation.

Jesus' response to evil involves both a rejection of evil and a refusal to adopt its methods. It involves an ability to see the potential goodness of the opponent, and an awareness of the potential goodness of a genuine relationship. In war, we label whole tribes and nations as animals who should be slaughtered. In politics, we mock the opposing parties as stupid, or greedy, or elitist, or uncaring, or weak. Even in our workplaces and neighbourhoods, we form resentful cliques and factions. But Jesus completely refused to settle for any of these divisive responses.

Instead, he said, 'Love your enemies and pray for those who persecute you.'[121] His advice for those facing evil was astonishing and radical:

> You have heard that it was said, 'An eye for an eye and a tooth
> for a tooth.' But I say to you, Do not resist an evildoer. But if
> anyone strikes you on the right cheek, turn the other also; and

---

121 Matthew 5.44

if anyone wants to sue you and take your coat, give your cloak
as well; and if anyone forces you to go one mile, go also the
second mile.[122]

This approach does not seek retribution, but nor does it simply
capitulate. It is third kind of response, which involves taking charge of
the situation through radical generosity. It neither seeks to gain power
through a violent struggle, nor does it simply surrender and accept
the power of the aggressor. Instead, it offers a completely unexpected
demonstration of love which may transform an angry encounter into
the beginnings of a new friendship. St Paul, quoting from the Book of
Proverbs, offers this similar advice:

'If your enemies are hungry, feed them; if they are thirsty, give
them something to drink; for by doing this you will heap
burning coals on their heads.' Do not be overcome by evil, but
overcome evil with good.[123]

Seeking to overcome evil with goodness is at the heart of Jesus'
teaching, his life and his death. It is more ambitious than an attempt
to destroy evil, for it is an attempt to redeem it. It is not a giving way
to evil, or an act of fearful appeasement, but rather the courageously
generous attempt to transform evil through love. It opens up the possibility that both sides will start to recognise what they have in common
and to respect their differences, and it opens up the possibility of trust
and a mutually beneficial relationship.

There is nothing weak or cowardly about this approach, which relies
on enough bravery and self-control to overcome our urgent instincts to
fight, surrender or run away. It refuses to let the aggressor take charge,
but it also refuses to use the methods of the aggressor. It is such a challenging idea that Christians have mostly preferred to ignore it. It comes
much more naturally to us to follow the example of the Emperor Con-
stantine, who at the Battle of Milvian Bridge in the year 312 inaugurated
the practice of painting Christian symbols onto weaponry. Theological
theories about just wars flourished during the following centuries while

122 Matthew 5.38–41
123 Romans 12.20–21

Europe was run by those claiming to follow Christ, most of whom failed to notice that their master had advocated something far more radical. Ironically, the modern rediscovery of Jesus' approach was led by a Hindu, Mahatma Gandhi (1869–1948), when he steered the non-violent protests that achieved Indian independence from the British Empire. His success then helped to inspire Baptist minister Martin Luther King to lead peaceful forms of civil disobedience in the campaign against racial segregation in America.

Seeking to overcome evil with goodness is very different from simply being nice, or weak or cowardly. Jesus himself was at times extremely fierce, as for example when turning over the tables of those making money unjustly in the Temple.[124] He denounced corrupt religious leaders as hypocrites, blind guides and broods of vipers because of the ways they were failing those in their care.[125] Even though he talked about the importance of being very generous in our willingness to forgive, he still advised that we should demand that those who have hurt us change their ways before we forgive them.[126] He was very blunt when pointing out the ways in which people were causing harm to each other, and very extravagant when advocating mercy for those who genuinely wanted to change.

Jesus' approach was not concerned with controlling other people, or being controlled by them. It was not about the establishment of any kind of hierarchy. It was an approach which aimed at the flourishing of individuals and communities, in honest relationships where the ways in which we hurt each other have been identified and put right.

These values can be seen in his teaching and in the details of his life, but they are seen most vividly in his death and in the events leading up to it. Christians understand the crucifixion to be the heart of God's response to the evil of the world, giving it a place of central importance in Christian doctrine. Over the centuries, various theories have therefore been developed about the significance of the death of Jesus, and I shall discuss some of them later. But these ideas have inevitably been

124 Mark 11.15
125 Matthew 23.1–36
126 Luke 17.3

shaped by the contexts of the hierarchical and mechanical views of the cosmos, and can now sound rather legalistic and mechanistic. The wonder of the cross is, above all, the story of what happened when the love of God collided head on with the evil of the world, and it is this narrative which forms a high proportion of the content of each of the four gospels. They present it as a dramatic clash between good and evil, an extraordinary victory, and as a great act of reconciliation which can heal the broken relationships between people and God.

THE NARRATIVE OF THE CRUCIFIXION

Wherever Jesus went, the tangled interactions of good and evil which shape our lives and our world became painfully, wonderfully obvious. The presence of such obvious goodness made the opposition of evil very evident. There was fear and opposition from religious and political leaders who were very comfortable with the way that things had been before he arrived. The powers of darkness cried out against him from the mouths of those affected by evil: 'Have you come to destroy us?'[127] Jesus' ministry built inexorably towards a terrifying collision between good and evil. Reality was unmasked: both the splendour of the goodness of God, and the horror of the darkness that likes to glory in its own pointless empire-building.

And so, at the time of the most holy festival of the Jewish year, Jesus arrived in Jerusalem from the east riding on a donkey, fulfilling an ancient prophecy for the coming of the Messiah. Everyone knew that something extraordinary was coming, but he knew that he was riding to his death. Living out his own teaching about turning the other cheek in response to evil, he willingly chose to offer the gift of his own life to those who hated him.

Jesus was cheered with great excitement by volatile crowds of pilgrims, who hoped that this remarkable man might be about to lead a violent revolution. He stormed into the great Temple, and threw out all the corrupt merchants who were making money out of those who came seeking the presence of God. And he preached with a new ferocity and

127 Mark 1.24

urgency, warning that evil would one day be judged and destroyed. But he remained always generous, compassionate, and free from violence, weeping over the situation of those who would not accept his message of reconciliation.

It was at this time that Judas Iscariot, one of his closest friends and supporters, made a deal with the hostile priests to betray Jesus to them in secret, away from the crowds, in exchange for thirty pieces of silver. He led a gang of thugs to where Jesus was praying late at night, in a quiet garden, and identified Jesus with a kiss. Jesus was arrested and his disciples fled in terror. And then came a series of futile interrogations and fake trials, in which those in power conspired to force his execution. While they bombarded him with false allegations, Jesus mostly remained patiently quiet. But the crowds, urged on by the conspirators, began to enjoy crying out for his blood.

And so began a murderous outpouring of evil from the nastiest depths of the human heart. It was the kind of sick instinct that offers us a refuge from our own problems by seeking a brief moment of power over another. We can take a twisted delight in contributing to pain and destruction, and find a twisted kind of togetherness in belonging to the winning side. And we can feel confident about it, because everyone else is doing it too. It can be hard for us to relate comfortably to great goodness, but our most primitive instincts can tell us how to join in with a killing. And there can be a brief moment of absolute clarity in the desire of the mob to wreak havoc and to destroy. So Jesus was tortured, and the crowds cried out for him to be crucified.

The soldiers stripped him naked, whipped him, mocked him, spat at him, hammered nails through his flesh, and lifted him up on a wooden cross to die. But throughout this time Jesus neither fought back nor showed any deference towards their power. He refused to argue. He refused to condemn. He refused to return in any way evil for evil. Even amidst his own agony, he spoke words of forgiveness, understanding and compassion. There, at the cross, the powers of darkness within human beings did their very worst. The Gospels describe this violent collision between the foulest evil and the purest goodness by saying that the midday sky turned to darkness.

Jesus, who had done no wrong, and who had only ever shown love to others, suffered one of the world's most vicious, barbaric executions. Crucifixion is an agonising slow death designed by the Romans to be a very public, brutal and humiliating sign of their supremacy. Alongside terrible physical pain, Jesus was abandoned and betrayed by friends, and endured the hatred of those he had come to help. He descended into the lowest depths of the human experience, overwhelmed by darkness and feeling utterly alone. And he cried out to God in those shocking words of protest from the Psalms: 'My God, my God, why have you forsaken me?'

But they could not make him hate. They did their very worst against him, and they could not make him hate. In all the triumph of their malice, they could neither make him become like them nor make him beg for their mercy. They could not make him despise them in return for all their violence, or cry out for vengeance, or plead for release. Instead, he showed his understanding and his respect for their humanity. 'Father, forgive them, for they do not know what they are doing,'[128] was his prayer for the soldiers who killed him. They broke his body, but his love remained strong. Although he died, he won the first part of a great victory over evil. The Roman centurion standing guard looked on in awe and said, 'Truly, this man was the Son of God.' They tried to destroy Jesus and all that he represented, but these events were so startling that this story is retold week by week in churches all over the world.

THE MEANING OF THE CRUCIFIXION
IN THE NEW TESTAMENT

The crucifixion is, above all, an event in history, and one which we encounter through the narratives of the four gospels. This event also inspires the central event of Christian worship, known to different churches as Holy Communion, the Mass, the Eucharist, the Lord's Supper or the Breaking of Bread. Worshippers re-enact the Last Supper, which took place shortly before Jesus' arrest. They recall how he gave another layer of significance to the Jewish celebration of the Passover

128 Luke 23.34

meal when he blessed bread and wine and shared it with his disciples. He spoke of his body, broken for them, and the blood of the New Covenant, poured out for the forgiveness of sins. Christians encounter Christ's offering up of his life by entering into this dramatic re-enactment of the Last Supper, and through the story in the gospels. The Eucharist makes the drama of the cross present for us, drawing in those who hear the words of the story and those who come to receive the bread and the wine.

Although the gospels primarily simply tell the story and enable us to encounter it, the Last Supper is one of three places where Jesus offers a few words of explanation about what his death will mean.[129] He speaks of his death bringing about a covenant, which is a close and committed relationship, like a marriage. It is, he says, a relationship based on forgiveness, showing that God's generous love and mercy has overcome the evil of the world. The bread and the wine convey Jesus' complete offering of himself to the human race, allowing us to break his body and to pour out his blood. He gives himself to angry, sinful human beings, allowing a cruel world to vent its hatred and cruelty on him. And through feeding on his limitless generosity, all can encounter the compassion and the forgiveness of God.

Elsewhere in Matthew, Mark and Luke, Jesus refers to his death in this way:

> Whoever wishes to become great among you must be your servant, and whoever wishes to be first among you must be slave of all. For the Son of Man came not to be served but to serve and to give his life a ransom for many.[130]

Mention of a ransom continues the imagery of slavery, referring to people who do not have the resources to obtain their own freedom. Jesus offers his life to set others free, rescuing us from a situation we could not escape from. As I shall discuss shortly, it is significant in the history of Christian theology that Jesus did not say to whom the ransom was paid. For now, I would suggest that Jesus' mention of a ransom is

---

129 Matthew 26.26–29; Mark 14.22–25; Luke 22.14–23; 1 Corinthians 11.23–26
130 Matthew 20.28 and Mark 10.45

consistent with the idea that he offered his own life to the evil of the world in order that he might break its grip on us.

Jesus' third description of his death is in John's Gospel, which offers a very confident account of the glory of the cross. Where the other gospels show the agony of Jesus' experience, John explores the extraordinary impact of his death. In John, Jesus describes how he will die, saying:

> Now is the judgment of this world; now the ruler of this world
> will be driven out. And I, when I am lifted up from the earth,
> will draw all people to myself.[131]

The two images of a victory over evil and an act of reconciliation are here again. The 'ruler of this world' indicates Satan, so Jesus is suggesting that the powers of evil will be provoked into leaving their dark hiding places and will come forth for a great confrontation, in which he will break their power and expel them. The crucifixion is therefore portrayed as a glorious victory, a lifting up of Jesus, which will capture the attention of the human race and draw us close to him.

Elsewhere in the New Testament, there is no one systematic account of purpose of the crucifixion. But a rich variety of language is used to explore aspects of the meaning of Jesus' death, including imagery from the sacrifices of the Old Testament. Jesus is, says John the Baptist, the 'Lamb of God who takes away the sins of the world.'[132] Meanwhile, St Paul explores the theme of a relationship restored by the generous love of God. He writes about justification, the act by which God shows that he forgives us and does not hold our sins against us. Paul describes Christ as one who sets us free from our guilty status as those who have failed to keep the rules.[133] All forces of judgementalism and legalism which might keep us away from God are disarmed and humiliated by the cross.[134]

The New Testament also describes ways in which people are changed by their encounter with the cross of Jesus, drawing on his

---

131 John 12:31–32
132 John 1.29
133 See especially his letters to the Galatians and the Romans
134 Colossians 2.14–15

teachings about turning the other cheek when confronted by evil. The First Letter of Peter describes how Jesus' own death had the effect of taking away our evil and transforming us.

> When he was abused, he did not return abuse; when he suffered, he did not threaten... He himself bore our sins in his body on the cross, so that, free from sins, we might live for righteousness; by his wounds you have been healed.[135]

The passage describes how Jesus was willing to suffer as an innocent man, bearing the onslaught of the rage and cruelty of the human race, in order to take that darkness away from us. He endured our sins in his body, so that we, free from those sins, might live for righteousness. Jesus, in his own body, takes away the sins of world, leaving us healed and free to live for God.

Christianity at its heart is saying that things have got completely messed up between people and God, but that the death of Jesus is the way that God began to sort it out. God made the first move, making himself vulnerable, and bridging the gap between him and us by coming right into the middle of our mess and our rage. He suffered all the painful consequences of that conflict himself in order to make a genuine relationship possible. Nevertheless, no attempt of mine to summarise the meaning of the cross will work. I have mentioned the various New Testament images of victory over evil, reconciliation, transformation, rescue, forgiveness, and a generosity that replaces legalism, and they all give insights into this event. But it remains something that can only be experienced in all its fullness in a personal way, through hearing the story and through sharing the bread and the wine.

THE MEANING OF THE CRUCIFIXION
IN THE HISTORY OF CHRISTIAN THEOLOGY

Down through history, the story has been told, and the bread and wine have been blessed and shared, and Jesus' offering of himself has touched the lives of billions. And Christian theologians have looked for ways to tell people about the wonder of the cross in terms which

---

135 1 Peter 2.18–25

were meaningful to the society of their own day. When successful, we theologians have offered the people of our own time a way of connecting to the narrative. But some of these explanations can sound odd to people in other times and contexts. Sometimes, Christians have turned the gripping story of a passionately generous act of reconciliation into something which may seem rather legalistic and baffling.

In the perilous early centuries of Christianity, theologians focussed as I have done on the theme of a victory over evil. But they were more enthusiastic than I have been in exploring the personal role of Satan. They put together Jesus' description of his death as a ransom with his description of his death as a driving out of the 'ruler of the world', and concluded that his death was a ransom payment made to the Devil. This is now known as the classic theory of the atonement, or the *Christus Victor* theory.[136] It says that our sins had allowed Satan to gain ownership of human beings, but that Christ offered himself to the powers of darkness in return for our release. The Devil gladly took the bait and made the exchange, but was then outwitted by Jesus' subsequent resurrection. This theory is not well known now, but it is part of the inspiration for C. S. Lewis's famous story *The Lion, the Witch and the Wardrobe*, in which Aslan hands himself over to be killed by the White Witch so that she will let Edmund go.

Later theologians were understandably not convinced by the great power attributed to Satan in this account. But, by then, Christianity had become deeply interwoven with the hierarchical view of the cosmos, and a powerful way emerged of making sense of the cross of Jesus within that society. It was defined in detail by St Anselm (c. 1033–1109), Archbishop of Canterbury, in his very influential book *Why God Became Man*.

A hierarchical social system depends on each person giving due respect and honour to those higher up the social scale. If this does not happen, then the whole system is disturbed, until steps are taken to put the offender firmly back in his place. One of my chickens who tries to rise above her place in the flock will alarm the others and will be sharply pecked until she remembers where she fits in the pecking order. Human

---

136 See Gustaf Aulen (1931) *Christus Victor: An Historical Survey of the Three Main Types of the Idea of Atonement* SPCK

societies often maintain social hierarchies through complex patterns of military salutes, hat-doffing, bowing, speech-making, processional orders, reserved seating, uniforms, titles and present-giving. Parking your car in the boss's space or laughing at a commanding officer leads to big trouble. In the 17th century, the very peaceful and radical early Quakers suffered great anger and violence simply as a result of their refusal to remove their hats in deference to anyone.

In the hierarchical society of Anselm's time, everyone knew their place, and everyone understood that a failure to respect one's superiors would threaten the stable order of society. Worst of all, clearly, would be a failure to give due honour to the figure at the very top of all hierarchies, namely God. More shocking than stealing from the Lord of the Manor, or pouring custard on the King, disrespecting God would throw the whole system into chaos until something very obvious was done to make up for the dishonour.

In Anselm's understanding, every human sin was an act of disrespect towards God. He wrote:

> There is nothing more intolerable in the universal order than that a creature should take away honour from the creator and not repay what he takes away.[137]

When the universal order is undermined in this way, God cannot simply overlook the offence. It is unthinkable that the person of highest honour could lose face in such a way. Anselm was adamant: 'It is not fitting for God to forgive a sin without punishment.'[138] In his understanding, the sinner owes a great debt of honour to God, and it is essential for the good order of all creation that this debt is seen to be repaid. But we already owe God all of our future obedience and respect, so we have nothing else to give, leaving us in a terrible predicament. Chaos looms for the universal order. The answer, of course, is Christ's offering of himself on our behalf. Jesus lives a sinless life, incurring no debts of honour towards God, but giving up his life in obedience to God in order to pay off the debts that we have accumulated.

137 Anselm Why God Became Man, book 1, chapter 13
138 Anselm Why God Became Man, book 1, chapter 12

Anselm therefore took the bold step of claiming that Jesus' death was a ransom paid not to the devil but to God, which I suspect is the most radical swapping of roles in the history of human thought. He said that 'Christ gave himself up to death for the sake of God's honour.'[139] Christ's death provides the big, public, dramatic event that makes up for all of the ways in which human sin disrespects God. And God is now able to forgive us, while retaining all of his honour, and the hierarchical structure of creation can continue peacefully as intended. The universal order is brought back into harmony and everyone can breathe a large sigh of relief. This understanding of the cross is called the satisfaction theory of the atonement, because it indicates that God's honour is seen to be satisfied through Jesus' death.

This preoccupation with God's dignity was a significant shift in Christian theology. Instead of seeing the evil of the world as a problem in itself, Christians now saw the real problem as being the dishonour caused to God by that evil. Cruelty, greed and apathy were understood to be bad primarily because of their effects on God's honour, not primarily because of their obvious destructive effects on human society. That was a small step to take in an age that believed that its social hierarchies were ordained by God, because human society and divine honour were so clearly linked. As I have been describing, they saw disrespect for God as the greatest possible threat to the good order of the whole world. For them, causing dishonour to God and causing chaos among people were two aspects of same thing. But, without the assumption that the whole cosmos is hierarchical, Anselm's theory can now seem very dubious. Now that we have dismantled all the pecking orders of Anselm's day, we are left only with the figure at the top of the hierarchy. God is marooned on high, fussing about his dignity, in a way which can seem very petty and detached from the real problems of evil.

There is, I think, a wrong turning in Anselm's approach, and it is much more evident now that we have lost the hierarchies of his time. It is evil which is the central problem, and evil is a problem in itself. When Anselm's approach focusses instead on God's dishonour

139 Anselm *Why God Became Man*, book 2, chapter 18

as the problem, this is for us a misleading reading of the Bible. The Biblical portraits of God present him as one who is loving, creative, and who wants to see his creation flourish, not as one who is primarily concerned with his own dignity. There are indeed many mentions of his anger in the Bible, but this anger is to do with the state of the world rather than with the state of his honour. In the Bible, God gets angry about the exploitation of the poor, the lack of care for the vulnerable, and religion which is just an outward show. But he is concerned about those things in themselves, and he is always ready to forgive all those who want to mend their ways. Even in the more disturbing parts of the Old Testament, mentions of divine discipline and punishment are generally aimed towards getting people to sort their lives out, rather than enabling God to save face. And the New Testament portrays the Son of God as having no qualms about being born among animals, washing his disciples' feet, and dying among convicted criminals. Jesus is not at all fussy about his honour.

But Christianity was shaped for the largest part of its history by this concern with hierarchies and their dignity. And so it became more and more a religion which was expressed through ideas about guilt and punishment. The emphasis on Christ's death, although it was seen as the answer to the problem of guilt, helped to establish that guilt as the central concern of people's spiritual journeys. Alongside Christ's supreme honour-restoring sacrifice, the medieval Church developed a complex set of spiritual disciplines based around the theme of sin and punishment. Christ's sacrifice overcame the need for people to face eternal punishment in hell for the human offence of original sin, but there would still be a long and painful journey through purgatory after death to pay off the smaller debts of many individual sins. The way to make progress in this life involved the confession of all but the most trivial sins to priests, doing penance, and ideally giving money to the Church to make up for our faults. It was a complex, and often exhausting, courtly dance of paying respect to God and his appointed representatives. Christian worship involved a lot of bowing, kneeling, apologising, and even attempts to bribe God.

When the Reformation began in the 16th century, Protestants started to tidy up some of this obsession with guilt and punishment. Martin Luther (1483–1546), the monk who began the rebellion against the Pope, found the religious system of his day terrifying and exhausting. He had been very zealous in confessing all of his sins, doing penance, and observing all the ceremonies of the Church. But he could find no peace in his heart until he discovered a much more direct message of God's love in the New Testament letters of St Paul. Luther concluded that God cares nothing for all of our legalistic attempts to be righteous, but simply wants us to trust him. There was no need for purgatory, no need for penance, no need for elaborate ceremonies or large donations. We are justified by faith, said Luther, echoing Paul, meaning that our relationship with God is completely put right simply by trusting in his love for us. We can rejoice in the knowledge that we are completely forgiven. And this experience is available to all directly from God, without reaching us through the hierarchies and ceremonies of the Church.

Luther's writing is very passionate, earthy and unsystematic. He greatly disliked the proud and fussy religious legalism that he saw in the New Testament accounts of the Pharisees of Jesus' time, and in the Catholic Church of his own day. But some later Protestants were much more systematic, and the most famous figure in the subsequent development of Protestantism was a former lawyer called John Calvin (1509–1564). The influence of his teachings flourished greatly alongside the rise of the mechanical view of the cosmos. As Protestantism grew, it helped to bring in an age which looked for fixed, universal, God-given laws in workings of nature and in the lives of people. And so a modified form of Anselm's theology came to dominate Protestant theology.

In place of Anselm's ideas of hierarchy and honour, Protestants advocated a mechanistic and universal principle of justice. It said that God, being perfectly just, is compelled to punish every single sin committed by human beings. We have all sinned, and therefore we are all doomed to eternal damnation. But God is also loving, and has therefore provided a way out. In the agony of the crucifixion,

Jesus Christ has borne the punishment of his followers on their behalf, allowing them to be set free from all guilt. Theologians call this idea 'penal substitution', although most of the people who believe in it are not familiar with that term. Traditionalist Evangelicals simply regard this understanding of the cross as the Gospel, the centre of Christianity. It is, however, the source of much fierce debate in today's Church. Much modern Protestant theology has sought to recover a greater sense of the breadth of imagery in the New Testament about the cross of Christ.

Penal substitution has found many supporters. Just as Anselm's satisfaction theory connected powerfully with a hierarchical view of the cosmos, so penal substitution has connected powerfully with a mechanical view of the cosmos. It has provided a very effective way for a great many people to connect with the story of Jesus, to take it seriously in a scientific age, and to start to make sense of it. For those who have found it helpful, it has conveyed very powerfully a sense of the love of God, a love which is greater than their guilt and which has a clear, objective and utterly reliable reality. It has enabled them to join up biblical ideas about the holiness and righteousness of God with biblical ideas about the grace and mercy of God. And it has inspired in them a deep sense of gratitude and love. Despite being inherently mechanistic, it has assisted many people to find a very personal sense of a loving relationship.

Nevertheless, I do not think that penal substitution is the most enlightening way of making sense of the Gospel of Jesus Christ, or of the whole message of the scriptures, or of the whole breadth of our experiences of reality. My reservations fall under two headings. Firstly, I think that Jesus' teachings are primarily concerned with the flourishing of people and relationships rather than with cosmic laws of justice. And, secondly, I think that the formation of human beings in this life involves much more than the avoidance of punishment.

There is nowhere in the entire Bible that endorses the idea that God is compelled to punish every sin. It simply is not a biblical idea. Instead, there are many instances when God freely chooses to forgive people, without seeming to need to displace their punishment onto anyone else. At the dedication of the Temple in Jerusalem, God says:

> If my people who are called by my name humble themselves,
> pray, seek my face, and turn from their wicked ways, then I
> will hear from heaven, and will forgive their sin and heal their
> land.[140]

Mentions of divine justice are intended to inspire people to mend their ways, rather than being inexorable cosmic principles. Much to the disgust of the prophet Jonah, God forgives the entire wicked population of Ninevah after they repent.

> When God saw what they did, how they turned from their evil
> ways, God changed his mind about the calamity that he had
> said he would bring upon them; and he did not do it.[141]

Again, there is no mention here of punishment being displaced onto anyone else. Nor is a displaced penalty mentioned in any of the situations where Jesus pronounced the forgiveness of sinners. Significantly, he never explained to anyone that he had come to bear the *punishment* for their sins, nor does any verse in the New Testament say that about him. Instead, Jesus interfered with the established principles of justice when he saved a woman from being punished for adultery, inviting any who had no sin to cast the first stone. When they had all gone, he simply said: 'Neither do I condemn you. Go your way, and from now on do not sin again.'[142]

Jesus taught that we should forgive each other in the way that God forgives us, and in both cases he was describing the offer of forgiveness to all those who repent. When someone genuinely seeks to change their ways and to repair a relationship, we should welcome them. Jesus explicitly links divine and human forgiveness in various places, such as the Lord's Prayer: 'Forgive us our trespasses, as we forgive those

---

140 2 Chronicles 7.14
141 Jonah 3.10
142 John 8.11

who trespass against us.'[143] There is no mention of either God or people needing to relocate a punishment.

The problem with penal substitution is that it diverts the cross from being a way of resolving a problem within the world and turns it into a way of resolving a problem within God. Jesus' death becomes the way in which God sorts out an internal contradiction within himself between his love and his justice. One person of the Holy Trinity punishes another in order that a divine law can be satisfied. It is an image which many people today find odd and unhelpful, and which leaves behind the problem of evil as a completely separate and unresolved question. Meanwhile, as I have described, the story told in the Gospels seems to present the cross as the way in which God makes himself vulnerable and confronts the evils of the world. Jesus came to change us and to reconcile us to God, not to change God.

In writing this Theology of Everything, my main hesitation about penal substitution is that it can so easily lead Christian theology down the disappointing road of becoming just one of those narrow areas of expertise that I mentioned in the first chapter. It gives in to that huge pressure on us all to become specialists. If the Gospel is understood in terms of penal substitution, it is an easy step for us to give up trying to talk about all of our experiences of reality and all of the ways in which people develop. Instead, Christianity becomes centred on the one question of whether or not an individual can escape eternal punishment and go to heaven. If that happens, then faith is no longer concerned with the whole of life, but only with a thing that can happen after we die. Theology becomes an account of the password for another reality, and ceases to be a way of making sense of this one.

Instead, I want to insist, as the New Testament does, that the cross of Jesus Christ is God's way of confronting the evil of the world, breaking its hold on us, and making it possible for us now to grow into relationships of love with him and with each other. It is God's way of turning the other cheek, and loving those who have become estranged from him. It is God's way of overcoming the shame and the guilt of those who

143 Matthew 6.12

hide away in the shadows. And it is God's way of coming alongside those in the very lowest depths of human experience.

The cross deals with *our* anger, *our* alienation and *our* internal contradictions, not God's. St Paul describes Jesus' role very beautifully in his cosmic vision of Christ as the one who holds everything together and who makes reconciliation possible for all:

> Jesus is the image of the invisible God, the firstborn of all creation... He himself is before all things, and in him all things hold together... For in him all the fullness of God was pleased to dwell, and through him God was pleased to reconcile to himself all things, whether on earth or in heaven, by making peace through the blood of his cross.[144]

All kinds of people have experienced the reconciliation brought by the crucifixion. Jürgen Moltmann (born 1926) writes this about his experiences of discovering faith as a young man:

> In 1945 I was imprisoned in a wretched prisoner-of-war camp in Belgium. The German Reich had collapsed. German civilization had been destroyed through Auschwitz. My home town Hamburg lay in ruins; and in my own self things looked no different. I felt abandoned by God and human beings, and the hopes of my youth died. I couldn't see any future ahead of me.

> In this situation an American chaplain put a Bible into my hands, and I began to read it. First of all the psalms of lament in the Old Testament: 'I have fallen dumb and have to eat up my suffering within myself... I am a stranger as all my fathers were' (Psalm 39).

> Then I was drawn to the story of the passion, and when I came to Jesus' death cry I knew: this is the one who understands you and is beside you when everyone else abandons you. 'My God, why have you forsaken me?' That was my cry for God too. I began to understand the suffering, assailed and God-forsaken Jesus, because I felt that he understood me. And I grasped that

144 Colossians 1.15, 17, 19–20

this Jesus is the divine Brother in our distress. He brings hope
to the prisoners and the abandoned. He is the one who delivers
us from the guilt that weighs us down and robs us of every
kind of future. And I became possessed by a hope when in
human terms there was little enough to hope for. I summoned
up the courage to live, at a point when one would perhaps
willingly have put an end to it all. This early companionship
with Jesus, the brother in suffering and the liberator from
guilt, has never left me since. The Christ for me is the crucified
Jesus.[145]

For Moltmann, it is Jesus' willingness to suffer and to die which is
the clearest window into the true nature and loving character of God,
not any dramatic exercise of power. He writes:

When the crucified Jesus is called 'the image of the invisible
God', the meaning is that *this* is God, and God is like *this*. God
is not greater than he is in this humiliation. God is not more
glorious than he is in this self-surrender. God is not more
powerful than he is in this helplessness. God is not more divine
than he is in this humanity.[146]

The Theology of Everything says that the greatest force in the universe is love, a love which is at the heart of reality, and a love that is
willing to be vulnerable and to suffer for the good of others. It is a love
which gives us the space to be ourselves, which watches and weeps over
the ways we go astray, which patiently endures our cruelty and our
selfishness, which comes alongside us in our shame and our isolation,
and which is always ready to embrace us, to forgive us and welcome
us home. Nothing is more enduring, more meaningful, more beautiful
or more true.

At the heart of Christianity's account of the personal nature of God
is the story that God came to dwell among us as one of us, in great
vulnerability and humility. He did not hide himself from the squalor
and the tyranny and the viciousness of the world. He identified himself
with the poor, the weak, the outsiders, the lonely and the despised. He

145 Jürgen Moltmann (1994) *Jesus Christ for Today's World* SCM, p. 2–3
146 Jürgen Moltmann (2001) *The Crucified God* SCM, p. 211

suffered and he died in order to bring a relationship of love that can be stronger than the darkest cruelty of the world.

In the centuries which have followed, churches have often sought status and influence by aligning themselves with the hierarchical forces of political power. But the heart of the message of Jesus Christ is something which is both astonishingly vulnerable and radically liberating. God came to redeem the world not by imposing martial law but by allowing us to nail him to a cross.

FROM SELFISHNESS TO LOVE: A SPIRITUAL JOURNEY

The impact of the death of Jesus on people like Moltmann is the supreme example of one of the very purposeful features of reality: the way that God seeks to inspire the emergence of goodness and hope out of evil and despair. Evil is always redeemable, and the harshest experiences of life can provide an inspiration for the growth of goodness and love. Moltmann's story is only one of a great multitude of accounts of people discovering hope within great darkness.

The presence of evil can be the challenge which enables us to grow in goodness. Faced with suffering and conflict, we can learn how to bring kindness and reconciliation. When we uncover injustice and cruelty, we can seek to build a fairer society and to defend the vulnerable. And the hardships we face can help us to empathise with others and to think carefully about our own priorities. An experience of darkness can lead to a dramatic recommitment to pursue what is good and life-affirming.

In this fragmented world of selfish individuals, genuine love and kindness does arise. Our freedom as conscious beings is a wonderful thing, but most wonderful of all are the ways in which we can learn to care for each other and to take delight in each other. Love is a vital part of reality, and to love is to participate in something which is as real as atoms, forces, energy, beauty, goodness and consciousness. As the New Testament says, God is love, and those who live in love live in God and God lives in them.[147] There is a special kind of knowledge that comes through friendship, laughter, empathy and community,

147 1 John 4.8

which is beyond anything that could be measured in a laboratory. Any one human being is a source of wonder, a complex character formed through a multitude of experiences, decisions, relationships, conflicts and discoveries. And we relate to each other in different ways, so that every friendship between human beings is different. There is a deep and surprising knowledge which one person can gain of another through friendship and love. To become a more loving person is to learn what human beings are truly meant to be.

The world is a training ground within which we may learn to love, if we so choose. It is a preparation for a better world which is still under construction. Here and now, we can learn to care about the well-being of other individual people and communities. And, through that, we can also learn to care about the whole divine purpose behind reality. We can gain an appreciation of the meaningfulness of life, and a desire to join in with the ways in which God's creation enables people to flourish. This transition from selfishness to love has been widely observed and is an important theme in many different faiths and philosophies. Buddhism and Hinduism describe the problems of the human ego and its unhealthy attachments. Sikhism advocates acts of selfless service to the community. And Stoic philosophy encourages a sense of global citizenship and of the equality of all people.

When Jesus Christ proclaimed the arrival of the kingdom of God, he called people to repentance and to a complete change of heart.[148] He said that to enter the kingdom of God would involve being reborn.[149] This rebirth is the change from a life centred on the selfish ego to a life which begins to overflow with love for God and for each other. It is a challenging process, which involves the gradual transformation of individuals by the Holy Spirit, the presence of God within them. Like the way that a tree grows slowly and eventually bears fruit, a person can gradually bring forth the qualities which St Paul described as the fruit of the Spirit: love, joy, peace, patience, kindness, goodness, gentleness, faithfulness and self-control.[150] They

148 Mark 1.14
149 John 3.3
150 Galatians 5.22–23

replace the selfishness and separateness which are the default state of human beings.

And so the transformation which Jesus described involves the willingness to see the selfish ego put to death, and the willingness to learn to love. He said that the two greatest commandments were to love God and to love other people as much as we love ourselves.[151] This, he said, was the way to real life, the eternal life of the kingdom of God. He criticised those who make a big public show of doing good deeds in order to impress others, and commended those who gave generously in secret.[152] True greatness, he taught, consisted in being the servant of all, not in trying to lord it over other people.[153] Many who are now first, he said, will be last in the kingdom of God. And the last will be first.[154] He knelt to wash his disciples' feet, and he said that he himself had come not to be served but to serve, and to give his life for others.[155]

He never lived in luxury, did not encourage the use of grand titles, and did not allow his disciples to protect him with weapons.[156] To be his follower, he said, would mean denying oneself and carrying a cross, a reference to his own journey towards his death.[157] It would mean being willing to see our old egoistical selves destroyed. Those who sought to save their lives would lose them, he said. But those who lost their lives for the sake of the good news of kingdom of God would save them. His words call into question so many of our normal dreams and ambitious. What good would it be, he asked, to gain the whole world and yet lose one's soul?

He was especially critical of those who put their trust in riches. Be on your guard, he said, against all kinds of greed, for one's life does not consist in the abundance of possessions.[158] We cannot, he warned, serve both God and wealth.[159] And it is harder for a rich person to

151 Matthew 22.34–39
152 Matthew 6.1–4
153 Mark 10.35–45
154 Mark 10.31
155 John 13.1–11, Mark 10.45
156 Matthew 8.20, Matthew 23.8–9, Matthew 26.52
157 Mark 8.34
158 Luke 12.15
159 Luke 16.13

enter the kingdom of heaven than for a camel to pass through the eye of a needle.[160] Possessions, he said, are always in danger from rust and moths and thieves, but true wealth comes from having a life which is rich towards God.[161] True riches are the relationships and strengths of character which we develop, the ways in which we grow in love. Those who pin all their hopes on amassing things are missing the point.

Jesus lived an extraordinary life of love, compassion and humble service. It is one which involved remarkable sacrifice. But surprisingly, he described his own calling as an easy one, even though it involved great hardship, sacrifice and physical pain. Humility and service are lighter burdens than the endless futile quest to satisfy the ego. He said:

> Come to me, all you that are weary and are carrying heavy
> burdens, and I will give you rest. Take my yoke upon you,
> and learn from me; for I am gentle and humble in heart, and
> you will find rest for your souls. For my yoke is easy, and my
> burden is light.[162]

He advocated a life of joyful, simple trust in God, rather than the endless striving of those who seek to amass unnecessary worldly treasures for themselves.

Jesus' teachings describe a great and wonderful paradox which is at the heart of life, and is one of the most significant human experiences of reality. If we believe that it is our selfish desires and insecurities which reveal our true identity, so that we devote our lives to seeking wealth, pleasure, power, status and affirmation for ourselves, then there will always be an aching emptiness at the core of our being. True happiness can never be found in fighting to satisfy every last greedy and fearful instinct that we happen to find within ourselves. If we do so, we will remain forever unfulfilled and insecure. It is a common human experience that the selfish goals we aim for, dreaming of earning wealth, status and the admiration of others, feel empty when we have achieved them. However much we brag about them, they soon feel hollow and meaningless. And we can only hide the emptiness within by quickly

160 Mark 10.23
161 Matthew 6.19–21
162 Matthew 11.28–30

racing on towards the next goal. Even if our self-centredness leads us to gain the whole world and reshape it around us, we lose our souls.

But if we forget about ourselves while caring for others, or while working with the aim of making the world a better place, we may suddenly find that life has become rewarding. If we are willing to live lives of humble generosity and enthusiastic service, while our egoism dies away, we may unexpectedly realise that we have found who we are truly meant to be. And we may discover that we have found a new sense of peace, hope and joy. Real happiness tends to arrive when we are not chasing frantically after it or worrying about ourselves. Those who lose themselves in living enthusiastically for the kingdom of God will find their identity, their place in the cosmos and the purpose of their lives. In losing themselves, they will find themselves. In taking up their cross and seeing their selfish nature put to death, they will rise to a new and more authentic way of life. It is an experience of being reborn.

I have been describing the cosmos as a very purposeful environment, which even in the midst of evil still brings forth the intended fruit of consciousness and love. I have one more theme to tackle, which is the question of the future of the cosmos. Where is all this creativity leading?

SUGGESTIONS FOR FURTHER READING

John Polkinghorne has a helpful chapter on evil in *Exploring Reality: The Intertwining of Science and Religion* (SPCK, 2005).

The most helpful account I know of different theories about the significance of the crucifixion is *Past Event and Present Salvation* by Paul S. Fiddes (DLT, 1989).

There is a great wealth of religious literature which explores the spiritual journey of transformation from selfishness to love. One example is *The Return of the Prodigal Son* by Henri Houwen (Darton, Longmann and Todd, 1994).

C. S Lewis's imagined correspondence from a senior to a junior demon, *The Screwtape Letters* (William Collins, 2012) has many amusing insights into human foibles and the nature of temptation.

Chapter Seven
The Promise Fulfilled

THE DEVELOPING UNIVERSE

One of the most misleading features of the mechanical view of the cosmos is the dull impression it gives that the universe will never do anything new. A perfect clockwork mechanism would keep ticking along in exactly the same predictable way forever, and it would never develop into something different. Science works by measuring the properties of the universe that we can currently detect, making the assumption that nature is like a mechanism that will always keep doing the same things. Scientists therefore get stuck within the idea that the phenomena evident today will be the only ones ever seen. Cosmologists, for example, attempt to deduce the future of the universe by extrapolating from the things that they can currently measure. They study gravity and the behaviour of the matter and energy of the universe, and try to calculate what happen in the distant future. They then try to work out whether today's observable properties will cause the cosmos to expand forever, or whether it will eventually collapse back on itself in a Big Crunch in billions of years' time.

This is a fascinating question, but the underlying assumption that the future universe will never display any new phenomena is deeply flawed. One of the most significant features of the history of the universe is that it is not just expanding in size but also in the range of things that it does. Past experience shows that it is far more likely to turn into a very different kind of place than to behave forever in the same way. The cosmos is like a growing plant which produces new flowers, fruits and branches in new seasons, rather than an endlessly-ticking mechanism.

The story of the universe is full of change and development, with a dramatic progression of surprising chapters. Like a tree producing blossom in the spring for the first time, there have been many times when something new has begun. There have been many times when an event has taken place which is part of a pattern never previously seen. There have been many times when a deeper part of the potential of the cosmos has been revealed.

The Big Bang is the earliest chapter that we know about, the moment of the birth of creation. And in its youth, the matter of the universe was found mostly in the form of clouds of hydrogen gas, composed of only the smallest and simplest of elements. Very little of the potential of the cosmos was then evident. But then a second chapter began. And those dull and unpromising clouds of gas gradually collected into greater concentrations to make the first generation of stars, so that the universe began to shine with a new light. Each star was a dazzling nuclear furnace, which fused atoms together to make larger elements, such as carbon, oxygen, nitrogen, iron and silicon: the building blocks which were later needed for rock, water, air and life. Until finally, when the fuel of these stars ran low and they began to fall apart, they dispersed those raw materials like seeds across galaxies.

Those first stars died, but they formed the ingredients which enabled the beginning of another chapter. In time, new generations of stars formed among the varied debris of the old. And the new stars were now circled by rocky planets, with winds and storms and flowing water. That is how our Earth began, although at first it was a lifeless place of volcanoes and lava flows. And so, for a time, stars burned and planets circled, with no eyes to see their raw beauty.

But there were more chapters of the story still to come. From our seas came organic molecules and then living cells which could reproduce, evolving into creatures which could swim and run and fly, tapping into deeper and deeper levels of the potential of the universe. There appeared bacteria, amoebae, plants, fish, amphibians, reptiles, birds and mammals, gaining strength and intelligence. And so there followed another new chapter: the beginning of consciousness. We do not know how many times and on how many planets this has happened. But there was a day, somewhere, when a living creature first became aware of its own thoughts and pondered the meaning of its own existence. And so on Earth there appeared human beings who gazed out into space in wonder. And there developed love, relationships, and the appreciation of beauty and the knowledge of good and evil.

Enthusiasts of the mechanical cosmos have tended to assume that it all ended there. That the universe had then seen all the new phenomena that there would ever be. That its matter held no further potential waiting to be revealed in the future. That from then onwards, its gears would simply tick along for billions of years of the same predictable clockwork behaviour, until finally the last of the stars grew dim and faded away, or the universe fell back into nothingness.

I believe that there is much more still to come. In fact, it seems to me highly irrational to assume that the cosmos will never exhibit any further revolutionary new phenomena. If we assert such a thing about the scientific patterns of matter then we deny the most fundamental and significant pattern of all: the way that the cosmos has kept on surpassing itself at an accelerating rate in all of its creative processes. Neither the first carbon atom, nor the first rocky planet, nor the first living cell, nor the first conscious thought could have been predicted on the basis of the processes previously occurring. And so it is highly illogical to assume that the future must be limited to an exact continuation of those phenomena that are evident at the moment.

There was a time when the Earth was a barren rock which gave no sign of the civilisations which would one day appear on its surface. But that ball of molten iron and lava has given rise to poetry, philosophy and friendship. Seawater and air have turned into dolphins. And bacteria have evolved into people who hug and laugh and write symphonies. It seems to me that the cosmos is configured to bring forth life and love in a long series of constructive developments. We are part of the way through the startling story of a life-giving, social cosmos which has repeatedly shown that it is bursting with creative potential. It is entirely rational to expect there to be further revolutionary developments in the story of this purposeful universe and of our lives within it.

To speculate about the future of a developing cosmos must take us beyond the realms of our current scientific knowledge, but there is a great weight of evidence which presses us to do so. The universe's history gives us very strong indications of its purpose and direction. If we go beyond our ability to make measurements, and engage our ability for discerning meaning, then there is much that we can notice. This is the environment within which life has evolved and consciousness has developed, within which human beings have been given space to develop character and virtue, and within which communities and civilisations have arisen.

The greatest of all the wonders that we have found within the universe are people. And the greatest of those people have always been the ones who have developed their own unique characters and talents to the full, who have resisted evil, and have learned to live in warm and supportive relationships with each other. Whatever their beliefs, they have been learning to live in harmony with God's constructive purposes.

Each previous chapter in the history of the cosmos has involved bringing together what has gone before and revealing another level of its potential. Hydrogen atoms joined together to make carbon, hydrogen, oxygen, nitrogen and silicon, the building blocks of planets and organic molecules. And organic molecules joined together to make microscopic single-celled organisms, such as bacteria and amoebae. And these single-celled organisms joined together to make complex multi-cellular organisms, which gradually evolved to become human beings. The universe is a constructive, life-giving, social environment. And my suggestion is that human beings are ourselves another kind of building block for the future. We are being drawn together through bonds of love to form a greater reality which is still to come.

The world as it is now is marred by the presence of evil, which exists as part of the choices which are open to human beings. But I believe that a day will come when all that is stubbornly evil will be removed. And then those who have been responding to the presence of goodness in the world, and who have been learning to live lives of compassion and generosity, will be drawn closer together in a new and closer community. Another chapter in the history of the universe will begin, and a greater set of possibilities for conscious life and loving relationships will be revealed.

Just as the first generation of stars made the atomic building blocks for planets and seas and life, this world has been forming the elements of human consciousness and relationship which are among the building blocks of the next stage of reality. And all that has been good in the world as it has existed so far will be brought together in a way which reveals a deeper level of the potential of the universe for consciousness, love, creativity, beauty and joy.

I have shown how the evidence discovered by scientists fits very well with a belief that the cosmos is a developing, life-giving, social environment. This picture also connects very well with the teachings of Jesus Christ, which offer further insights into the next stage of the development of creation.

JESUS CHRIST AND THE
RESURRECTION OF THE DEAD

Jesus described a day in the future when people from all over the world would join together in a great banquet, along with figures from previous ages. He said that 'many will come from east and west, and will eat with Abraham and Isaac and Jacob in the kingdom of heaven.'[163] This is an image of celebration, of community, and of the shared enjoyment of all that is good in life. Such themes are prominent in the hope described in the New Testament, which often talks of a new relationship between people and God and of a reconciliation between divided groups of people.[164]

In the imagery used in the Bible, this future age involves the resurrection of the dead here on earth. A bodily resurrection contrasts with the idea of being some kind of ghost, and it is also not meant to suggest some kind of reanimated corpse or restless zombie. It means being fully alive in mind, body and spirit; being all that we are now, and more so. Jesus' description of a great banquet suggests people who

163 Matthew 8.11
164 e.g. Ephesians 2.11–21

can embrace each other, and look into each other's eyes, and listen to music, and taste wine and breathe in the aromas of fine cooking. But it also means being freed from the sicknesses and frailties of our current mortal bodies. St Paul writes, therefore, of receiving an immortal body which is imperishable.[165]

The New Testament describes the whole world being renewed[166] and the dead being remade in new bodies, at some unknown point in the future. It says very little about what happens between death and resurrection. But Christian spirituality has inevitably turned its attention to the current state of our departed loved ones, and has developed a complex set of ideas about the present situation of souls in heaven, purgatory or hell. There are disagreements about the details of this intermediate state, such as the rejection by most Protestants of the Catholic belief in purgatory. But all the main Christian churches still officially share that original New Testament hope of a future resurrection on earth, even if our hymns do not always get round to mentioning it.

I have described a whole series of constructive new developments in the history of the universe: stars forming the materials for rocky planets, organic molecules forming the building blocks of life, cells joining together to make plants and animals, and people acquiring intelligence, consciousness, and growing in virtue and love. Christian theology suggests that the next stage involves the bringing together of these people in a new kind of life and a new kind of community. In the imagery of the Bible, this involves resurrection, the gathering together of all who have ever lived. Jesus himself is presented as the pioneer of that resurrection, described by St Paul as 'the first fruits of those who have died.'[167]

The Gospels report that Jesus rose from the dead two days after his crucifixion. In his resurrected form, he had the familiar abilities of a human being, and yet also transcended our physical limitations. He was able to share meals with his disciples, but could also appear and disappear unexpectedly. Christians understand his resurrection

165 1 Corinthians 15.35–58
166 Revelation 21.1
167 1 Corinthians 15.23

as the completion of the great victory of the crucifixion, the defeat of evil and death. His overcoming of mortality is also the first appearance of the phenomenon which will one day renew the whole world. He is the 'firstborn from the dead.'[168] His resurrection was the first time that we have seen a deeper level of the potential of life which will one day become widespread.

At particular decisive moments in the history of our universe, there developed the first ever carbon atom, and the first ever planet, and the first ever living cell, and the first ever conscious thought. All of those revolutionary developments were then continued on a much wider scale and had a huge significance. The risen Christ is the first appearance of another new phenomenon, one which will in the future remake human life and community.

Until then, St Paul writes that the whole of creation is now 'groaning in labour pains', waiting for the glory which is to be revealed.[169] Just as the discomforts of pregnancy and the pains of childbirth lead up to the joy of new life, so the conflicts and struggles of the world as it is now lead up to the wonder of an age which is still to come. This will happen when the kingdom of heaven is fully established on earth.

Some passages in the Bible seem to describe the coming of the kingdom of God as a gradual process of change which is happening now, while others suggest that a more revolutionary transformation is still to come.[170] It seems to me to be rather like comparing the world as it is now to a building site. At present, there is noise, dust, mess, ugliness and occasional exciting signs of progress and glimpses of grandeur. But the day will come when the scaffolding will come down, the plastic sheets will be removed, the dust will be swept up, and all that has been under construction for so long will be seen in all its glory. The same is true, I think, of this world and of all the people who have ever taken shape within it. The day will come when the evil of the world will pass away, and the true glory of life in the universe will be revealed.

---

168 Colossians 1.18, Revelation 1.5

169 Romans 8.18–25

170 Compare the parable of the mustard seed (Matthew 13.33) with the description of the new heaven and the new earth (Revelation 21.1).

JUDGEMENT

The teachings of Jesus describe a time when God will draw together all that is and has ever been good in the world and use it to make a better future. Inevitably, this transformation involves some kind of sorting process. Jesus therefore spoke of a coming judgement, when the complex mixture of good and evil in the world will be carefully sifted. All that is good will be gathered up and brought forward into the next age, and all that is evil will be removed. He compared this to the way in which fishermen might draw in a net full of fish of every kind, put the good ones in baskets and throw out the bad.[171] In another parable, he talked of wheat and weeds growing in a field, all tangled up together. After the harvest they are separated out. The wheat is gathered into barns, but the weeds are thrown away and burned.[172]

Similarly, he said that the angels would at the end of the age 'collect out of his kingdom all causes of sin and all evildoers and throw them into the furnace of fire.' And then he said that 'the righteous will shine like the sun in the kingdom of their Father.'[173] This is very dramatic imagery, and it is also famously disturbing. These descriptions of the Last Judgement are the strongest biblical basis for the Christian preoccupation with punishment that I discussed in the previous chapter. And mention of a furnace of fire brings to mind the traditional image of hell as a place where people will be tormented eternally.

However, the dominant theme in Jesus' teachings about judgement is the constructive work of collecting together goodness and clearing evil out of the way. It is not the wrath of God, or the honour of God, or divine vengeance, or a principle of justice. It is about getting rid of the weeds, not about furiously stamping on them forever and making them pay. The central idea in Jesus' teachings about judgement seems to be simply a dramatic warning that the days are numbered for those aspects of creation which are not suited to the closer relationships of the kingdom of God. The word commonly translated as 'hell' in the Gospels is 'Gehenna', which was the name of a rubbish tip outside

171 Matthew 13.33
172 Matthew 13.24–30
173 Matthew 13:40–43

Jerusalem. Fires burned there as the most efficient way of destroying unwanted waste.

Gehenna is undoubtedly a rude and shocking image of the fate of the unrepentantly wicked, but does not convey any sense that God is a vicious tyrant who enjoys making people suffer for eternity. Jesus described Gehenna as a place where body and soul are destroyed,[174] not as a previously unknown kind of fire which causes torment while preserving people eternally alive and conscious. Nor do Jesus' teachings suggest that God is a cold-hearted magistrate who dispenses set quotas of punishment. The weeding out of evil and the bringing together of goodness is all part of God's good, loving and creative plans to see his creation flourish.

In the time of the hierarchical view of the cosmos, ideas of honour and punishment seemed deeply important and highly moral. And threats of retribution from the very top of the hierarchy helped to stabilise the rest of the system. Powerful men also used threats of everlasting punishment to increase their own power, seeking a way of frightening others into obedience. And their arrogance has often distorted people's image of God into something very cruel and sadistic. But, since the 19th century, ideas of eternal punishment have been rejected by many theologians, who have sought to re-emphasise the love and the creativity of God. It is love which is the fundamental character of God. The New Testament picture of God is more of one who loves us, who opposes evil, and who longs for people to join in with the project of building a better future. But, as part of that love, God gives us freedom, respects our human dignity and honours our choices, as I have been describing in the previous two chapters. God does not force anyone to respond to his vision of the world to come. Nor is he some kind of cosmic stalker who relentlessly and eternally pursues those who do not wish to know him. In the end, he respects the decisions which people have made. And any who are convinced that there can be nothing more to life than a few decades of greed and selfishness will, ultimately, get what they have expected and chosen: an unfulfilling existence which comes to a permanent end.

174 Matthew 10.28

This is not a gleeful act of vengeance, and those later Christians who suggested that the saints would enjoy watching the torments of the damned have shamefully missed the point. Jesus' own attitude to judgement is seen very movingly at the end of a ferocious passage where he berates religious leaders for their murderous hypocrisy and implores them to change their ways. His exasperation leads him ultimately to words not of revenge but of deep sorrow:

> Jerusalem, Jerusalem, the city that kills the prophets and stones those who are sent to it! How often have I desired to gather your children together as a hen gathers her brood under her wings, and you were not willing! See, your house is left to you, desolate.[175]

Those who have repeatedly refused to respond to God's invitations to gather together in his kingdom will ultimately be abandoned, as they have chosen. But there are many who have begun to join in with the meaningful divine work of reconciling people and gathering them together, and many who have started to grow in love for God and for each other. The kingdom of heaven begins here and now, alongside the evils and ambiguities of this life, but the time will come when it fills the world and transforms it. And all those, present and past, who have begun to learn to live as part of the kingdom, will enter a glorious new chapter of their existence. And all the ways in which present and past generations have grown in love and used their gifts for the common good will be brought together to remake the world. Many people will be utterly delighted to see the coming of the kingdom of God, recognising within it the fulfilment of all the glimpses of beauty, goodness, love and truth which they have sought after in their lives. But others will be disappointed and furious to find that a more powerful force than their own egos is sweeping aside their own limited plans.

So who exactly are the wicked people and the righteous people mentioned in Jesus' parables? The boundary around the set of those who love God does not match the boundary of any particular religious

175 Matthew 23.37–38

institution. And Jesus' parables seem to indicate a judgement which has many surprises. Christians have often wanted to tidy this up, and to insist that anyone who conforms to some particular set of Christian beliefs or practices must thereby officially be one of the righteous, while all others are utterly lost. But Jesus' descriptions of the day of judgement seem to be designed to unsettle those who are arrogant about any kind of religiosity. He said:

> On that day many will say to me, 'Lord, Lord, did we not prophesy in your name, and cast out demons in your name, and do many deeds of power in your name?' Then I will declare to them, 'I never knew you; go away from me, you evildoers.'

People who have been busy preaching dramatically and claiming all kinds of miraculous powers may still have just been serving their own egos, and failing to follow their true calling with love and humility. Even official Christian leaders may not be truly a part of the kingdom. God's vision for reconciliation may turn out to be very different from the small sectarian empires they were eagerly building up. Many actions done in the name of Jesus or beliefs proclaimed about him will turn out to have had nothing to do with him at all.

However, Jesus also spoke of others who would discover at the judgement that they had been serving him without realising it. He said that he would thank them for feeding him when he was hungry, for welcoming him when he was a stranger, for clothing him when he was naked, for taking care of him when he was sick, and for visiting him in prison. These people will be bewildered and delighted to discover that they had been unknowingly following him through their experiences of love and goodness. Matthew's account continues:

> Then the righteous will answer him, 'Lord, when was it that we saw you hungry and gave you food, or thirsty and gave you something to drink? And when was it that we saw you a stranger and welcomed you, or naked and gave you clothing? And when was it that we saw you sick or in prison and visited you?' And the king will answer them, 'Truly I tell you,

just as you did it to one of the least of these who are members
of my family, you did it to me.'[176]

Kindness and humility count for far more than grand displays
of religiosity. But, as people who have often sat tests and exams, we
probably find ourselves wondering if there is some kind of pass mark,
some kind of necessary quota of good deeds which we are supposed
to achieve to earn our admittance to the kingdom of God. In the passage just quoted, those who are identified as righteous are not those
who have been deliberately trying to pass some kind of test, but those
who have been genuinely loving without any thought of reward. They
have been happy to help those who are of low status, without drawing
attention to themselves. The transition from ego to love means that we
become less and less preoccupied with trying to impress people with
our achievements.

What seems to matter most to Jesus is not some remarkable list of
accomplishments, but a humble sense of our own need of God. Being a
proud member of a religious tradition has no value in itself; it is much
more important to have an honest awareness of our own problems,
our need for forgiveness and an openness to the ways in which God
wants us to grow. In another parable, Jesus contrasts the attitude of a
religious leader with that of a notorious sinner:

> He also told this parable to some who trusted in themselves
> that they were righteous and regarded others with contempt:
> 'Two men went up to the temple to pray, one a Pharisee and the
> other a tax collector. The Pharisee, standing by himself, was
> praying thus, "God, I thank you that I am not like other people:
> thieves, rogues, adulterers, or even like this tax collector. I
> fast twice a week; I give a tenth of all my income." But the tax
> collector, standing far off, would not even look up to heaven,
> but was beating his breast and saying, "God, be merciful to me,
> a sinner!" I tell you, this man went down to his home justified
> rather than the other; for all who exalt themselves will be
> humbled, but all who humble themselves will be exalted."[177]

176 Matthew 25:37–40
177 Luke 18:9–14

'Justified' here means declared to be in a true relationship with God. The very religious Pharisee's pride is a barrier between him and God, and his prayer is a lonely exercise in self-congratulation. However, the tax-collector's earnest cry shows a clearer understanding of his own spiritual state and a genuine openness to God. Therefore he is the one who enjoys a real connection with God, not the Pharisee.

A similar situation involves one of the thieves crucified alongside Jesus. At the very end of his life, the thief confesses his guilt, accepts that he deserves his fate, but asks Jesus to remember him in his kingdom. And Jesus comforts him by promising him a place in paradise.[178] To be part of the kingdom requires not an impressive CV full of dazzling achievements, but a humble willingness to accept the reality about ourselves and God, and a genuine repentance. We cannot earn a place in the world to come, but our decisions and actions, up to the very end of our lives, show whether or not we would be happy to learn to live in harmony with all that is good. A change of heart is possible even in our last moments.

But someone who leads a life of cruelty and who only regrets it just before death will be far less well prepared for the kingdom of heaven than someone who has lived seventy years of adventurous generosity and humble service. Jesus often referred to the fact that some would be first and some last in the kingdom and that people would experience different rewards.[179] This suggests that there is more to our involvement in the kingdom than just the yes/no response of whether or not we join in with it. There is a journey of learning and transformation which some have travelled much further along than others. Some become very well trained in the ways of goodness by the time they die, while others may still be beginners.

A LOVE THAT KEEPS ON GROWING

The idea that there might be different experiences of reward in the afterlife may surprise some people, who expect it to consist of a uniform experience of heavenly perfection. Their understanding owes a

178 Luke 23.39–43
179 E.g. Matthew 19.27–30 and Luke 14.12–14, and see 1 Corinthians 3.10–15

lot to the Platonist philosophy that envisages a spiritual realm which is unchanging because it is utterly perfect. But the narrative approach found in the Bible seems to suggest that our experience of the future life is a continuing story of growth and development.

I know that I am not the only one who thinks that an unchanging state of perfection sounds rather dull, and also rather baffling. How could there be any kind of ceiling to mark a maximum level of goodness? Why cannot the love of God keep on overflowing with new possibilities? And how could there be any kind of limit to creativity, goodness and love? If I know and love a number of people today, and next week I know and love one more, then love is still growing. If an artist has painted a number of beautiful landscapes, and then next week has painted another, then beauty is still growing. I do not see why that should ever cease to be the case. God may, for example, continue to create and redeem whole worlds of people. Why ever stop? I imagine the kingdom of God as a place where the growth of love accelerates, rather than suddenly hitting an upper limit. It seems to me, therefore, to be a place where those who are novices in the ways of the kingdom can learn and grow alongside those who are experts. And those who are more experienced can help to guide and train those who are beginners.

In fact, Jesus' parables describe a view of the kingdom of God which is very dynamic. They suggest a continuing experience of activity which follows on from our current experience and which is different for different people. Jesus' parable of the pounds illuminates these themes especially well.[180] He describes a nobleman going away to receive a kingdom, leaving his servants to look after his money and to do business with it. He entrusts different amounts to different servants, and returns to find that they have made use of it in very different ways. Some have traded it and earned much more money, while one has simply hidden it away. With his new royal authority, the ruler distributes new responsibilities in his kingdom according to how faithfully his staff have served him during his absence. To one, he says, 'Well done, good servant! Because you have been trustworthy in a very little, take

180 Luke 19.11–27

charge of ten cities.' He puts another in charge of five cities, but takes the money away from the servant who has done nothing.

Jesus' parable suggests that there is much more *work* to be done in the kingdom of God. Those who have learned to serve God in small ways in this life may be put in charge of cities in the world to come. This image suggests that life now is a kind of training ground, in which we have the opportunity to put to work the talents which God has given us. We have the opportunity to use them faithfully, lovingly, humbly in the service of our divine guide. If we do that, then we grow into the kinds of people the universe was created for. And God will then be able to draw out more of our potential by putting us to work in positions of far greater responsibility. And, if we have grown into people who love to do good, then we will take great delight in having new opportunities and new challenges.

The things that we learn now and the ways that our characters develop now are important. The talents and virtues we develop now are of great significance. We are on the first stage in a journey of discovery, love, adventure and service which can continue beyond this life. If we are happy to put our talents and our energies to good use, then there are far greater labours and rewards still to come. The transition from looking after ten pounds to looking after ten cities is a big leap. So the promised future is not a state of unchanging perfection, or of uneventful rest, but one of continuing activity, growth and discovery. There will still be problems to solve, plans to make, places to explore, buildings to construct. Other places in the New Testament talk of a future in which Jesus' followers reign with him on earth.[181] That image suggests that there are decisions to make, projects to manage, people to guide, teach and take care of. The process of learning, doing and loving will continue.

It is a future which I think will be far greater than anything I can describe, but I cannot resist trying to imagine it. I like to picture the whole world being brought into a new and greater harmony with God, in which sickness, death, and addiction to sin are no longer possible. All those who would prefer to be resolutely selfish, unforgiving,

181 1 Tim 2.12, Rev 5.10, Rev 22.5

untrustworthy, hateful or tyrannical have gone. And the good, kind, loving, faithful people from former times have returned, ready to continue using their talents for the common good, in grateful thanks for all that they have been given. Many who were previously beaten down by cruel circumstances now find new opportunities to flourish. A great many self-seeking, pompous, arrogant officials are removed from positions of power, and their responsibilities are given to people who actually have taken the time to learn wisdom, vision and compassion. Lots of people who have previously worked quietly and devotedly to help others are now given exciting new roles. While others who have mostly worked very noisily to enhance their own status and comfort now begin to enjoy learning how to serve others in simple and humble ways.

The environment is cleaned up, animals are treated with respect and compassion, communities and cultures which previously distrusted each other now learn to understand and care for each other. New friendships become possible, and people create amazing new works of art, music, literature, architecture, science and engineering. We discover a joy and a delight in relationships with each other and with God which makes our current experiences of sexuality, companionship and worship seem drab and dismal in comparison. The possessiveness and insecurity of our couples and cliques are replaced by warm communities which love to form new relationships. And then what? Perhaps we explore the galaxy. Perhaps we become the angels for other, younger worlds. Perhaps we join up with beings on distant planets. Perhaps there are new projects, new adventures which go far beyond anything we have currently dreamed of. Whatever happens, I am sure it will far exceed these imaginings of mine. I long to find out.

If there are such revolutionary changes in store for us, what do they mean for us now? I think that life now is our opportunity to become part of the kingdom of God, to learn to love, to learn to serve humbly, to develop our characters, and to encourage and nurture others in the ways of compassion and wisdom. In doing so, we will be preparing the ingredients for a greater future world, and our actions will have an eternal significance. The more that we adopt the values of the kingdom of God now, the more that God will be able to work through our acts of generosity, kindness, creativity and love. And then the ways in which we affect other people's lives for the better will be caught up in the transformation of the world which is the coming of the kingdom.

At the end of the Book of Revelation, the final book of the Bible, the coming of the kingdom of God on earth is represented by the image of a beautiful city coming down from heaven to earth. The city will be decorated with every precious stone, with a radiance like a very rare jewel, and will be illuminated by the shining brightness of the glory of God. People and God will live together in a new and wonderful harmony. It is a poetic account of perfect, divine beauty being revealed on earth, as the glory of God blazes forth for all to see. But this divine glory does not simply overwhelm the works of human beings, for the same passage says that the kings of the earth will bring their glory into the holy city, and people will bring into it the glory and the honour of the nations. It is an amazing image which suggests, I think, that all that is good and true and beautiful in our world will be gathered up into this holy, divine city, and then used to transform the world. God's glory does not obliterate the beauty which we see in our own work and in our creativity; it embraces it. God rejoices to see the ways in which our lives can grow to reflect his glory. And all the good things of this world will be caught up into the wonder of the kingdom of God.

In my own imaginative speculations, I like to picture the Queen arriving in her finest gold carriage at the jewelled gates of the holy city, and laying the crown jewels at the feet of Jesus, including her crown and her 530-carat diamond sceptre. And then I imagine a huge procession turning up with the entire contents of the National Gallery, with centuries of amazing artistic treasures. And then I picture all the nations of the world offering all the fruits of human creativity to God, from illuminated manuscripts to spaceships. Every human achievement which draws out the good potential of God's universe will be offered back to him and joined to the source of all beauty. And then the music of the voices and instruments of countless people from all centuries and all nations will join together in a surge of ecstatic praise and celebration.

And the beauty of God will be echoed by the beauty of his creation, as all are united within the dazzling splendour of his glory.

I think that is the kind of future which God invites us to, and we anticipate that future whenever we do something beautiful for God; whenever we make something, or sing something, or do something which will be joyfully included in the holy city; whenever we gladly serve God and work with him to build for the kingdom of God. We anticipate that future whenever we help others to see the beauty of the Lord; whenever we can bring hope and comfort and dignity and joy to those who face hardship and fear; whenever we learn to look after each other and to care for God's creation wisely. All our acts of goodness join in with God's work of building his kingdom, and all that is good has a lasting place within it.

That vision of the future can therefore inspire our approach to the present. It shows that working for our own status and glory is empty, meaningless and of no lasting value. As Jesus often said, many who are now first will be last, and many who are last will be first. Many powerful dictators, glamorous celebrities and wealthy businessmen will find that their splendid selfishness has been a waste of time. But many who have learned kindness and integrity amidst hardship and poverty will find that their faithfulness and strength of character has been aligned with the creative purposes of God. Many who have quietly served God will rejoice to see that their work has a lasting place in the glory of the kingdom. They will be like delighted children finding that their paintings have been framed in gold and brought together in a display of great beauty.

EPILOGUE: THREE VIEWS OF THE COSMOS

This journey across the breadth of human experience has explored two well-known pictures of reality and suggested a third which can engage with better theology and better science. The hierarchical view of the cosmos clearly establishes the significance of human beings and human relationships, giving a vivid picture of a meaningful world in which everyone has a particular role to play. It portrays God as the ruler and sustainer of all, the source of all life and goodness and beauty. But it is a static picture which lacks a sense of the development of the cosmos. And it is built around a fixed set of relationships of power which emphasise the privileges of a minority. Its account of divine and human relationships says too little about love, and too much about honour and punishment. People have found it to be oppressive, and have had good reason to rebel against it.

The mechanical view of the cosmos undermines these traditional hierarchies, allowing a very helpful sense of the equality and freedom of human beings to emerge. But it emphasises the measurable properties of matter so much that it misses the importance of our experiences of beauty, meaning, consciousness, goodness, love and spirituality. It frequently loses sight of the significance of human beings and relationships, and only notices an optional place for God as the watchmaker and law-giver at the beginning of time. It is regarded as a scientific worldview, but it has been undermined by quantum physics, and it fails to notice the significance of scientific discoveries about the development of the cosmos. It has enabled human beings to function very inventively as experts, but it fails to bring all of our experiences together in one coherent picture. And it objectifies nature in a way which facilitates commercial exploitation instead of love and wisdom.

However, our many discoveries have provided the necessary pieces for a much better view of the cosmos. And theology can redevelop its traditional role of offering a framework which can fit them all together. It can serve all other endeavours by illuminating their true importance, and can help us to take seriously the full range of our experiences.

God is not the top of a hierarchy or a long-departed engineer, but is a Trinity of love who shapes the universe to be life-giving and social.

The rational scientific structures of creation provide an environment which is perfectly balanced for the evolution of rational creatures. It is a place where we can understand the consequences of our actions, and can grow in virtue. The beauty of the cosmos calls to us with an invitation to respond to God in thankfulness and love, and to explore creation with curiosity and wonder. Our freedom gives us the opportunity to find our own way in life, and the space to develop relationships that are genuine, honest and equal, if we choose to do so. And our sense of meaning invites us to join in with the divine project of helping people to grow in character and to develop compassionate civilisations.

God's way of drawing us into relationships centres on the reconciling work of Jesus Christ. He became a vulnerable human being, lived as one of us, and was willing to suffer death in order to overcome the evil of the world with love and to make peace with us. His resurrection overcame death and gave a foretaste of the next stage of the development of the cosmos, when all that has ever been good and loving will be drawn together to renew the world.

This social picture of reality gives a very significant place to human beings, who have evolved as a microcosm of the universe. It is time to take seriously the whole range of our experiences of reality and to rejoice in the dignity of our calling. We are not meant to submit blindly to hierarchies, or to function as cogs in a meaningless machine. Nor should we be content to rule possessively over our own narrow domains of expert knowledge, or to optimise our ability to consume resources. We need another Renaissance, in which we celebrate the full breadth of the privilege of being human beings in this cosmos of wonders. To us has been given our delight in the beauty of nature, our deep sense of the meaningfulness of life, the fascination of our experiences of inventiveness, exploration and creativity, the invitation to address our creator in words of total honesty, the opportunity to experience the reconciling grace of God, the challenge of meeting evil with love, and the transforming joy of learning to live with compassion and generosity.

SUGGESTIONS FOR FURTHER READING

Tom Wright's *Surprised by Hope* (SPCK, 2007) is an excellent discussion of the Christian theology of resurrection. He explores very thoroughly the theme that God is primarily seeking to redeem and transform this world.

Similar ideas are also found in *The Coming of God: Christian Eschatology* by Jürgen Moltmann (SCM Press, 1996).

John Polkinghorne brings together ideas from science in theology about the future of the cosmos in *The God of Hope and the End of the World* (SPCK, 2002).

Lightning Source UK Ltd.
Milton Keynes UK
UKOW01f0114080817
306884UK00002B/185/P